the

INVENTION

of

HeteroSEXUALITY

Jonathan Ned Katz

---

the

INVENTION

of

HeteroSEXUALITY

Foreword by Gore Vidal
Afterword by Lisa Duggan

A DUTTON BOOK

DUTTON

Published by the Penguin Group
Penguin Books USA Inc., 375 Hudson Street, New York, New York 10014, U.S.A.
Penguin Books Ltd, 27 Wrights Lane, London W8 5TZ, England
Penguin Books Australia Ltd, Ringwood, Victoria, Australia
Penguin Books Canada Ltd, 10 Alcorn Avenue, Toronto, Ontario, Canada M4V 3B2
Penguin Books (N.Z.) Ltd, 182–190 Wairau Road, Auckland 10, New Zealand

Penguin Books Ltd, Registered Offices:
Harmondsworth, Middlesex, England

First published by Dutton, an imprint of Dutton Signet,
a division of Penguin Books USA Inc.
Distributed in Canada by McClelland & Stewart Inc.

First Printing, March, 1995
10   9   8   7   6   5   4   3   2

 REGISTERED TRADEMARK—MARCA REGISTRADA

LIBRARY OF CONGRESS CATALOGING-IN-PUBLICATION DATA:
Katz, Jonathan.
        The invention of heterosexuality / Jonathan Katz ; foreword by Gore Vidal ; afterword by
Lisa Duggan.
        p.   cm.
    ISBN 0-525-93845-1 (acid-free paper)
    1. Heterosexuality–Psychological aspects. 2. Homosexuality–Psychological aspects.
I. Title.
HQ23.K315   1995
306.76'4—dc20
                                                                                    94-32650
                                                                                        CIP

Printed in the United States of America
Set in New Baskerville and Gill Sans

Designed by Steven N. Stathakis

CONTENTS

FOREWORD

by Gore Vidal

As the Freudian gulag finally implodes like the former Yugoslavia, it is heartening that the learned and constitutionally irreverent Jonathan Ned Katz should be on hand to drive, as it were, a wooden stake through the expiring gulag's heart. Heterosexuality, a weird concept of recent origin but terrible consequences, is, of course, central to those very strange notions of human sexuality with which Freud and his apostles saddled us for a century.

According to the Prophet, one begins by being born—this was to be the last plain fact that he dealt in; then, baby has erotic longings for the parent of opposite gender; next, baby fears incest as soon as the subject has been explained to him or her, so he/she represses *as best he/she can a passionate longing to couple sexually with parent; later in life, due to this repression, the adult (heir to baby) suffers from anomie, asthma, dandruff . . . until he consults with a member of the Freudian priesthood, who will tell him that although he repressed (did he, though?) his basic incestuous drives, he will be cured, once he rec-*

ognizes that he had wanted to screw his old Mom just as Oedipus did.
Characteristically, Freud managed to muddle even that classical allu-
sion: Oedipus killed his father and screwed his mother without knowing who either was; so, perhaps uniquely in Freudian history,
Oedipus the king did not suffer from the complex that bears his name.

 Freud was a romantic, school-of-Nietzsche, would-be novelist of
the modernist-symbolist school (his "case history" of Leonardo
da Vinci is historical fiction worthy of Rafael Sabatini) who put together a crackpot religion that would never have got off the ground
had it not been for his personal brilliance and imperturbable megalo-
mania. Along the way, he developed a theory of human sexual development that rests, as is usual with him, on a series of false hypotheses.
Baby moves, if lucky, from incestuous desires to a longing for self
(masturbation) and then for others like himself—the dread abomina-
tion that the Leviticus Committee denounced in old Babylon—and
then, with luck, and the intervention, perhaps, of a brilliant Jewish
burgher from old Vienna, he will, as an adult, ascend to the happy
plateau of "heterosexuality" where Mom and Pop do their thing in the
happy knowledge that they are following, if not God's scenario, the
rather more important one of S. Freud, inventor of psychoanalysis
(sensibly he often slept while his patients babbled on the sofa at his
side) and no matter what was plaguing a girl, he was there to tell her
that it was just plain hysteria, and touching her clitoris was a no-no
since maturity meant vaginal orgasm, something that does not exist
but he believed that it did, and so he even managed to get wrong the
very anatomy that he had so firmly declared was destiny. Certainly he
never saw anything in human nature that he himself, rather like an
absentminded God, had not put there.

 For some years now, long before the Freudian religion began to
crumble, Katz has been questioning its essential foundation: heterosexuality, as the grail, the ultimate in human maturity and happiness.
As I write that last word, I think of Freudian slips or misunderstand-
ings. Prime Minister and Mrs. Harold Macmillan were having lunch
with General and Mrs. de Gaulle in Paris. Macmillan and de Gaulle
discussed what each would do when he ceased to lead his country.
Each said he would write a book. Politely Macmillan asked Mrs. de
Gaulle what she wanted after the limelight faded and the trumpets fell

silent. Mrs. de Gaulle's English was not good. "I would like," she said solemnly, "a penis."

The unflappable Macmillan assured her that this was a very sensible thing to want. The general, however, realizing his wife's mistake, said, in his somewhat better English, "Madame means 'app-penis."

Freudians were never able to come up with a proper word (instead of a hybrid Greek-Latin one) for heterosexuality because the Greeks didn't know what it was. They knew about reproduction. They knew about lust and love. They knew about the intensity of sexual desire between men and men, women and women, but for them, Lesbos was just an island off the coast of Asia Minor while Sappho was your average Pulitzer Prize winning poet. Unfortunately, as a Vienna burgher of the late nineteenth century, Freud had powerful Old Testament ideas about what was good and what was bad behavior. He was also no fool (though, arguably, he was an evil man in many respects) and so he accepted the bisexuality of human behavior. As a classics buff, he knew Greek history and culture. He had not missed the ultimate wrath of Achilles triggered by his lover's death. But, finally, the Old Testament natural lawyer in him won out. Cock plus cunt equals baby is what it's all about. He took that as bedrock even though he himself had sex with his sister-in-law, and no baby-making was on either adulterer's mind. The invention of the word "heterosexuality" occurred at about this time (I leave to Katz the essential date).

At first heterosexuality meant an unseemly interest in the opposite sex—in other words, baby usually got douched away. At the turn of the century, the rising middle class was into nonmature sex and, lacking a Greek concept, they came up with a Latin-Greek neologism to describe something that every other culture described simply as "sex." Meanwhile, as the brain is binary (source of our either/or way of "thinking"), there had to be another word to denote the opposite, and thus "homosexuality" was invented and Katz now shows how the words got frozen into their present usage. Good team: hetero. Bad team: homo. Straight versus gay. Either one or the other; no Mr. In-Between. This division has led to endless trouble for many men and women while giving vast joy to the rulers of those lands that accept these unnatural categories—for they can then proscribe the bad team, *thus maintaining control over much of the population, the aim of every government everywhere in every history we know.*

By analyzing the stages by which these sloppy words became concepts that then became "facts," Katz nicely undermines the whole false division. I have often—perhaps too often—made the point that there are no homosexual people and no heterosexual people, only hetero or homo acts, and most people, at one time or another, despite horrendous taboos, mess around, as we used to call it in my Washington, D.C. boyhood. Katz, rather wearily, repeats my monotonous refrain, noting that this was also the general view of Dr. Kinsey, whose report on sexual behavior in the male was published a month or two after my novel The City *and the* Pillar, *in which two "straight" boys have a love affair with dire results, thanks to the time and place where they were living: the United States, once hailed by Spiro Agnew as "the greatest nation in the country."*

I do take some exception to the reverence with which Katz handles the "thoughts" of that eminent preacher and friend of mine, James Baldwin. In 1949 Baldwin did indeed have some sensible things to say about the ridiculousness of one-dimensionalizing human personality: "It is quite impossible to write a worth-while novel about a Jew or a Gentile or a Homosexual, for people refuse, unhappily, to function in so neat and one-dimensional fashion." As the French say, this goes without saying. But then he assaults my novel of the previous year in which the "avowed homosexual . . . murders his first and only perfect love when at length they meet again, for he cannot bear to kill instead that desolate and impossible dream of love." This nicely misses the point. The City and the Pillar. *Biblical title.* What city? Sodom. Fag life. Pillar? *Lot's wife could have been saved from Sodom's destruction if she had not looked behind her for one last glimpse of glamorous old Sodom. She takes a peek. Is turned into a pillar of salt. My protagonist, Jim Willard, is not "an avowed homosexual"—Baldwin was not the most attentive critic of our time—Willard hated fairies and only hustled to stay alive until he was reunited with his "first and only perfect love." I agree with Baldwin that this was probably "impossible," but hardly "desolate." It was high romanticism taken to a terrible extreme. Instead of moving on (no,* not *to Freud's mysterious high good place, heterosexuality, where the air is too thin for too many to breathe), he spent his life looking backward to a perfect conjunction with another boy, and, when he does meet him again, he finds that the other is now living where the air is thin, and so rejects him and, in the best obsessive romantic tradition, the perfect lover is killed. Even the title of the book is a warning to the romantic temperament. But Baldwin sees this violent resolution as "compelled by a panic which is close to madness. These novels [Charles Jackson's* The Fall of Valor *is included] are not concerned with homosexuality but with the ever-present danger of sexual activity between men." This might be true of Jackson but not of me. I argue throughout the book that homosexual acts are a very good thing indeed and for some men and women, permanently preferable to heterosexual acts. This was a new concept in 1948. But romantic heroes usually come to tragic ends, as Shakespeare demonstrates with his two intellectually challenged teenagers from Verona. In any case, a few years after Baldwin's assault on me for "panic," exactly the wrong word, he wrote* Giovanni's Room, *a perfect panic of a book that ends with the beloved one's head chopped off in Paris.*

Katz not only has a good time with all this but he manages to deconstruct two nouns whose invention created false categories, thus making it possible to control the people at large through legal taboos that must now be revoked, as any nonsuperstitious reader of Katz will conclude.

1

THE GENEALOGY OF A SEX CONCEPT

From Homosexual History to Heterosexual History

In the early 1970s numbers of homosexuals began an exuberant move out of our old secret lives. Forging a new, open way of living our lusts and loves, we passed from one historical ordering of homosexuality to another. Observing the change we'd lived, we perceived homosexuality with a double vision—the view of our closeted love lives past, the sight of our unveiled gayness present. Breaking with the old, static, psychological model of homosexuality, some of us became fascinated with exploring homosexuality's changing history—and then, slowly, without premeditation, heterosexuality's.

In that era many of us moved from the shamefully "homosexual" to the affirmatively "gay" and "lesbian," making the power of those words one focus of our political agitating.

Fifteen years earlier, with a new and dawning horror, I had first consciously applied the word *homosexual* to my feelings for men—the morning after I first slept with one. He was a high school friend, it was June 1956, and I was a tender, anxious eighteen. Even now, after all these years, I still recall the dread that the word *homosexual* evoked on that conformist fifties morn.

I also recall the later, humiliating sting of "Fag!" and the mortifying punch of "Queer!" hurled at me for looking one second too long at the wrong straight guy.

These collisions with words explain, in part, this book's exploration of the history, power, and social uses of language. First, as a victim of words, I felt their ability to wound. Here, as historian, I dissect and question them, to understand them, and subvert their force.

Following that fateful fifties morning, I spent the next fifteen years shamed and isolated, tortured by the word *homosexual,* and by my homosexual feelings. Deeply imbued with a rebellious spirit, however, I closely interrogated the Great Books of the anti-establishment canon. The closet encouraged reading. In the early 1960s I marched for peace in Vietnam, and applauded (from the sidelines) the black civil rights struggle and, later, the rise of the black power movement.

But in the late 1960s, hearing occasional reports of demonstrations by fledgling homosexual-rights groups, I was deeply discomforted. Homosexuals were psychological anomalies, freaks. Why didn't they shut up and keep their embarrassing problem to themselves? I heard nothing at all about the Stonewall uprising of June 1969—the closet muffled the sounds of change coming from the world outside.

In September 1970 *Harper's* magazine published Joseph Epstein's "Homo/Hetero: The Struggle for Sexual Identity," and a sweet straight man with whom I shared group therapy gave me a copy. Epstein's article had a profound impact on me.[1]

His essay may be studied now as a rich personal document of heterosexual history at a moment of new, self-conscious defensiveness. Heterosexuals were facing an unaccustomed challenge: "of late homosexuals seem to have taken to the attack against heterosexuality as a way of life." Among the new militants, it seems, was one Elliot, "the hairdresser of a lady friend of mine":

> "Don't tell me about the glories and joys of married life," Elliot says. "I know something about those from the women I work on." And of course, in a sense, he is right. Heterosexuality has not been without its own special horrors. Over the past few years I have witnessed my own once marvelous marriage crumble, fall, and dissolve into divorce. I look around me and see so few good marriages: I know of so many people . . . who, if they thought they could bring it off, would not return this evening to the person they are married to.[2]

Epstein's hordes of heterosexuals, chained through endless disenchanted evenings to insignificant others, were indeed a dismal sight.

"Yet if heterosexual life has come to seem impossibly difficult," Epstein reassured his readers—and himself— "homosexual life still seems more nearly impossible." Writing within that genre that awards loathing packaged as sincerity, Epstein confessed abhorrence: "I do think homosexuality an anathema, and hence homosexuals cursed. . . ."[3] Homosexuals are "cursed," Epstein later repeated, "struck by an unexplained injury . . . whose origin is so unclear as to be, finally, a mystery."[4] That homosexuals are injured by essays just like this was a mystery only to its author.

Near the conclusion of this smug confessional, Epstein declares:

> If I had the power to do so, I would wish homosexuality off the face of this earth. I would do so because I think it brings infinitely more pain than pleasure to those who are forced to live with it; because I think there is no resolution for this pain in our lifetime, only, for the overwhelming majority of

homosexuals, more pain and various degrees of ex-
acerbating adjustment; and because wholly selfishly, I
find myself completely incapable of coming to terms
with it.[5]

Reading Epstein's words in 1970 I experienced with new
and stunning force the depth of antihomosexual hatred. I
noted later that wishing is the single thing all of us can always
do. So Epstein's conditional, "I would wish homosexuality off
the face of this earth," is a lie. He actually *did* wish homosexuality (and homosexuals) "off the face of the earth," but
couldn't quite say so. Genocidal desire is embarrassing in a
Jew.

The hate fueling Epstein's essay also had a revelatory effect on me. I understood: My homosexual feelings made me
and others objects of "prejudice"—subject to stigma as a
group, like black people, like women. Strange to say, this was
a new idea.

Slowly, that dawning consciousness carried me into the
world. With fear and trembling I began to explore New York
City's recently founded gay liberation groups. The eloquent
oratory of gay leaders rang in my ears. I saw the world with
fresh eyes. I participated in public actions, and took part in
intense private discussion groups. I marched with a poster
that proclaimed: "Homosexuals Are Revolting. You Bet We
Are!"

In the winter of 1971, at the age of thirty-three, I was feeling rather better about myself after years of psychotherapy
with a kind, humane heterosexual who, as a boy, had ob-
served Nazi hatred at first hand. Years before, he'd rejected
my opening complaint that homosexuality was my problem.
Now, I began attending the raucous weekly meetings of New
York City's Gay Activists Alliance and, in just a few months,
weathered a destabilizing change. I came home from those
wildly exhilarating meetings exhausted and reeling from the
intense, abrupt shift in understanding and emotion I was so
quickly undergoing.[6]

My experience of that historic shift was, I think, typical of many middle-class homosexuals who became adults before the Stonewall uprising of 1969. We experienced a fundamental alteration—from a sense of ourselves as individual monster-freaks to a new, shared sense of ourselves as outraged resisters.[7] In the gay movement I affirmed my affectionate and erotic feelings for men, the particular emotions for which my society put me down—and for which, for so many years, I put myself down.

Although I then casually identified myself as "a gay man," in my mind I was affirming my feelings for men, not any gay "self." In the early seventies, though I did not use these terms, I began to embrace a politics of feeling and pleasure, not of identity.[8]

My participation in the gay movement soon led to my first imagining such a thing as homosexual history. At a meeting of the Gay Activists Alliance's media committee we talked of ways to portray our new movement, and I resolved to research a documentary theater piece on gay and lesbian life and liberation. This would employ American historical and literary materials to evoke dramatically our changing situation, emotions, and understanding.[9]

The research for my theater piece began "with only a presumption—that Gay American history must exist."[10] The idea of gay history was presumption indeed—homosexuality was then so thoroughly reduced to the psychological. The agitation-propaganda theater piece, *Coming Out!*, was produced by the Gay Activists Alliance in June 1972, and re-produced the following June in a tiny Chelsea theater.[11] Martin Duberman's comments on that production, on the front page of *The New York Times* Sunday drama section, encouraged a publisher to give me a contract for a book of documents on homosexual history, and *Gay American History: Lesbians and Gay Men in the U.S.A.* was published three years later, at the end of 1976.

That title announced a tome right for its time: The *Gay* heralded its liberationist viewpoint, the *American* brought the homos home, and the *History* proclaimed its recovery of an unknown past. That title appealed emotionally and intellectually to the many men and women eager to discover their obscure "roots," and avid to affirm their gay and lesbian feelings.

That book's goal, immodestly proclaimed by me in the militant manner of the day, was nothing less than "to revolutionize the traditional concept of homosexuality." Because that "concept is so profoundly ahistorical," I say, "the very existence of Gay history may be met with disbelief."[12] In 1976, the phrase "Gay history" sounded strange indeed. Though in retrospect a surprising number of books and articles had begun to touch on changing attitudes toward homosexuals in history, the existence of "Gay American history" was still in doubt. Even this gay militant historian found the phrase daunting.

Near the end of the book's move toward publication, long after I'd piled up stacks of documents, I recall sitting on a Hudson River pier with a former boyfriend, asking him if I really dared call the book *Gay American History*. My concern had nothing at all to do with the flattening, difference-denying, universalizing effect of referring to four hundred years of history as "gay." The title *Gay American History,* I worried, too boldly affirmed the existence of a history I was not sure I had the courage to so blatantly assert.

Among the publications that made homosexual history seem possible, and less strange, were the new books and articles then appearing on women's history—usually, heterosexual women were the assumed subjects. I recall the tremendous excitement I felt when the problems encountered and insights offered by those early, daring feminist historians of heterosexual women kept paralleling and illuminating lesbian and gay history.

Already, also, a basic destabilizing of the heterosexual/homosexual dichotomy was under way. In the early seventies a number of manifestos by radical gay and lesbian liberationists were envisioning a future in which the heterosexual/

homosexual distinction would be repealed.[13] In 1970, a group of "Radicalesbians" declared: "In a society in which men do not oppress women, and sexual expression is allowed to follow feelings, the categories of homosexuality and heterosexuality would disappear."[14] In 1971, in Dennis Altman's *Homosexual Oppression and Liberation,* that Australian professor of politics said: "The vision of liberation that I hold is precisely one that would make the homo/hetero distinction irrelevant."[15] In that heady, hopeful, exhilarating dawn of gay and lesbian liberation, the abolition of heterosexuality, and the end of homosexuality, were in the air. We dared to imagine a radically free and different sexual future. We had yet to imagine a radically different sexual past.

Gay American History touches fleetingly on the idea that "homosexual" *and* "heterosexual" relations have changing historical "traits."[16] But that's about as far as I then took heterosexual history—not far. My main goal back then was to demonstrate the existence of vast quantities of original, eye-opening, entertaining homosexual history materials, and to stimulate research and analysis of an untold story.

I do, however, suggest that it's not a good idea "to 'fit' past relations into one pole or the other of the traditional hetero-homo dichotomy." A year earlier, historian Carroll Smith-Rosenberg had published a pathbreaking article on nineteenth-century American women's intense, eros-filled friendships, "The Female World of Love and Ritual." To understand those intimacies, she suggested, we need to go beyond the either/or, heterosexual/homosexual division, and embrace the idea of a "continuum" of such relations. That continuum, she imagined (following Alfred Kinsey's 1948 lead), had a "committed heterosexuality" at one pole, an "uncompromising homosexuality" at the other.[17]

In 1976, amending Smith-Rosenberg's formulation, I suggested that "Categorizing human relations as homosexual or heterosexual should be replaced by research aimed at revealing the multiple aspects of the particular relations under study."[18] With others, I was beginning to sense the distorting effect of employing the heterosexual/homosexual distinction in retrospective historical analysis.[19]

As I and most others understood it then, a timeless, universal homosexuality and heterosexuality take different historical forms. At the moment I was writing, no one I knew was worrying much about the distorting effect of hypothesizing an eternal homosexual essence. Even less did we worry about an ageless heterosexuality. Today, after two decades of investigation, the idea of varying historical forms of an essential homosexuality and heterosexuality still functions as the dominant working notion, even of historically oriented researchers. In 1988, for example, under the clock-stopping hand of this essentialism, the author of a huge, scholarly history of "the social construction of homosexuality" refers to "homosexuality" in the period "Before Homosexuality," not, apparently, bothered by the contradiction.[20] How to transcend the notion of an unchanging heterosexual (and homosexual) essence is a problem I struggle with in this book.

In 1977, with huge excitement, I eagerly read the first social history of the English gay and lesbian emancipation struggle, Jeffrey Weeks's *Coming Out: Homosexual Politics in Britain, from the Nineteenth Century to the Present.* That book confirmed the direction of my own thinking, creatively stimulating and encouraging my work.[21] I immediately wrote to Weeks, eager to contact a like-minded gay historian of the left, pleased that a small international group of gay and lesbian conspirators was quietly starting homosexual history recovery work.

Pioneering research on lesbian and gay history was also beginning to be published by a number of scholars, encouraging further work on the subject from inside and outside academia.[22] In 1980 the prestigious University of Chicago Press published John Boswell's monumental *Christianity, Social Tolerance, and Homosexuality: Gay People in West Europe from the Beginning of the Christian Era to the Fourteenth Century.*[23] That author's flaunted footnote fetish, his command of multitudinous languages, his wealth of empirical data on a subject of great interest to many, and his book's positive, prominent reviews and large sales constituted an important legitimating event in the development of sexual history research in general, and homosexual history research in particular. The following year Lillian Faderman's *Surpassing the Love of Men: Romantic Friendship and Love Between Women from the Renaissance to the Present* newly validated the study of lesbian history.[24]

But a specifically heterosexual history still usually remained unmarked and unremarked. A few feminist historians, however, were just beginning to bring heterosexuality explicitly into time. One of these was Mary P. Ryan, in her *Womanhood in America: From Colonial Times to the Present.*[25]

In the winter of 1977 I reviewed Ryan's book in the gay press, fascinated by this historian's "simple conceptual innovation." This was her casual reference to "heterosexual relations" and "heterosexual women," rather than the usual "sexual relations" and "women." Her specifying of heterosexuality made it stand out newly as a problem. I commented: "The existence of such a particular thing as heterosexual history, along with homosexual history, has not yet been generally recognized, its implications analyzed."[26] Naming "heterosexual history" asserted the existence of such a thing, a necessary move toward analyzing it.

The following year, 1978, at a New York University conference on "Power and Sexuality," my opening talk focused on the empirical and theoretical problems emerging in recent work on homosexual history. That research, I said,[27]

> suggests that existence of a heterosexual history which needs to be recognized and explored, rather than simply taken for granted.

I elaborated:

> Research on the homosexual past inspires us to question the necessity of the present division of persons, activities, and feelings into heterosexual and homosexual. Even Kinsey's famous continuum of sexual

activities and feelings maintains the now dominant and traditional hetero-homo division. Research into past "same"-sex relations questions the applicability of this hetero-homo model to societies which did not recognize this polarity. If we have trouble imagining a world without heterosexuals or homosexuals, a historical perspective is useful. The term "homosexual" was only invented in 1869 [the year's now been moved back to '68]. The first use of "heterosexual" listed in the *Oxford English Dictionary Supplement* dates to 1901. [The most recent *Oxford English Dictionary Supplement* takes the date back to 1892, and "heterosexual" has also been traced to 1868.][28] The terms heterosexual and homosexual apparently came into common use only in the first quarter of this century; before that time, if words are clues to concepts, people did not conceive of a social universe polarized into heteros and homos. If we do not wish to impose our modern vision on the past, we need, first, to ask what terms and concepts the people of a particular era used to refer to sexual and affectional relations between women and between men. We need to transcend the hetero-homo division.[29]

Since the 1978 translation of the first volume of Michel Foucault's *The History of Sexuality,* the work of this thinker has profoundly influenced the interpretation of sexual history by English-speaking researchers.[30] As I'll later make clear, my analysis of homosexual and heterosexual history owes much to Foucault. But, since younger scholars now often write as if Foucault initiated sexual history research from his chair on high in the French academy, I note that homosexual history research owes its main impetus to the gay, lesbian, and feminist movements, not to this one great man.[31]

Foucault's influence is clear in the widely read "Sexual Matters: On Conceptualizing Sexuality in History" (1979), by Robert A. Padgug, who warned: "Sexual categories which seem so obvious to us, those which divide humanity into 'heterosexuals' and 'homosexuals,' seem unknown to the ancient Greeks."[32] This author warned that we need to avoid projecting our present categories on past societies, which organized people and sexuality along very different lines. The need to avoid anachronism in reading and writing sexual history—repeatedly reiterated by numbers of authors—indicates a strong tendency to such misleading retrospective projections.

Padgug also specifically criticized the common notion that "sexual essences" define *persons* called the homosexual and the heterosexual. In ancient Greek society, he said, " 'Homosexuals' and 'heterosexuals' in the modern sense did not exist." That phrasing allowed that heteros and homos in some ancient sense might have existed.

He also questioned, ambiguously, the application of homo- and heterosexual to ancient Greek *acts*. For the Greeks of the classical period, "Homosexuality and heterosexuality . . . were indeed groups of . . . acts," but "not necessarily very closely related acts. . . ."[33]

This historian finally denied that heterosexual and homosexual had any operative existence in ancient Greece: Those "categories themselves . . . had no meaning in antiquity."[34] Such formulations encouraged my interest in category questioning.

By 1981 I had heard a young feminist historian and friend, Lisa Duggan, read a draft of a paper on women, American society in the 1920s, and "the social enforcement of heterosexuality."[35] A few days later Duggan's phrase set off in my head a flash of illumination. It suddenly came to me, and I even muttered out loud to myself: "Heterosexuality wasn't only 'enforced,' it was 'invented.' " A few months after that epiphany, I read to our small sex-in-history study group the first version of a paper, "The Invention of Heterosexuality," exploring the hypothesis that heterosexuality, like homosexuality, is a social-historical construction.[36] The group urged me on.

Comment on heterosexuality's historical "invention" was

incorporated into three analytical essays in my second book on homosexual American history. But when *Gay/Lesbian Almanac* appeared in 1983, few readers seemed as excited as I by its most surprising revelation: The historical discourse on "heterosexuality" was a modern fabrication. Our term *heterosexuality*, assumed to describe a sex-love older than Methuselah, was of quite recent origin, and had a history of changing, contested definitions.[37]

My ideas about heterosexuality's invention had first come into clearer focus in the early 1980s as I looked closely at some medical journal articles of the 1890s. In these, psychiatrists first described the "homosexual." I began to notice that a number of these doctors also referred to the "heterosexual"—but as a pervert![38] Only gradually, I noted, did the word *heterosexual* come to signify the assumed, different-sex erotic ideal we know today. Pursuing the making of homosexuality over time, I had stumbled, unexpectedly, upon another primal scene, a previously unremarked seminal event, the occasion on which heterosexuality was conceived.

In the early eighties I hypothesized that the terms *heterosexuality* and *homosexuality* signify historically specific ways of naming, thinking about, valuing, and socially organizing the sexes and their pleasures. This book argues my case.

It's dangerous to introduce this book about heterosexual history with the personal story of "a homosexual," about "homosexual history." I may lend ammunition to those eager to shoot down this history as the biased rant of a "special interest"—as if a heterosexually inclined writer would tell this story from the viewpoint of the universal. Given this book's confessional opening, it may be perceived as really being about homosexuality. It's not.

I focus this story on the mundane materiality of the word *heterosexual* because talk of different-sex eroticism so often and so easily glides off into talk of homosexuality, leaving heterosexuality—once again—forgotten. Sticking closely to the word *heterosexual*, I try to stick to that elusive subject. The term *het-*

erosexual provides concrete evidence of surprising changes in the heterosexual idea and ideal—the ways that sex-love has been understood and valued.[39] And because, since the late-nineteenth century, the heterosexual and homosexual have danced in close dialectical embrace, I touch as well on the homosexual's story.

I also focus on the seemingly simple word *heterosexual* because any discussion of heterosexuality threatens to expand, dauntingly, to include everything about women's and men's relationships. The intimidating notion that heterosexuality refers to everything differently sexed and gendered and eroticized is, it turns out, one of the conceptual dodges that keeps heterosexuality from becoming the focus of sustained, critical analysis. You can't analyze everything.

I concede right off that my reference to heterosexuality as "invented" may well strike some readers as crackpot. Though the word *heterosexual* may be recently invented, surely the feelings and acts are not. Questioning our belief in a universal heterosexuality goes completely against today's common sense.[40] Still, I speak of heterosexuality's historical invention to contest head-on our usual assumption of an eternal heterosexuality, to suggest the unstable, relative, and historical status of an idea and a sexuality we usually assume were carved long ago in stone.

Heterosexuality, we usually assume, is as old as procreation, as ancient as the lust of the fallen Eve and Adam, as eternal as the sex and gender difference of that first lady and initial gentleman. Heterosexuality, we imagine, is essential, unchanging: ahistorical. That hypothesis is our ordinary, unexamined starting point when we think about heterosexuality—*if* we think about it.

When challenged we most likely support with three arguments our idea of an age-old heterosexuality:

(1) a procreate-or-perish imperative makes heterosexuality a necessity everlasting;

(2) all societies recognize basic distinctions between

human females and males, girls and boys, women and men—those biological and cultural differences are the source of an immortal sexuality that is hetero;

(3) the bodily pleasure generated by female and male conjunctions remains the unchanging basis of an eternal heterosexuality.

By this book's end I hope to unsettle your conviction that those arguments are simple, obvious, and unquestionable. Despite what we've been told, I'll suggest that heterosexuality is not identical to the reproductive intercourse of the sexes; heterosexuality is not the same as sex distinctions and gender differences; heterosexuality does not equal the eroticism of women and men. Heterosexuality, I argue, signifies one particular historical arrangement of the sexes and their pleasures.

To be sure, a reproductive necessity, distinctions between the sexes, and eroticism among the sexes have been around for a long time. But sexual reproduction, sex difference, and sexual pleasure have been produced and combined in different social systems in radically different ways. Not until a hundred years ago, I'll argue, were those ways heterosexual. I'll present evidence that sex-difference (the hetero) and sex-pleasure (the sexual) have not always defined the socially authorized essence of the sexes' unions. An official, dominant, different-sex erotic ideal—a heterosexual ethic—is not ancient at all, but a modern invention. Our mystical belief in an eternal heterosexuality—our heterosexual hypothesis—is an idea distributed widely only in the last three-quarters of the twentieth century.

I grant you, the idea of a primordial heterosexuality is powerful in our society, a potent sign under whose influence all of us still work out our lives, wherever we take pleasures.[41] Unlike the discredited Victorian theory of a dangerous, life-threatening masturbation, a depleting self-abuse, the late-nineteenth-century hypothesis of a universal male-female pleasure-sex still represents to most of us a timeless, living truth. For that very reason the history of the sexual and hetero idea is a particularly startling and enlightening one to trace.

But destabilizing our conventional sexual wisdom is a difficult task. Rarely do we focus for long on the riddle of heterosexuality—our gaze turns quickly to "the problem of homosexuality." The problem of heterosexuality resists problematizing as resolutely as several other peculiar ways of feeling, acting, speaking, and thinking.

We name and talk of a problematic "transvestism," the desire to dress in the clothes of the other sex. We do not usually name and speak of the strong desire to dress in the clothes of one's own sex.[42] But why would most of us feel intense anxiety at dressing publicly in the clothes of the other sex? Does not our fervid desire to dress in the clothes of our own sex suggest a mystery to be explained?

We name and speak of a troublesome "transsexualism," the feeling of being the other sex, the desire to inhabit the body of that other sex. We do not name and talk much about the feeling of being the same sex—the sex we think we are, the sex most of us desire to stay. But does not our feeling relatively comfortable with our sex, and our intense desire to maintain the integrity of our sex, indicate something that needs to be explained, as much as "transsexualism"?

We name and speak of "race" and most often specify "African Americans" or "black people," not "white people." We name a "black American history," but rarely a "white American history." Being of the "white race" and from a "white" cultural tradition have only recently been made objects of systematic inquiry in the way that being from an African-American tradition is now studied—after a long, hard struggle for visibility. Although most history has been written as the history of white people, it has not often focused on the changing, historical ordering of whiteness, its uses and abuses. That dominant racial category and power structure continues to be privileged, normalized, naturalized, and forgotten, like heterosexuality.[43]

We talk of women's history, but less often of men's. For men's story has failed to stir the same questions as women's, stimulated recently by the compensatory research push of feminists. Because most past history writing has focused on men's activities and ignored women's, the initial impulse of feminists has stressed the recapture of women's history. Only recently is the changing social organization of maleness and manhood beginning to receive the same close, historical scrutiny.[44]

Unless pressed by powerful, insistent voices, we fail to name the "norm," the "normal," and the social process of "normalization," much less consider them perplexing, fit subjects for probing questions.[45] Analysis of the "abnormal," the "deviant," the "different" and "other," "minority" cultures has seemingly held much greater charm.

Yet the deep desire possessing some of us to dress in the clothes of our own sex, and the profound conviction of some of us that we feel like the sex we are—if we think about these emotions—are quite as puzzling and complex as transvestism and transsexualism. Why should external norms of dress and sex have such deep, powerful internal holds on so many of us? What, after all, does our sex feel like? How are we to know? Do we really think there are emotions specific to one sex and not the other? Who says so? And why does it matter, and matter so much? We need to know more, it seems, about the social and historical production of sexed feelings, sexed bodies, and sexed clothes.

In-depth, critical study of the social and historical institution of whiteness and maleness will also, I believe, reveal much about the social construction of white supremacy and male domination—as much as the critical study of different-sex erotic history will reveal about the cultural creation of heterosexual dominion. Examination of these formerly unquestioned, socially institutionalized norms and systems may provide a startling new view of a previously invisible, taken-for-granted, "normal" social universe coexistent with the more deeply pondered "deviant" world—perhaps even unsettle forever our idea of norm and deviance.

By this time, practicing heterosexuals may be nervous that a book challenging traditional assumptions about heterosexuality also questions the legitimacy of their heterosexual emotions, behaviors, relationships, and identities. Let me state, therefore: This book does *not* doubt the value of anyone's heterosexuality. Nor does this book represent the homosexual's revenge, an exercise in reverse denigration.

Another of the anxieties I speak to here is that the history of a socially constructed heterosexuality is perceived to debunk heterosexuality. That fear arises because the biological determinists have convinced many of us that an individual's "real" sexual feeling is physiologically and immutably grounded, therefore "natural," "normal," and good.

Similarly, some sexologists have insisted that an individual's erotic emotions, though only focused after birth in a process of social interactions, are set at an early age and for life—and, thus, we imagine, are authentic and good. The idea that hetero and homo feelings are *legitimated* via such biological or social determinisms constitutes a widely held late-twentieth-century U.S. folk belief.

The idea that heterosexuality and homosexuality are historically constructed seems to many to challenge the reality, profundity, and value of their desires. That perception, I believe, is wrong. The emotional quality, the aesthetic and ethical value, and the cultural and personal worth of any eros is independent of biology, and of its socially and individually constructed origins.

I focus in this book on two major periods in the history of heterosexuality. The first is the late-nineteenth-century era, when that term and concept were first created and were still unstable. The second is that epoch, starting in the 1960s, when heterosexuality was again destabilized—this time, by feminists, then by gay and lesbian liberationists.

I also focus on the influence of a number of men on the

manufacture of the heterosexual idea and ideal. Because Karl Maria Kertbeny, Richard von Krafft-Ebing, Sigmund Freud, and most other pioneering theorists of heterosexuality were men, it seems not unlikely that the particular social standpoint of that gender profoundly influenced their—and our— ideas about heterosexuality. I therefore raise the issue of how these male doctors' (and, later, female feminists') theories of heterosexuality affected their different ideas of female and of male heterosexuality.[46]

Each of heterosexuality's founding fathers was also "white," and since Western European and Anglo-American society has insistently divided people of different colors and cultures by "race," the residue of a white perspective may also be found within theories of heterosexuality. Freud's association of "civilization" and heterosexuality, the "primitive" and homosexuality, comes to mind, and the complex intersections of race and heterosexuality are hinted at.[47]

This small book on a large subject makes a first, exploratory attempt to bring to light the implications of a historically specific heterosexuality.[48] I sketch here the rough, tentative story of a heterosexual history still needing detailed empirical research and extended analysis. My aim is to further the critical analysis of heterosexuality begun in the 1960s and 1970s by feminists and gay and lesbian liberationists. I'll be pleased if this work stimulates further historical investigations of heterosexuality, and new interpretations based on that radical reviewing—even if that research reviews and revises my own conclusions.

But if heterosexuality was, as I say, invented, who were its inventors? Where did they go about their work? When was it invented? How was it invented? What, exactly, was invented? And, lastly—the most difficult question— why?

While we look at evidence and explore some answers to those questions, I ask you to suspend, temporarily, our usual universalizing heterosexual hypothesis. Come with me now on a journey into the sexes' sexual past, to observe and ponder the invention of heterosexuality.

2

THE DEBUT OF THE HETEROSEXUAL

*Richard von Krafft-Ebing
and the Mind Doctors*

In the United States, in the 1890s, the "sexual instinct" was generally identified as a *procreative* desire of men and women. But that reproductive ideal was beginning to be challenged, quietly but insistently, in practice and theory, by a new *different-sex pleasure* ethic. According to that radically new standard, the "sexual instinct" referred to men's and women's erotic desire for each other, *irrespective of its procreative potential.* Those two, fundamentally opposed, sexual moralities informed the earliest American definitions of "heterosexuals" and "homosexuals." Under the old procreative standard, the new term *heterosexual* did not, at first, always signify the normal and good.

The earliest-known use of the word *heterosexual* in the United States occurs in an article by Dr. James G. Kiernan, published in a Chicago medical journal in May 1892.[1]

Heterosexual was not equated here with normal sex, but

with perversion—a definitional tradition that lasted in middle-class culture into the 1920s. Kiernan linked heterosexual to one of several "abnormal manifestations of the sexual appetite"—in a list of "sexual perversions proper"—in an article on "Sexual Perversion." Kiernan's brief note on depraved heterosexuals attributed their definition (incorrectly, as we'll see) to Dr. Richard von Krafft-Ebing of Vienna.

These heterosexuals were associated with a mental condition, "psychical hermaphroditism." This syndrome assumed that feelings had a biological sex. Heterosexuals experienced so-called male erotic attraction to females *and* so-called female erotic attraction to males. That is, these heterosexuals periodically felt "inclinations to both sexes."[2] The hetero in these heterosexuals referred *not* to their interest in *a different sex,* but to their desire for *two different sexes.* Feeling desire inappropriate, supposedly, for their sex, these heterosexuals were guilty of what we now think of as gender and erotic deviance.

Heterosexuals were also guilty of reproductive deviance. That is, they betrayed inclinations to "abnormal methods of gratification"—modes of ensuring pleasure without reproducing the species. They also demonstrated "traces of the normal sexual appetite"—a touch of the desire to reproduce.

Dr. Kiernan's article also included the earliest-known U.S. publication of the word *homosexual.* The "pure homosexuals" he cited were persons whose "general mental state is that of the opposite sex." These homosexuals were defined explicitly as gender benders, rebels from proper masculinity and femininity. In contrast, his heterosexuals deviated explicitly from gender, erotic, and procreative norms. In their American debut, the abnormality of heterosexuals appeared to be thrice that of homosexuals.[3]

Though Kiernan's article employed the new terms *heterosexual* and *homosexual,* their meaning was ruled by an old, absolute reproductive ideal. His heterosexual described a mixed person and compound urge—at once sex-differentiated, eros-oriented, and reproductive. In Kiernan's essay, heterosexuals' ambivalent procreative desire made them absolutely abnormal. This first exercise in heterosexual definition described an unequivocal pervert.

KRAFFT-EBING'S *PSYCHOPATHIA SEXUALIS*

The new term *hetero-sexual* next appeared early in 1893, in the first U.S. publication, in English, of *Psychopathia Sexualis, with Especial Reference to Contrary Sexual Instinct: A Medico-Legal Study,* by Richard von Krafft-Ebing, "Professor of Psychiatry and Neurology at the University of Vienna."[4] This book would appear in numerous later U.S. editions, becoming one of the most famous, influential texts on "pathological" sexuality.[5] Its disturbing (and fascinating) examples of a sex called sick began quietly to define a new idea of a sex perceived as healthy.[6]

In this primer, the "pathological sexual instinct" and "contrary sexual instinct" are major terms referring to nonprocreative desire. Their opposite, called, simply, "sexual instinct," is reproductive. But that old procreative norm was no longer as absolute for Krafft-Ebing as it was for Kiernan. Conspicuously *absent* from the Viennese doctor's large tome on all varieties of sick sex is any reference to what some other doctors called "conjugal onanism," or "frauds in the accomplishment of the generative function"—birth control.[7]

In the heat of different-sex lust, declares Krafft-Ebing, men and women are not usually thinking of baby making: "In sexual love the real purpose of the instinct, the propagation of the species, does not enter into consciousness."[8] An unconscious procreative "purpose" informs his idea of "sexual love." His sexual instinct is a predisposition with a built-in reproductive aim. That instinct is procreative—whatever the men and women engaged in heterosexual acts are busily desiring. Placing the reproductive aside in the unconscious, Krafft-Ebing created a small, obscure space in which a new pleasure norm began to grow.

Krafft-Ebing's procreative, sex-differentiated, and erotic "sexual instinct" was present by definition in his term *heterosexual*—his book introduced that word to many Americans. A hyphen between Krafft-Ebing's "hetero" and "sexual" newly spliced sex-difference and eroticism to constitute a pleasure defined explicitly by the different sexes of its parties. His hetero-sexual, unlike Kiernan's, does not desire two sexes, only one, different, sex.

Krafft-Ebing's term *hetero-sexual* makes no *explicit* reference to reproduction, though it always *implicitly* includes reproductive desire. Always, therefore, his hetero-sexual implicitly signifies erotic normality. His twin term, *homo-sexual,* always signifies a same-sex desire, pathological because non-reproductive.

Contrary to Kiernan's earlier attribution, Krafft-Ebing consistently uses hetero-sexual to mean normal sex. In contrast, for Kiernan, and some other late-nineteenth- and early-twentieth-century sexologists, a simple reproductive standard was absolute: The hetero-sexuals in Krafft-Ebing's text appeared guilty of procreative ambiguity, thus of perversion.

These distinctions between sexual terms and definitions are historically important, but complex, and may be difficult for us to grasp. Our own society's particular, dominant heterosexual norm also helps to cloud our minds to other ways of categorizing.

Readers such as Dr. Kiernan might also understand Krafft-Ebing's hetero-sexuals to be perverts by association. For the word *hetero-sexual,* though signifying normality, appears often in the Viennese doctor's book linked with the non-procreative perverse—coupled with "contrary sexual instinct," "psychical hermaphroditism," "homo-sexuality," and "fetichism."

For example, Krafft-Ebing's first use of "hetero-sexual" occurs in a discussion of several case histories of "hetero- and homo-sexuality" in which "a certain kind of attire becomes a fetich."[9] The hetero-sexual premieres, with the homo-sexual, as clothes fetishist.

The second hetero-sexual introduced has a "handkerchief fetich." Krafft-Ebing quotes a report on "this impulse in hetero-sexual individuals" by Dr. Albert Moll, another influential early sexologist. The Victorian lady's handkerchief apparently packed an erotic wallop for a number of that era's men. An intense attraction to ladies' hankies might, it seems, even temporarily undermine patriarchal power. A "passion for [women's] handkerchiefs may go so far that the man is entirely under their [women's] control," Dr. Moll warns his endangered fellows.

This reversal of the customary male-female power relationship might not be displeasing to the Victorian woman who found herself—and her hanky—the object of a male fetishist's interest. Moll quotes such a woman:

> "I know a certain gentleman, and when I see him at a distance I only need to draw out my handkerchief so that it peeps out of my pocket, and I am certain that he will follow me as a dog follows its master. Go where I please, this gentleman will follow me. He may be riding in a carriage or engaged in important business, and yet, when he sees my handkerchief he drops everything in order to follow me,—i.e., my handkerchief."[10]

In the above examples, the term *hetero-sexual* signifies a normal different-sex eroticism, though associated closely with fetishism and the nonprocreative perverse. In the following examples, Krafft-Ebing's normal hetero-sexual is associated, as it most often is, with the "perversion" he calls "homosexuality" and "contrary sexual instinct."

Mr. Z

The case history of a Mr. Z, aged 36, a Hollander, is titled "Contrary Sexual Instinct—with Sexual Satisfaction in Hetero-Sexual Intercourse."[11]

For "reasons of family and business," Mr. Z has to marry, and consults Krafft-Ebing, anxious about his future "virility as a husband." Mr. Z's family and class duties conflict with his erotic inclinations. In fantasy, Mr. Z tells the doctor, his "greatest pleasure" is to embrace and "press himself" on a working-class man.

The "beauty of the female form," reports Krafft-Ebing, makes "no impression" on Mr. Z. Despite his aesthetic failing, this client is said to "enjoy the act of coitus" with female prostitutes. He regularly visits brothels—"to cure himself," it's said, "of masturbation, and to thoroughly satisfy his libido."[12]

By way of therapy Krafft-Ebing assures Mr. Z that he is "virile" and will "probably be so in conjugal intercourse" with his future wife. The patriarchal scientific authority of this doctor's exhortations to virility are clearly part of the medicine he prescribes. Mr. Z is urged to wage war on his erotic feelings for men, abstain completely from masturbation, and to exercise his "normal sexual desires"—continue his brothel trips, apparently. Mr. Z is also urged to try hypnotism, hydrotherapy (baths), and faradization (the application to the body of small electric currents).

Other uses of "hetero-sexual" by Krafft-Ebing link it to the form of "perversion" called "psychical hermaphroditism"—erotic desire for both sexes.[13] Discussing treatment prospects, the doctor notes that individuals erotically attracted to both sexes are the best candidates for conversion to heterosexual normality. This point's obviousness did not keep it from being repeated as profound insight by numbers of later psychiatrists.

For clients with *some* clear interest in hetero-sexual lust, doctors felt that supporting that potential was especially pressing. Psychiatrists therefore subjected clients inclined to both sexes to especially severe moral censure when they continued, willfully, to follow their same-sex desires.

Mr. von X

Because he "has hetero-sexual feelings," Krafft-Ebing evidences a partiality for Mr. von X, described as "not a complete and hopeless urning" (another name for

"homo-sexual"). Mr. von X's sex troubles began after his eighteenth year when he became a "source of anxiety to his highly
respected parents." He then started "a love affair with a male
writer, who fleeced him and made him an object of remark
and ridicule." At home, Mr. von X "consorted with servants,"
got into and out of a blackmail attempt and, says this censo-
rious therapist, continued to exhibit "disgraceful inclinations
toward men."

Sent to Krafft-Ebing "to be cured of his fatal peculiarity,"
Mr. von X assures the doctor that he wants to be cured. He
adds, however, that "he had never regarded his inclination to
his own sex as abnormal." The doctor sets out to convince Mr.
von X otherwise.

Since von X displays "rudiments of hetero-sexual feelings," Krafft-Ebing begins hypnosis, suggesting to his client:

1. I abhor onanism, because it makes me sick and
   miserable.
2. I no longer have inclinations toward men; for love
   of men is against religion, nature, and law.
3. I feel an inclination toward women; for woman is
   lovely and desirable, and created for man.[14]

Several years after this brainwashing, the patient reports:

he still had sympathetic feeling for some men, but
never anything like love. He occasionally had pleasurable coitus with women, and now thought of
marriage.[15]

Numbers of Krafft-Ebing's treatment histories end with wedding bells—or, at least, the "thought of marriage."

Mr. von Z

Strong social pressure to marry plays a large role in several of
Krafft-Ebing's conversions. Mr. von Z's visit to the psychiatrist

is motivated by external pressure to tie the knot, not by the client's own desire for exclusive heterosexuality.[16]

Mr. von Z, age 29, a "tall, slim man, of aristocratic and decidedly masculine manners," consults Krafft-Ebing, "pained" by his sexual feelings for men—and "especially because he is urged by his family to marry." Mr. von Z is "interested in women only mentally, not physically," and dreams only of men. His sexual activity includes "passive or mutual masturbation with men" and "solitary onanism."

Mr. von Z's pain elicits Krafft-Ebing's sympathy. With this client, "so worthy of compassion," the doctor also tries hypnosis, suggesting to Mr. von Z:

> ever despise onanism and male love; find women beautiful and dream of them.[17]

So ordered, Mr. von Z finds he can resist "homo-sexual desire."

Reforming his eroticism, Mr. Von Z quickly goes on to straighten up his gender—and his house, clothes, and books. His

> former *boudoir* became a work-room; instead of adornment and frivolous reading, he gave himself to walks in the mountains and forests.[18]

Because a premature "fiasco" in intercourse with a woman might sabotage Mr. von Z's treatment prospects, "the initiative in hetero-sexual attempts was left to the patient."[19] After the fourteenth week of hypnosis, says Krafft-Ebing, Mr. von Z ventured intercourse with a woman, was "perfectly successful," became "happy, and sound in body and mind," and even had "thoughts of marriage."[20]

Feeling "perfectly normal in hetero-sexual intercourse," the patient stopped treatment. When Krafft-Ebing saw his client a year or so later, Mr. von Z still regarded his sex life as "perfectly normal; for he had coitus regularly with pleasure and full virility, dreamed only of women, and had no inclination to masturbation."

After intercourse, however, Mr. von Z did admit that he still frequently felt passing inclinations for men, though he easily controlled them. "He thought he was lastingly cured," and was (still) "occupied with thoughts of marriage."[21] The client's desire to tell the doctor what he wanted to hear certainly colors such reports.

Mr. R

Marriage is a "phenomenal" treatment result in the case of Mr. R, cited by Krafft-Ebing as reported by Dr. von Schrenk-Notzing, an early specialist in hypnosis as a cure for nonprocreative desire.[22] Of Mr. R, Krafft-Ebing says: "I consider the hetero-sexual instinct of the patient to be the artificial creation of his excellent physician." Though usually considered inborn, hetero-sexual desire might, it seems, sometimes be artificially induced—invented. The ingenuity of doctors knew no bounds.

Mr. R, an official, age 28, reported that "in sexual relations I feel myself to be completely feminine." Feeling feminine meant: "Since my earliest youth, in my sexual acts and fantasies, I have always had before my eyes only images of masculine beings and masculine genitals."[23] Feeling, here, is considered to be sexed and gendered.

After a few sittings with Schrenk-Notzing, "somnambulism" was induced, indifference to men and interest in women was suggested. Mr. R then felt "pleasure at the sight of women." At the seventh sitting, "successful coitus was suggested; this was fulfilled."

After three months of commanded coitus, however, Mr. R had "a relapse," induced, it's said, by his male companion. At the next session with his doctor Mr. R felt "remorse and shame." As "expiation" he later performed "coitus with a woman in the presence of his [male] seducer." This "expia-

tion" apparently included the unconscious homoerotic pleasure of his male friend's gaze.

After forty-five treatments, says Schrenk-Notzing, Mr. R:

> considered himself cured. Treatment ceased. He be-
> came engaged to a young lady some weeks later, and
> presented himself again, after six months, as a happy
> bridegroom.[24]

The mechanical, psychologically unconvincing quality of
these transfigurative hetero copulations is typical of many reported in later psychological texts—a form of conversion
literature.

Without rejecting the old reproductive norm, Krafft-Ebing introduced the new heterosexual term. This came, in the twentieth century, to signify a different-sex sexuality completely
free from any tie to reproduction. His use of the term heterosexual began to move his sex text away from the Victorian reproductive ideal toward the modern different-sex erotic
norm. His text is transitional, inhabiting a space between the
Victorian and the modern.

Krafft-Ebing's use of the word *hetero-sexual* to mean a normal different-sex eroticism marked in discourse a first historic
shift away from the centuries-old procreative norm. His use of
the terms *hetero-sexual* and *homo-sexual* helped to make sex difference and eros the basic distinguishing features of a new
linguistic, conceptual, and social ordering of desire. His
hetero-sexual and homo-sexual offered the modern world two
sex-differentiated eroticisms, one normal and good, one abnormal and bad, a division which would come to dominate
our twentieth-century vision of the sexual universe.

Because I focus on Krafft-Ebing's *Psychopathia Sexualis* as a
founding text of heterosexuality, readers may assume that the
word *hetero-sexual* dominates his book. But in this 436-page
tome the term *hetero-sexual* appears only twenty-four times,
and is not considered important enough to be indexed.[25] Het-

erosexuals are of less explicit interest to this doctor than the nonprocreative perverts who are his focus.

This text on the pathological sexual impulse begins to argue for a new idea of the healthy sexual instinct. Speaking of nonprocreative pathology, he distinguishes between acts supposedly caused by an inborn, biological anomaly—*congenital sexual perversion*—and voluntary acts constituting an *acquired sexual perversity*. That distinction between biologically determined acts and individually authored acts served an ethical and legal end.

According to this moral-biological theorizing, individuals are not responsible for their inborn nonprocreative sexual perversion—*or, by implication, their innate, procreation-oriented erotic attraction to the other sex*. The idea of a given, physiological sexual orientation ("healthy" or "sick," "normal" or "abnormal") became a dominant hypothesis of modern sexual theory. In the twentieth century, this deterministic bio-ethic proclaims heterosexuality an immutable fact of nature—a naturally given norm.

Krafft-Ebing's transitional model of sexuality was equivocal about pleasure—a basic conflict over the value of eroticism is evident in this and many later defining texts of heterosexuality.

On the one hand, on the first page of *Psychopathia Sexualis*, Krafft-Ebing refers rather positively to the enjoyment associated with the expression of the procreative sexual instinct:

> In the gratification of this natural impulse are found not only sensual pleasure and sources of physical well-being, but also higher feelings of satisfaction in perpetuating the single, perishable existence, by the transmission of mental and physical attributes to a new being.[26]

"The bliss which the sexual sentiment creates in fancy," he adds, "seems incomparable and infinite in contrast with all other pleasurable feelings."[27]

On the other hand, his first page also sounds an ominous note: "In coarse, sensual love, in the lustful impulse to satisfy this natural instinct, man stands on a level with the animal." This is a low level indeed. Only by a great effort of control can civilized human beings distinguish themselves from sensual beasts and conquer natural lusts.

The "natural" here is, by no means, the good. "Man" can "raise himself to a height where this natural instinct no longer makes him a slave." On this moral pinnacle, "nobler feelings are awakened, which, notwithstanding their sensual origin, expand into a world of beauty, sublimity, and morality."

By controlling sensual impulses, this doctor suggests, "man overcomes his natural instinct, and from an inexhaustible spring draws material and inspiration for higher enjoyment, for more earnest work, and the attainment of the ideal."[28] The proper productive channeling of natural sensuality was an individual and social responsibility.

A moral hierarchy is hard at work here, with sensual pleasure judged a lowly emotion, a lust-free spirituality judged heavenly. From early-colonial New England through our own day, a value system that condemns hedonism and the joys of the flesh has contended with a pro-pleasure principle.

The introduction of the heterosexual term proclaimed "sexuality"—the sensual pleasure of men and women—an essential element of their intimacy. But our society has rarely, without equivocating, affirmed the independent value of sensual pleasure. So the heterosexual ideal displays, from its inception, a fundamental tension. Heterosexual affirmation encounters a basic conflict between the pleasures of the flesh and the yearning for a pure, fleshless spirit. The sexual in the hetero ideal was a troublemaker from the start.

"Opposite sex" desire is another essential element of Krafft-Ebing's theorizing of the hetero in his hetero-sexual. He repeatedly refers to males and females as "opposite"— anatomical, genital differences signify an all-encompassing, fundamental contrariety. Just as he conceives of homosexual desire as "contrary sexual instinct," so he conceives of women and men as "contrary" sexes. Human males and females are not just different in some biological structures and functions, similar in others, depending on one's standard of evaluation. This doctor's two sexes are antithetical. This alleged opposition appears repeatedly in heterosexual history, inspiring various ingenious explanations of how such contrary sexes ever manage to get together.[29]

Although Krafft-Ebing speaks of women's and men's "equality," his concept of the sexes' essential difference makes women separate and unequal.[30] Men are his primary, active subjects; his viewpoint is unselfconsciously a man's.[31] Women readers are relegated by this doctor to another, purer sphere, out of earshot of his disturbing case histories. This paternalistic patriarch shelters women from the world's exciting, complex, dangerous sensuality.

One of the essential differences between women and men is exemplified for this doctor by the relative strength of their erotic desire. "Undoubtedly," he says, "man has a much more intense sexual appetite than woman"—a dominant, though not universal, nineteenth-century notion. Krafft-Ebing suggests that *he* typically "loves sensually," *she* usually loves spiritually. He is "aggressive and violent in his wooing":

> With a woman it is quite otherwise. If she is normally developed mentally, and well bred, her sexual desire is small. If this were not so the whole world would become a brothel and marriage and a family impossible.[32]

Women and men are also essentially different in other ways. Woman, he says, "remains passive." Her innate passivity "lies in her sexual organization [nature], and is not founded merely on the dictates of good breeding [nurture]."[33] The "need for love" is also alleged to be innately greater in woman than in man. And women's love is not necessarily a sex-love: "Sensuality disappears" in a "mother's love," claims Krafft-

Ebing.[34] Such differences of the sexes extend to "all the sexual functions and desires."[35]

The innate dissimilarity of men's and women's eroticism means that each sex starts off from a different place in relation to the new and developing heterosexual norm. Because of their supposed greater eroticism, men are considered closer to heterosexuality. When women moved toward erotic parity with men in the twentieth century, they became more heterosexual and, supposedly, more manlike in their lusts. Because of their disparate positions with regard to hetero pleasure, the histories of male heterosexuality and female heterosexuality differ significantly throughout the twentieth century.

Krafft-Ebing's discourse on the hetero-sexual reveals a late-nineteenth-century theorist during the first stage of heterosexualization, a construction to which his own work was a major, transitional contribution.

The brief era of heterosexual American history discussed here, the last years of the nineteenth century, represents the first years of the heterosexual epoch. In this period, doctors of the mind, some still flying fertility's flag, some pushing tentatively beyond it, first publicly formulated the idea of *heterosexual* and *homosexual.*

But what earlier sex-historical developments led to those new terms, and that new way of valuing? Let's take a look backward.

3

BEFORE HETEROSEXUALITY

Looking Backward

If the word *heterosexual* did not exist in the United States until 1892, how did Americans talk and think about, and socially organize the sexes' differences and their sexuality? Did they employ equivalent terms, or wield an altogether different language? Is it possible that, before the debut of the term *heterosexual*, nineteenth-century Americans arranged sex-differences, eroticism, and reproduction in ways substantially different from the way we do? Dare we imagine that they constituted a qualitatively distinct sexual system—a society not appropriately described by our modern term *heterosexual*?

From the present, looking back on past eras before the use of the term *heterosexual*, we can, of course, find well-documented examples of different-sex erotic acts and emotions. Yet, from the standpoint of those who lived, loved, and lusted in the past, those same acts and emotions may not have referred in any essential way to the same combination of sex and gender difference and eroticism that we call heterosexuality. Ways of ordering the sexes, genders, and sexualities have varied radically. That variation challenges our usual assumption that an unchanging, essential heterosexuality takes qualitatively different historical forms. The word *heterosexual,* I propose, itself signifies one timebound historical form—one historically specific way of organizing the sexes and their pleasures.

EARTHLY LOVE AND HEAVENLY LOVE

One example of a nonheterosexual society is ancient Greece, as analyzed by the late French historian Michel Foucault, a discussion that includes his most explicit, extensive comments on heterosexuality.[1]

Foucault repeatedly warns present-day readers of the danger of projecting our heterosexual and homosexual categories on the past. The specific past he refers to is ancient Greece, as represented in those texts that discuss free men's problematic, pleasurable intimacies with women and with boys.

In a passage appraising a famous speech by Pausanias in Plato's *Symposium,* Foucault says that one finds there

> a theory of two loves, the second of which—Urania, the heavenly love—is directed [by free men] exclusively to boys. But the distinction that is made *is not between a heterosexual love and a homosexual love* [emphasis added]. Pausanias draws the dividing line between "the love which the baser sort of men feel"—its object is both women and boys, it only looks to the act itself (*to diaprattesthai*)—and the more ancient, nobler, and more reasonable love that is drawn to what has the most vigor and intelligence, which obviously can only mean [for free men] the male sex.[2]

Pausanias, Foucault stresses, employed a hierarchical distinction between free men's lower, *earthly love,* focused on acts, and free men's higher, *heavenly love*, defined by a feeling for the beauty of boys, a superior object. That distinction between earthly and heavenly love is substantially different from our contrast between heterosexual and homosexual.

Discussing ancient Greek society, Foucault generalizes, "The notion of homosexuality is plainly inadequate as a means of referring to an experience, forms of valuation, and a system of categorization so different from ours." Our homosexual/heterosexual polarity does not match these ancient Greek men's views. Our distinction is based on sexed difference and sexuality:

> The Greeks did not see love for one's own sex and love for the other sex as opposites, as two exclusive choices, two radically different types of behavior. The dividing lines did not follow that kind of boundary.[3]

According to Foucault, ancient Greek writers might sometimes recognize that one man's inclinations usually favored women, another man's, boys. But those emotional tendencies were not embedded within the same social organization of sexed difference and eroticism that gives rise to our own heterosexual/homosexual pair. Neither Greek men's inclination for women, nor their desire for boys, was any "more likely than the other, and the two could easily coexist in the same individual."[4] He asks:

> Were the Greeks bisexual then? Yes, if we mean by this that a Greek [free man] could, simultaneously or in turn, be enamored by a boy or a girl. . . . But if we wish to turn our attention to the way in which they conceived of this dual practice, we need to take note of the fact that they did not recognize two kinds of "desire," two different or competing "drives," each claiming a share of men's hearts or appetites. We can talk about their "bisexuality," thinking of the

free choice they allowed themselves between the two
sexes, but for them this option was not referred to a
dual, ambivalent, and "bisexual" structure of desire.
To their way of thinking, what made it possible to desire a man or a woman was simply the appetite that
nature had implanted in man's heart for "beautiful"
human beings, whatever their sex. . . .[5]

We can take a retrospective look at the ancestry of our
own society's sexual terms and organization—their "genealogy," Foucault calls it. But we should not, he suggests, employ
our terms *bisexuality, homosexuality,* and *heterosexuality,* in a way
to suggest that these were the concepts past subjects used.

Foucault fears his readers' projection on the past of their
own society's sexual categories and arrangements because
such projections unconsciously and unjustifiably affirm the
similarity of present and past. His readers will thereby be pre-
vented from perceiving *dissimilarity* and *change*—the historically specific character of ancient prescriptions about free
men's pleasure, and the historically particular social organization of eroticism that gave rise to them.

The French historian's sexual relativity theory points us
to a basic "presentist" bias in readers' and scholars' vision of
sexualities and pleasures past—that is, we necessarily view
them from a particular position in the present.

It's significant that Foucault thought it necessary to
provide even fairly sophisticated, intellectual readers with repeated cautions against anachronistic projections—a well-
known historical blunder.[6] His and others' reiterated warnings
against anachronism in sexual history analysis testify not so
much to the primitive level of sex history interpreters, or their
readers, as to the continuing, enormous power of our present
dominant concepts of sexuality. Without realizing it, usually,
we are all deeply embedded in a living, institutionalized
heterosexual/homosexual distinction.

MAXIMIZED PROCREATION AND SODOMITICAL SIN

For a second example of a society not ordered along heterosexual lines we can turn to a culture nearer home—the New
England colonies in the years 1607 to 1740.[7]

In these formative years, the New England organization
of the sexes and their erotic activity was dominated by a reproductive imperative. These fragile, undeveloped agricul-
tural economies were desperate to increase their numbers,
and their labor force. So the early colonial mode of procreation was structured to optimize the production of New Englanders. The New England settlers married earlier than Old
Englanders, and their ordering of maximized reproduction
created a colonial birth rate higher than in England or Europe at the time.

This intensive populating was incited by religious exhortations to multiply, and by legal retributions for acts thought
to interfere with procreation (such as sodomy, bestiality, and
masturbation) or the dominant reproductive order (such as
adultery). In early colonial Boston, after confessing to adultery with twelve men, the eighteen-year-old Mary Latham was
hanged with one of her lovers. At least two other early New
Englanders were hanged for extramarital acts, thereby serving, according to one historian, "as graphic reminders" of the
punishment that could befall those "violating the sexual exclusivity" of marriage. Although all the early New England colonies prescribed death for adultery, very few executions
actually occurred under these statutes. (Perhaps, since the
crime was "one of the most common," the death penalty
would have done more to disrupt the procreative economy
than to support it.) But more than three hundred women and
men found guilty of adultery in early New England were seriously punished with twenty to thirty-nine lashes. (A married
man was severely punished only if he committed adultery with
a woman pledged or married to another man. An engaged or
married woman was considered to have committed adultery
whatever the marital status of her partner.)[8]

Sodomy should be punished by death, declared the Reverend John Rayner, even though it might not involve the same "degree of sinning against the family and posterity" as some other "capital sins of uncleanness." William Plaine deserved death for sodomy in England, and for inciting the youth of Guilford, in the New Haven Colony, to "masturbations," John Winthrop explained. For Plaine's crimes frustrated the marriage ordinance and hindered "the generation of mankind."[9]

The death penalty for sodomy prevailing in all the colonies, and the public execution of a few men for this crime, violently signified the profound sinfulness of any eros thought hostile to reproduction. The operative contrast in this society was between fruitfulness and barrenness, not between different-sex and same-sex eroticism.

Women and men were constituted within this mode of procreation as essentially different and unequal. Specifically, the procreative man was constructed as seminal, a seed source. The procreative woman was constituted as seed holder and ripener, a relatively "weaker vessel." For a man to "waste his seed" in nonprocreative, pleasurable acts was to squander a precious, limited procreative resource, as crucial to community survival as the crops the colonists planted in the earth. Although women were perceived to have "seed," a woman's erotic acts with another woman were not apparently thought of as wasting it, or as squandering her seed-ripening ability. So these were lesser violations of the procreative order.

Men and women were, however, regarded as equal in lust. As the Reverend Thomas Shepard sermonized: "Every natural man and woman is born full of sin," their hearts brimming with "atheism, sodomy, blasphemy, murder, whoredom, adultery, witchcraft, [and] buggery. . . ." As a universal temptation, not a minority impulse, a man's erotic desire for another man did not constitute him as a particular kind of person, a buggerer or sodomite.[10] Individuals might lust consistently toward one sex or another and be recognized, sometimes, as so lusting. But this society did not give rise to a subject defined essentially by an attraction to a same sex or an appetite for a different sex.

Within the early New England organization of pleasure, carnal desire commonly included the mutual lust of man and woman and the occasional lust of man for man. A dominant colonial figure of speech opposed lust for an earthly "creature" to love for an other-worldly God. In these colonies, erotic desire for members of a same sex was not constructed as deviant because erotic desire for a different sex was not construed as a norm. Even within marriage, no other-sex erotic object was completely legitimate, in and of itself.

In this New England, the human body's capacity to function as means of earthly pleasure represented a deeply problematic distraction from a heavenly God, a diversion to which men's and women's bodies were equally prone. Within New England's dominant mode of procreation the body's "private parts" were officially constituted as generative organs, not as hetero pleasure tools.

In a sermon on the "sins of Sodom," the Reverend Samuel Danforth linked "sodomy" and idleness. Using energy in reproductive acts, an important form of production, kept one from wasting energy in unproductive sin. In contrast, since the first quarter of the twentieth century, our society's dominant order of different-sex pleasure has encouraged the use of energy in a variety of heteroerotic activities. This stimulation of hetero pleasures completely apart from procreation constructs a heterosexuality increasingly congruent with homosexuality. In early New England, sodomy stood as perverse paradigm of energy wasted in unproductive pleasure.

The reproductive and erotic acts of New England's women and men were among those productive activities thought of as fundamentally affecting the community's labor force, its security and survival. In contrast, in the twentieth century, the erotic activity of women and men was officially located in the realm of private life, in the separate sphere of dating, courtship, romantic love, marriage, domesticity and family. Until Kate Millett and other feminists questioned this ideological separation of the sexual and political spheres, heterosexuality was thought to inhabit a private realm of intimacy distinct from the often alienated public world of work.

In early New England the eroticism of women and men was publicly linked to sodomy and bestiality in a realm of tempting sinful pleasures. Colonial lust was located in an arena of judgments, an avowedly moral universe. Heterosexuality is located, supposedly, in the realm of nature, biology, hormones, and genes—a matter of physiological fact, a truth of the flesh. Only secretly is heterosexuality a value and a norm, a matter of morality and taste, of politics and power.

The "traditional values" of early colonial New England, its ordering of the sexes, their eroticism, and their reproduction, provides a nice, quintessentially American example of a society not dominated by a heterosexual/homosexual distinction.

THE EARLY-NINETEENTH-CENTURY ORGANIZATION OF TRUE LOVE

Nineteenth-century America, from about 1820 to 1850, is a third society not organized according to our heterosexual law. Neither, it turns out, was it the prudish society of stereotype. The evidence offered recently by historians challenges the common notion of nineteenth-century middle-class society as sexually repressed. The rise of the pro-heterosexual principle can't be explained, then, simply as a sharp break with an antisexual Victorian past. Though recent historians don't always distinguish adequately between early and late nineteenth-century developments, their analyses can help us understand the social origins of the heterosexual as a historically specific term and relationship.

In early-nineteenth-century America, I'll argue, the urban middle class was still struggling to distinguish itself from the supposedly decadent upper orders and supposedly sensual lower orders. The middling sort claimed sexual purity as a major distinguishing characteristic. No middle-class sexual ethic then validated different-sex lust apart from men's and women's love and reproduction. Only in the late nineteenth century did the middle class achieve the power and stability that freed it to publicly affirm, in the name of nature, its own "heterosexuality." The making of the middle class and the invention of heterosexuality went hand in hand.[11]

Ellen Rothman, in her *Hands and Hearts: A History of Courtship in America,* contests the antisexual Victorian stereotype.[12] She analyzes the diaries, love letters, and reminiscences of 350 white, Protestant, middle-class American women and men living in the settled areas of the North who came of courting age between 1770 and 1920. She concludes that courting couples in the early nineteenth century defined "romantic love so that it included sexual attraction but excluded coitus." That particular courtship custom she names the "invention of petting."[13] This common courting convention, she maintains, allowed the middle class quite a lot of private erotic expression short of intercourse. She stresses: "Couples courting in the 1820s and 1830s were comfortable with a wide range of sexually expressive behavior."[14]

In her book *Searching the Heart: Women, Men, and Romantic Love in Nineteenth-Century America,* Karen Lystra also marshals lots of sexy verbal intercourse from nineteenth-century love letters, arguing forcefully against the twentieth-century stereotype of the Victorians. She analyzes the intimate letters of one hundred middle-class and upper-class white couples, and sexual-advice literature of the 1830s through the 1890s.[15] She demonstrates that, under the powerful legitimizing influence of "love," middle- and upper-class women and men, in their *private* behavior and conversations with each other, affirmed a wide range of erotic feelings and activities—though not usually intercourse before marriage.

Summing up the Victorians' "approval of sex when associated with love," Lystra declares,

The highest values of individual expression and autonomous self-hood were heaped upon the erotic.
Victorians did not denigrate sex; they guarded it.[16]

She emphasizes, "Sex had a place of honor and prominence in
Victorian culture."[17] She reiterates: "Victorians reveled in the
physicality of sex when they believed that the flesh was an expression of the spirit."[18] The idea of eroticism as "a romantically
inspired religious experience, a sacrament of love" was, she says,
"perhaps the most culturally significant meaning attached to Victorian sexuality."[19] Her sex-positive view of the Victorians is also
borne out, she claims, by research in more than fifty nineteenth-
century advice books. Mainstream advisers of that day, she
claims, encouraged an active eroticism *as an expression of love.*[20]

For a small group of sexual enthusiasts, the radicals of their
day, true love was a free love. John D'Emilio and Estelle B.
Freedman's *Intimate Matters: A History of Sexuality in America* describes free lovers daringly justifying erotic expression *even outside
of marriage.*[21] Free lovers challenged the respectable idea that legal matrimony was necessary to license the erotic intercourse of
the sexes. Free love, free lovers argued—not the church, not the
state—freely legitimated conjugal unions. Arch-romantics that
they were, however, free lovers did not advocate eros unaccom-
panied by love. Just as this era's mainstream strongly condemned
sensuality detached from legal matrimony and love, so its free
lovers condemned sensuality detached from romance.[22]

Steven Seidman, a historically oriented sociologist, qualifies somewhat the revisionist historians' view of nineteenth-
century eroticism. A note in his own study, *Romantic Longings:
Love in America, 1830–1980,* rejects Lystra's argument that the
eroticism of Victorian women and men was unambiguously
legitimated as symbol of love.[23] Although "all" nineteenth-
century sexual advisors, Seidman admits,

acknowledged the beneficial role of sex in marriage,
love was construed as essentially spiritual. Sex, at
best, symbolized a spiritual union or functioned as a

spiritual act. *In none of these discourses . . . was eroticism
ever framed as essential to the meaning of intimacy or as a
basis of love* [emphasis added].

Lystra's stress on the Victorians' active appreciation of eroticism is, he thinks, "grossly overstated."[24]

Certainly, an eroticism needing to be sanctified by love
was originally unhallowed. Among middle-class Victorians,
"sensuality" was a dirty word. Lystra occasionally admits this:
"Sex was wholeheartedly approved as an act of love and
wholeheartedly condemned by the Victorian mainstream
when bodily pleasures were not privileged acts of self-
disclosure"—that is, when erotic pleasure was not the expression of love.[25] Lust *not* sanctified by love, she concedes here,
was utterly condemned.[26] Her interpretation of nineteenth-
century sensuality as legitimized by love does dispel the usual
stereotype, though she constructs a counter-myth of erotic
Victorians.

In his own book, Seidman usefully stresses the historically
specific character of the heterosexual/homosexual opposition. During most of the nineteenth century, he says, "the
term *heterosexuality* and what we today take as its natural antithesis, *homosexuality,* were absent" from discourses on gender
and eroticism.[27] The heterosexual and homosexual were not
thought of "as mutually exclusive categories of desire, identity
and love."[28] Only in the early twentieth century did "the concepts of heterosexuality and homosexuality" emerge "as the
master categories of a sexual regime that defined the individual's sexual and personal identity and normatively regulated
intimate desire and behavior."[29]

As noted, the revisionist historians of nineteenth-century
American sexuality typically fail to distinguish carefully between early and late developments. A closer look at early-
nineteenth-century society clarifies its difference from that
late-nineteenth-century order which gave rise to the heterosexual category.

The early nineteenth century prescribed particular ideals

of manhood and womanhood, founding a cult of the true man and true woman. The "Cult of True Womanhood" is said by historian Barbara Welter to mandate "purity"—meaning asexuality—for respectable, middle-class women.[30] More recent historians contest this interpretation of "purity." Karen Lystra, for example, quotes numbers of letters in which women's and men's erotic expression is referred to as "pure" by association—that is, by lust's link with "love." Purifying lust was, in fact, an important function of the middle-class true-love ideal. In this view, the special purity claimed for this era's true women referred not to asexuality but to middle-class women's better control than men over their carnal impulses, often conceived of as weaker than men's. True men, thought to live closer to carnality, and in less control of it, ideally aspired to the same rational regulation of concupiscence as did respectable true women.[31]

The ideal of true men and true women was closely linked to another term, "true love," used repeatedly in this era. Holding strictly to true love was an important way in which the middle class distinguished itself from the allegedly promiscuous upper class and animalistic lower class. Those lust-ridden lower classes included a supposedly vicious foreign element (often Irish, Italian, and Asian) and a supposedly sensual dark-skinned racial group shipped to America from Africa as slaves.[32]

True love was a hierarchical system, topped by an intense spiritual feeling powerful enough to justify marriage, reproduction, and an otherwise unhallowed sensuality. The reigning sexual standard distinguished, not between different- and same-sex eroticism, but between true love and false love—a feeling not sufficiently deep, permanent, and serious enough to justify the usual sensual courtship practices, or the usual well-nigh immutable marriage.

Given the powerful legitimating influence of true love, many of the letter writers quoted by Lystra, Rothman, and the other revisionists spend much energy trying to prove the trueness of their love. Assuring one's beloved of love's truth was, in fact, a major function of these letters.[33]

In this era, the human body was thought of as directly constituting the true man and true woman, and their feelings. No distinction was made between biologically given sex and socially constructed masculinity and femininity. Under true love's dominion, the human body was perceived as means of love's expression. Under the early-nineteenth-century rule of reproduction (as in early New England), penis and vagina were means of procreation—"generative organs"—not pleasure parts. Only after marriage could they mesh as love parts.

Human energy, thought of as a closed and severely limited system subject to exhaustion, was to be used in work, in producing children, and in sustaining love and family, not wasted on unproductive, libidinous pleasures.

The location of love's labors, the site of engendering and procreating and feeling, was the sacred sanctum of early-nineteenth-century true love, the home of the true man and true woman. This temple of pure, spiritual love was threatened *from within* by the monster masturbator, that archetypal early Victorian cult figure of illicit-because-loveless, non-procreative lust.[34]

The home front was threatened *from without* by the female prostitute, another archetypal figure of lust divorced from love. (Men who slept with men for money do not seem to have been common, stock figures of the early- nineteenth-century middle-class imagination, probably because there weren't many of them, and they weren't thought of as a major threat to the love of men and women.)[35]

Only rarely was reference made to those other illicit erotic figures, the "sodomite" and "sapphist" (unlike the later "homosexual," these were persons with no "heterosexual" opposite, terms with no antonyms). State sodomy laws defined a particular, obscure act, referred to in a limited legalese, not a common criminal, medical, or psychological type of person, not a personal, self-defined "identity" and, until the nineteenth century's end, not a particular sexual group.[36]

Because the early-nineteenth-century middle-class mind was not commonly focused on dreams of legitimate different-sex pleasures, neither was it haunted by nightmares of perverted same-sex satisfactions. The sexual pervert did not emerge as an obsession of society's new-born, fledgling normal sexuals until the nineteenth century's last decades. Though the early-nineteenth century middle-class might be worried by erotic thoughts unhitched from love, this group was not yet preoccupied by an ideal of an essential, normal, different-sex sexuality.

In early-nineteenth-century America no universal eros was thought to constitute the fundamental nucleus of all passionate intimacies. In this pre-Freudian world, love did not imply eros. So respectable Victorian women and men referred often and explicitly to their "passionate" feelings with little thought that those intense emotions were a close relation of sensuality. Proper middle-class women might often speak of their intense "passion" for each other without feeling compromised by eroticism.[37] Unlike post-Freudian passion, early-nineteenth-century passion inhabited a universe separate and distinct from the hot-house world of sensuality.

Given the early-nineteenth-century distinction between the moral character of passionate love and the immoral character of sensual lust, intense, passion-filled romantic friendships could flourish erotically between members of the same sex without great fear that they bordered on the sodomitical or sapphic. Those terms' rare use suggests the lack of any public link between sensuality and same-sex passion. Same-sex romantic friendships might even enjoy an uncomplicated existence unknown to many different-sex relations—haunted as these might be by the very gender difference that constituted the sexes as opposite—therefore as potential love and marriage objects for each other, therefore as potential sensual partners. "Until the 1880s," say the historians of American sexuality, John D'Emilio and Estelle B. Freedman, most same-sex "romantic friendships were thought to be devoid of sexual content." The "modern terms *homosexuality* and *heterosexuality* do not apply to an era that had not yet articulated these distinctions."[38]

Spiritual love and passion inhabited an abode far from the earthly, earthy home of sexuality. True love was enacted legitimately only within marriage, the legal mode of proper procreation. Intercourse, as sign of love's "consummation," held a special, deep significance. The intercourse of penis and vagina, men and women commonly agreed, was the one move they could not make before marriage and still remain respectable. Intercourse distinguished the true and virtuous woman from the fallen. Refraining from intercourse was the final test of the true man's manliness, his status as genteel, Christian gentleman.

The early-nineteenth-century middle-class fixation on penis-vagina coitus implied that numerous pleasurable acts *not* involving the "penetration" of this specific female part by this specific male part were *not* thought of as prohibited, or even as "sexual." Quite a lot of erotic activity then passed as permissible in a love relationship precisely because it wasn't "intercourse."

This cult of intercourse was formulated most clearly by the more restrictionist ideologists of sex, as discussed by Lystra: the promoters of a procreative ethic. But they were waging a losing battle. The number of "legitimate" births per middle-class family shows a continuous sharp decline during the nineteenth century.[39] By the late nineteenth century the old true-love standard was giving way to a new, different-sex erotic ideal termed *normal* and *heterosexual*. A close look at that late-nineteenth-century era suggests how it came to terms.

THE LATE-NINETEENTH-CENTURY CONSTRUCTION OF SEXUAL INSTINCT

Each of the revisionist historians of nineteenth-century sexuality presents one or several memorable examples of lust-loving, male-female couples. The most enthusiastic sensualists they offer typically date to the late nineteenth century, though often serving generalizations about "Victorian" sexuality or "nineteenth-century" eroticism.

One of Ellen Rothman's featured couples is Lester Ward and Lizzie Vought. In 1860, in Myersburg, Pennsylvania, the nineteen-year-old Lester (later, a well-known sociologist) began keeping a diary of his and Lizzie's courtship. This record suggests that Lizzie was as active in the couple's sexual explorations as her diarist boyfriend.[40]

In 1861, when Lester and "the girl" (as he called her) were often separated, his diary indicates that Lizzie made sure that, when they could, the two got together in private. After a Saturday spent with the girl and friends, Lester stayed on to spend "a happy night" with Lizzie:

> Closely held in loving arms we lay, embraced, and kissed all night (not going to bed until five in the morning). We have never acted in such a way before. All that we did I shall not tell here, but it was all very sweet and loving and nothing infamous.[41]

Lester's "I shall not tell here," his refusal to put into words all of the couple's erotic doings, and his defensive "nothing infamous," are telling. Even this easygoing enthusiast of bodily love evidently felt the judgmental power of a strict standard of sexual propriety.

Six months later the still-courting couple first "tasted the joys of love and happiness which only belong to a married life." The phrasing suggests that their initial coupling was perceived as breaking a well-known intercourse ban.

About a year later, in 1862, Lester and Lizzie married. Lester Ward's diary, says Rothman, suggests that this couple experienced little emotional conflict over their sexual explorations, even their atypical premarital intercourse.[42] Lester and Lizzie stand in Rothman's text for a revised vision of Victorians as privately erotic, publicly reticent.

In 1860, the same year that Lester Ward began his diary,

an eloquent, embattled exponent of the new male-female lust-iness, Walt Whitman, was publishing his third edition of *Leaves of Grass.* That year's version first included a section, "Children of Adam," publicly evoking and promoting the procreational-erotic intercourse of men and women. As a pio-neering sex radical, Whitman broke with the early-nineteenth-century idea that women's passion for motherhood included no eros. Whitman's poems publicly proclaimed women's lusty, enthusiastic participation with men in the act of conceiving robust babies. Another of Whitman's new sections, "Cala-mus," vividly detailed acts of erotic communion between men.

As research by Michael Lynch stresses, Whitman bor-rowed terms from his day's pop psychologists, the phrenolo-gists, naming and evoking hot "amative" relations between men and women, and sizzling "adhesive" intimacies between men.[43] In the perspective of heterosexual history, Whitman's titling of these amative and adhesive intimacies was an at-tempt to position male-female and male-male eroticisms to-gether as a "natural," "healthy" division of human erotic responses. (Along with most other writers of the time, Whit-man almost completely ignored eros between women—a pow-erful indication of phallic rule: erotic acts not involving a penis were insignificant.) Though now perhaps better known as man-lover, Whitman is also a late-Victorian trailblazer of a publicly silenced, often vilified lust between the sexes.[44]

Historian Peter Gay's first two hefty volumes on *The Bour-geois Experience* in nineteenth-century Western Europe and the U.S. constitute a mammoth defense—980 pages of text and notes—of the middle class, its *Education of the Senses* and its *Tender Passion* (as these volumes are subtitled). Gay sets out to restore the Victorian middle class's erotic reputation, so often characterized as "repressed" or "hypocritical."

Personalizing Gay's presentation of the Victorians as ar-dent champions of eros (even sex athletes) is his discussion of the "Erotic Record" documenting the 1877 courtship, later marriage and enthusiastic adultery of Mabel Loomis and Da-vid Todd. The story of Mabel and her men is, significantly, a late-nineteenth-century tale, though Gay doesn't emphasize this point.

This end-of-the-century story includes Mabel's thirteen-year, graphically detailed, doubly adulterous affair with Austin Dickinson (Emily's married brother) in Amherst, the outwardly staid, inwardly steaming New England college town.[45] Peter Gay employs the tale of Mabel and David and Austin to counter the typecasting of Victorians as prudes. Like other revisionists, he insists that the nineteenth century middle class was secretly sexual, though publicly prudish.[46]

Evidence offered by Gay and the other revisionists suggests that, as the nineteenth century went on, the private pleasure practices of the middle class were diverging more and more from the public ideal of true love. By the end of the century, as the middle class secured its social place, its members felt less need to distinguish their class's sexual purity from the eroticism of the rich and the sensuality of the poor, the colored, and the foreign.[47] In the late nineteenth century, as the white Protestant middle class pursued its earthly happiness, its attitude toward work shifted in favor of pleasurable consumption. By century's end the ideal of true love conflicted more and more with middle-class sensuous activity. Lust was bustin' out all over.

Peter Gay mentions Mabel Loomis Todd's need "to find expressive equivalents for her erotic emotions, manifested by her diary keeping."[48] That need of Mabel's was, I think, typical of her class. In the late nineteenth century, Mabel's personal letters and diaries provided a private place for putting into words and justifying—literally, coming to terms with—middle-class practices which could not be talked of publicly without censure. Like Mabel, the late-nineteenth-century middle class needed to name and justify the private erotic practices that were growing more prevalent, and more open, by century's end. That class's special interest would find expression in the proclamation of a universal heterosexuality. The invention of heterosexuality publicly named, scientifically normalized, and ethically justified the middle-class practice of different-sex pleasure.[49]

COMING TO TERMS

The heterosexual and homosexual did not appear out of the blue in 1892. Those two sex-differentiated, erotic categories were in the making from the 1860s to the end of the century. In late-nineteenth-century Germany, England, France, and Italy, and in America, our modern, historically specific idea of the heterosexual began to be constructed; the experience of a proper, middle-class, different-sex lust began to be publicly named and documented.

In the initial strand of the heterosexual category's history we may be surprised to discover the prominent part played by early theorists and defenders of same-sex love. In 1862 in Germany, one of these pioneers, the writer Karl Heinrich Ulrichs, began to produce new sexual names and theories defending the love of the man who loved men, the *Uranier* (or "Urning"). The Urning's opposite, the true man (the man who loved women), he called a *Dionäer* (or "Dioning"). His theory later included the *Urninde,* the woman "with a masculine love-drive"—his phrase for the woman with male feelings—that is, the woman who loved women.

The Urning's erotic desire for a true man, Ulrichs argued, was as natural as the "Dioning-love" of true man and true woman. His Dioning and Urning are the foreparents of the heterosexual and homosexual. Starting in 1864, Ulrichs presented his theories in twelve books with the collective title *Researches on the Riddle of Love Between Men,* written and printed at his own expense.[50]

In Ulrichs's eroticized update of the early Victorian true man, the real man possessed a male body and a male sex-love for women. The Urning was a true man with the feelings of a true woman. The Urning posssessed a male body and the female's sex-love for men.

As we've seen, the Victorian concept of the "true" mechanically linked biology with psychology. Feelings were thought of as female or male in exactly the same sense as penis or clitoris: anatomy equaled psychology, sex physiology determined the sex of feelings. Sex-love for a female was a male feeling, sex-love for a male was a female feeling. A female sex-love could inhabit a male body, a male sex-love could inhabit a female body.

According to this theory there existed only *one* sexual desire, focused on the other sex. (In today's terms, there was only one different-sex "sexual orientation," not two distinct "heterosexual" and "homosexual" desires.) Within this conceptual system, a (male) Urning felt a woman's erotic love for men, a (female) Urninde experienced a man's attraction to women. In each case, the desire for a different-sex was felt by a person of the "wrong" sex. Their desire was therefore "contrary" to the one, normative "sexual instinct." Ulrichs accepted this one-instinct idea, but argued that the emotions of Urnings were biologically inborn, therefore natural for them, and so their acts should not be punished by any law against "unnatural fornication."

In a letter to Ulrichs on May 6, 1868, another early sex-law reformer, the writer Karl Maria Kertbeny, is first known to have privately used four new terms he had coined: *"Monosexual; Homosexual; Heterosexual; und Heterogenit"*—the debut of homosexual and heterosexual, and two now forgotten terms.[51] Though Kertbeny's letter did not define his foursome, his other writings indicate that "Monosexual" refers to masturbation, practiced by both sexes. "Heterogenit" refers to erotic acts of human beings with animals. "Homosexual" refers to erotic acts performed by men with men and women with women. And "Heterosexual" refers to erotic acts of men and women, as did another of his new terms, "Normalsexualität," normal sexuality.

Heterosexuality and normal sexuality he defined as the innate form of sexual satisfaction of the majority of the population. That emphasis on numbers as the foundation of the normal marks a historic break with the old qualitative, procreative standard.

But Kertbeny's heterosexual, and his normal sexual, are by no means normative. Both the heterosexual and normal sexual are characterized by their "unfettered capacity for degeneracy"—he who coins the terms loads the dice.[52] The sex "drive" of normal sexuals is said to be stronger than that of masturbators, bestialists, or homosexuals, and this explains normal sexuals' laxity, license, and "unfetteredness." Kertbeny's heterosexual men and women participate with each other

> in so-called natural [procreative] as well as unnatural [nonprocreative] coitus. They are also capable of giving themselves over to same-sex excesses. Additionally, normally-sexed individuals are no less likely to engage in self-defilement [masturbation] if there is insufficient opportunity to satisfy one's sex drive. And they are equally likely to assault male but especially female minors . . . ; to indulge in incest; to engage in bestiality . . . ; and even to behave depravedly with corpses if their moral self-control does not control their lust. And it is only amongst the normally-sexed that the special breed of so-called "bleeders" occurs, those who, thirsting for blood, can only satisfy their passion by wounding and torturing.[53]

Kertbeny's heterosexuals and normal sexuals are certainly no paragons of virtue. Considering psychiatrists' later cooptation of the term *heterosexual* to affirm the superiority of different-sex eroticism, Kertbeny's coinage of *heterosexual* in the service of homosexual emancipation is one of sex history's grand ironies.

Kertbeny first publicly used his new term *homosexuality* in the fall of 1869, in an anonymous leaflet against the adoption of the "unnatural fornication" law throughout a united Germany.[54] The public proclamation of the homosexual's existence preceded the public unveiling of the heterosexual. The first public use of Kertbeny's word *heterosexual* occurred in Germany in 1880, in a published defense of homosexuality, in a book by a zoologist on *The Discovery of the Soul.*[55] *Heterosexual* next made four public appearances in 1889, all in the fourth German edition of Krafft-Ebing's *Psychopathia Sexualis.*[56] Via Krafft-Ebing, *heterosexual* passed in three years into English, as I've noted, first reaching America in 1892. That year, Dr. Kiernan's article on "Sexual Perversion" spoke of Krafft-Ebing's "heterosexuals," associating them with nonprocreative perversion.[57]

Influenced, partly, by Ulrichs's years of public agitation for sodomy-law reform and the rights of Urnings, in 1869 psychiatrists began to play their own distinct role in the public naming and theorizing of sexual normality and abnormality. Although medical-legal articles on sexual crime appeared in the 1850s, only at the end of the 1860s did medical professionals begin to assert a new proprietary claim to a special expertise on sex-difference and eroticism, and begin to name the object of their concern. A mini-history of the psychiatric labeling of "abnormal sexuality" suggests how these doctors' explicit specifying of "sexual perversion" furthered their implicit theorizing of "normal sexuality."[58]

In August 1869, a German medical journal published an article by Dr. K.F.O. Westphal that first named an emotion he called "Die conträre Sexualempfindung" ("contrary sexual feeling"). That emotion was "contrary" to the proper, procreative "sexual feeling" of men and women.[59] Westphal's contrary sexual feeling was the first, and became one of the best known, contenders in the late-nineteenth-century name-that-perversion contest.

In 1871, an anonymous review of Westphal's essay in the London *Journal of Mental Science* first translated the German *contrary sexual feeling* into English as "inverted sexual proclivity." That urge inverted the proper, procreative "sexual proclivity" of men and women.[60]

In 1878, an article in an Italian medical review, by a Dr.

Tamassia, first used the phrase "inversione sessuale." Translated into English, "sexual inversion" became a second prominent contender in the fin de siècle aberration-labeling sweepstakes.[61]

In 1897, the medically trained Havelock Ellis first used "sexual inversion" in a publicly printed English work. As liberal sex reformer, Ellis tried to appropriate medical terms and concepts for the cause of sexual expression.[62]

Before the invention of "heterosexuality," the term "contrary sexual feeling" presupposed the existence of a noncontrary "sexual feeling," the term "sexual inversion" presupposed a noninverted sexual desire. From the start of this medicalizing, "contrary" and "inverted" sexuality were problematized, "sexual feeling" was taken for granted. This inaugurated a hundred-year tradition in which the abnormal and the homosexual were posed as riddle, the normal and heterosexual were assumed.

In the last decades of the nineteenth century, the new term *heterosexual* moved into the world, sometimes linked with nonprocreative "perversion," sometimes with "normal," procreative, different-sex eroticism. The theorizing of Sigmund Freud played an influential role in stabilizing, publicizing, and normalizing the new heterosexual ideal.

4

MAKING THE HETEROSEXUAL MYSTIQUE

Sigmund Freud's Seminal Conceptions

Journeying from heterosexuality's formulation by Krafft-Ebing to its classic conception by Freud, we travel from a relatively simple, outdated sex theory to one of the most complex and still influential. Freud's works provide the heterosexual canon with some of its most intellectually developed, and double-edged, texts. For Freud functions as major modern maker of heterosexuality's ahistorical medical model *and* as subversive theorist of heterosexuality's social construction—its historical invention. His theories provide the most complex support of heterosexual rule *and* important tools for challenging hetero-sexual dominion.

Freud's subjects—male and female, adult and child, het-erosexual and homosexual—all seek satisfaction of erotic desire. When their pleasure pursuit clashes with society's rules, the pressure to conform causes sparks to fly.

"Dora," for example (actually Ida Bauer, the young subject of one of Freud's most fascinating case histories), inhabits a world electrified with conflicting lusts—radiating from her and to her.[1] The eighteen-year-old Dora, in Freud's entranced description—"in the first bloom of youth—a girl of intelligence and engaging looks"—is buffeted by her own libidinous wishes, conscious and unconscious.[2] Dora's and others' longing for sensual gratification—and basic doubt about such yearning—make for intense, contentious intimacies.

Freud's detailed history of Dora illustrates his active role as master heterosexual norm builder, illuminating the effect on one young woman of heterosexual presumption. It's no big surprise that Freud was guilty of heterosexual bias in his therapeutic work with Dora. But his part in the making of that heterosexual presumption is less well known.

Freud's history of Dora particularizes his vision of life as a melodrama featuring a vivid cast of conflict-ridden pleasure seekers:

Dora, says Freud, is unconsciously attracted to her father, a heteroerotic feeling mirrored by the attachment of Dora's brother to their mother.[3] For her father's love Dora rivals a Frau K, with whom he is having what jealous Dora calls a "common love-affair."[4]

Dora, stresses Freud, is also attracted to Frau K's husband, Herr K, described by the admiring Freud as "still quite young" and "prepossessing." This Herr K has twice made sexual advances to Dora, the first when she was thirteen.[5]

Toward the "young and beautiful" Frau K, Dora harbors homoerotic feelings, sharing a close intimacy in which the two often share a room and bed, and discuss sex, Herr K, and the possibility of the Ks' divorce.[6]

The young governess of the Ks' children tells Dora that Herr K has made sexual advances to her and, following their success, rejected her, inspiring the woman's—and Dora's—fury.[7]

As the astute Dora realizes, her own governess—who secretly reads advanced sex books, and shares them with Dora, warning her that all men are "frivolous and unworthy"—is in love with Dora's father.[8]

Dora has also been fond of and "had taken as her model" her father's sister, who died after a life "weighted down by an unhappy marriage."[9]

In addition, Dora's strong positive and negative feelings for Freud himself are analyzed by the world's first psychoanalyst, though Freud's complex feelings for Dora go unremarked.[10]

Freud interprets Dora's presenting symptoms—among them, a cough, throat constriction and inability to speak, "fainting-fits," and a half-hearted suicide threat, as signs of psychological conflict over her complex, unconscious erotic desires.[11] Freud set out as psychic truce-maker in Dora's and his other clients' distress over their conflicted, libidinous passions.

Moving from Krafft-Ebing and his reproductive "sexual instinct" to Freud and his lusting "libido," we experience the historic shift from the late-Victorian procreation ethic to the modern "pleasure principle."[12]

Sexual pleasure is going up in value in Freud's middle-class universe and reproduction is going down—the falling birthrate indicates a historic rejection of the old procreation ethic. By the end of the nineteenth century, Freud explicitly suggests, the imperative to beget had already lost much of its old hold over the private practices of the middle class:

> If one makes a broad survey of the sexual life of our time and in particular of the classes who sustain human civilization, one is tempted to declare that it is only with reluctance that the majority of those alive today obey the command to propagate. . . .[13]

As secret advocate of those nonpropagating civilized classes, the scientist Freud promotes, not an ethic, but a sexual "instinct" or "drive," one which does "not originally serve the purpose of reproduction at all but has as its aim the gaining of particular kinds of pleasure."[14] The built-in goal of Freud's "sexual instinct" is satisfaction, not increase. The focus on fertility, he stresses, is a late, secondary development in life's long pursuit of happiness.[15] "Pleasure," Freud emphasizes, is the "main purpose" of "our mental apparatus"—a machine with satisfaction as its mission.[16]

Freud attributes pleasure, a valued human end, to body, mind, and desire. Freud's mind is that of a moralist, though he presents himself to the world as nonjudgmental observer. As closest moralist, Freud offers descriptions of the mind's work that slide often into normative judgments about how that mind *should* work.

In numerous texts Freud suggests that "perverse" impulses are those which arouse "unpleasurable feelings"—*not* those which frustrate breeding.[17] Freud's "sexual instinct" breaks with the remnants of Krafft-Ebing's reproductive standard. The "essence of perversions," Freud explains, lies "solely in the *exclusiveness* with which these deviations are carried out and as a result of which the sexual act serving the purpose of reproduction is put to one side" (emphasis mine).[18] According to this exclusivity standard, acts must turn *completely* from reproduction before they turn perverse—a generous reproductive standard indeed.[19]

Enjoyment is posited by Freud as the essential core of human intimacy, of marriage, family life, and even of "civilization," though civilized satisfactions are fenced in by society's restrictions. The terms *pleasure, satisfaction,* and *gratification* float throughout his texts, signifying his commitment to the secular pursuit of this-worldly happiness—qualified, to be sure, by his belief in the necessity and satisfaction of sublimation.

The centrality of the erotic is assumed by Freud, and since his day the importance of pleasure has become a modern Western ethical axiom—one, I later argue, we could do more to honor in practice. As a prime mover of sexual modernization Freud rejects the early Victorian ethic in which the bad "fleshly" opposed the good "spiritual"—the invidious body/soul distinction. Physical and psychological fulfillment, erotic and other—and the impediments to such satisfaction—are Freud's conscious concern.

Freud forges a new, broad concept of sexual yearning as "libido," "drive," "instinct," or "impulse"—the desire for psychic satisfaction experienced in the flesh. This pleasure wish, suggests Freud in perhaps his most subversive innovation, is detached from any innate link to procreation or to any particular act—and detached, even, from any particular object or specific sex.

Freud innovatively proposes the original and complete independence of erotic desire and erotic object. The sexual instinct's only built-in aim is its own satisfaction. The erotic instinct yearns innately not for generation, not for intercourse, neither for male or female, but only for fulfillment. For Freud's hungering libido the whole body becomes a potential field of pleasures. Freud plays an important role in transmuting sex from productive duty to act of pleasurable consumption.

Yet Freud is no unqualified pleasure advocate.[20] He speaks censoriously of those "enslaved to hedonism."[21] The sex theorist who made a problematic "repression" and a difficult "sublimation" common terms of standard English, by no means advocated the end of all erotic inhibitions. He typically urges the social curbing and channeling of the original, natural, free-ranging libido. Given Freud's reputation and actual influence as sexual liberationist, it's startling to find him arguing sometimes for the positive virtues of "shame" and "disgust."[22]

Freud does sharply criticize the excessive, unnecessary repressions that so commonly in "our Western civilization" cause deep psychic pain:

> the choice of an object is restricted to the opposite sex, and most extra-genital satisfactions are forbidden as perversions. The requirement . . . that there shall be a single kind of sexual life for everyone, dis-

regards the dissimilarities, whether innate or acquired, in the sexual constitution of human beings;
it cuts off a fair number of them from sexual enjoyment, and so becomes the source of serious in-
justice. . . . heterosexual genital love, which has
remained exempt from outlawry is itself restricted by
further limitations, in the shape of insistence upon
legitimacy [legal marriage] and monogamy. Present-
day civilization makes it plain . . . that it does not like
sexuality as a source of pleasure in its own right and
is only prepared to tolerate it because there is so far
no substitute for it as a means of propagating the human race.[23]

Freud cautions only against those extreme repressions and
twisted sublimations that cause profound, distressing conflict.[24]

He speaks in favor of exchanging unconscious repression
for a conscious overseer: conscience. Psychoanalysis, he says at
one point,

replaces the process of repression, which is an auto-
matic and excessive one, by a temperate and pur-
poseful control on the part of the highest agencies
of the mind.[25]

Freud's endorsement of the pleasure principle is tempered by
his approval of an ethic of conformity to society's dominant
norms. This is vividly illustrated in his counseling of Dora.

PRIVATE PLEASURES, PUBLIC SILENCE

The centrality of the eroticism of men and women with each
other was assumed by Freud and most other medical model-
ers of heterosexuality. Freud was by no means alone as advocate of the heteroerotic. But in speaking publicly in defense
of men's and women's satisfying sexual relationships he saw

himself as battling the upholders of a traditional silence. At the dawn of the heterosexual epoch, Freud and the other promoters of a new, public heterosex talk were vehemently condemned by the advocates of a proper reticence. It wasn't only homosex talk that was censored. Freud's famous "talking cure," and his publications and teaching, were designed to break a general genteel hush.

In Dora's world, neither the heteroerotic nor homoerotic were often publicly discussed. Dora's troubles arose, in part, from her inability to talk about all those eroticisms swirling confusingly in the air around her. Only in Dora's therapy with Freud—and in Freud's medical report on Dora—does eros begin to be openly, even enthusiastically, discussed. Freud, with Dora's and his other clients' assistance, helped to create one of the first semipublic scientific forums (the psychoanalytic session), and one of the earliest semipublic and respectable literary genres (the psychoanalytic report), in which sex talk was insistently demanded.

The active resistance to public heterosex talk is well-documented in Freud's history of Dora. When this young woman did begin to speak out, accusing her father of an affair with Frau K, and charging Herr K with attempted seduction, Dora's father and Herr K together accused her of lying. She is "handed over" to Freud by her father, who asks the doctor "to bring her to reason"—that is, to shut the damn girl up. Herr K charges Dora with overexcitement due to illicit reading of erotic books and to improper discussions about sex. Aimed at a young woman of the respectable classes, these were serious accusations.

The difficulty of talking openly about sex—even heterosex—is documented in one revealingly confused passage in which Freud analyzes a dream of Dora's. This dream exposes, Freud claims, Dora's fantasy that her father is impotent, and another fantasy about his particular heterosexual activity with Frau K.

Freud asks Dora how, if she imagines that her father is impotent, he could have an affair with Frau K. Dora responds:

"She knew very well . . . that there was more than one way of obtaining sexual gratification." Freud asks Dora if "she referred to the use of organs other than the genitals for the purpose of sexual intercourse, and she replied in the affirmative." Freud tells Dora that she "must be thinking of precisely those parts of the body which in her case were in a state of irritation—her throat and mouth. Dora at first denies oral-genital fantasies, but later, Freud claims, she accepted his interpretation, and that, a "very short time after," Dora's "cough vanished."

Freud tells his readers that young Dora imagined Frau K performing oral sex on Dora's father. The possibility that Dora fantasized her father performing oral sex on Frau K is not considered, and cunnilingus is never explicitly mentioned in any of Freud's published works (women's sexual pleasure is subordinate to men's).

Freud had started by asking Dora what kind of sexual satisfaction her supposedly impotent father could provide Frau K. Freud ends by discussing the kind of sex *he fantasizes* Frau K provides Dora's father.

His sex talk will cause "the medical reader . . . feelings of astonishment and horror," Freud nervously anticipates. Penises in mouths was strong stuff. The idea that an "inexperienced girl could know about practices of such a kind and could occupy her imagination with them" may arouse "horror" in his readers, Freud reiterates.[26] Defending himself, Freud argues that his sex talk with Dora only translates "into conscious ideas what was already known in the unconscious."[27] The treatment of hysteria, in particular, says Freud, absolutely requires that sexuality be spoken of.

Freud admonishes his fellow physicians: We "must learn to speak without indignation of what we call the sexual perversions."[28] The difficulty of speaking without indignation is illustrated by Freud's own reference to "this excessively repulsive and perverted phantasy of sucking at a penis."[29] The therapeutic necessity of speaking about a problematic sexual "perversion" served Freud as rationale for beginning to publicly speak about a new, "normal" male-female eroticism.

FREUD ON HETEROSEXUALITY

But what does Freud say explicitly about heterosexuality? And why does this matter? Why focus on Freud's use of the term *heterosexual* when his deployment of the idea and ideal would seem to be more important?

Freud's explicit comments on heterosexuality provide one material clue to the history of heterosexual discourse. And that history provides an insight into the normalizing of different-sex eroticism apart from reproduction.

The first published use of "heterosexual" by Freud appears in 1905, in his *Three Essays on the Theory of Sexuality.* Speaking of the causes of sexual "deviations," Freud mentions that the "dangers of heterosexual intercourse" (VD, apparently) may result in a "fixation" of "homosexuality."[30]

Freud employs "heterosexual" here and elsewhere without explanation, suggesting that the term was already in fairly common use among doctors.[31] The great rapidity with which that word was integrated into doctor discourse suggests that the term *heterosexual* signaled an idea and ideal whose time had come—a norm that medical men were eager to adopt.

The initial appearance of "heterosexual" in a discussion of homosexuality is a typical practice of Freud's that later becomes typical of others. Heterosexuals, it turns out, most often owe the explicit, public mention of their existence to talk of homosexuals. Though the heterosexual category came to signify the dominant standard, it remained oddly dependent on the subordinate homosexual category. Heterosexual and homosexual appeared in public as Siamese twins, the first good, the second bad, bound together for life in unalterable, antagonistic symbiosis.

In Freud's discussion, homosexual functions as scare term, heterosexual is what one's scared away from. Homosexuality may result from the "dangers of heterosexual intercourse." In the twentieth century the threat of homosexuality was often used by sex liberals as argument for sex education and greater heterosexual freedom.[32]

Freud uses *heterosexual* to refer to an emotion, a variety of erotic "drive," "instinct," or "desire," and a kind of "love." Freud's *heterosexual* also refers to a kind of activity and a type of person.

Those uses tend to make feeling, not act, define the heterosexual. This contrasts with the earlier reproductive model which had focused on *acts*. In Freud's modern usage, hetero *feeling* defines hetero *being*, whether or not one *acts* heterosexually. Freud furthered the making of a heterosexual identity. This doctor also helped to constitute our belief in the existence of a unitary, monolithic thing with a life and determining power of its own: "heterosexuality."[33]

Freud's explicit uses of the word *heterosexual* helped to constitute a different-sex eroticism as modern society's influential, dominant norm.

Though his uses of the word *heterosexual* are revealing, they are limited, surprisingly, in frequency. The *Concordance* to the twenty-four volumes of Freud's complete writings indicates that he uses "hetero-eroticism," "heterosexual," or "heterosexuality" twenty-nine times. In comparison, he uses some version of "homosexual" 316 times.[34]

How do we explain the relative scarcity of the word *heterosexual* in texts absolutely central to heterosexual definition?

Freud introduced the heterosexual norm quietly, as that which all modern sexual sophisticates presume. Under the spell of this peculiar silence, heterosexuality became the ruling ghost, the absent presence, that haunted this and other modern sex texts. For most of the hundred-plus years of the historically specific heterosexual norm, a verbal taboo banned most explicit talk about heterosexuality, making it another of the loves that dared not speak its name.

The taboo on heterosex talk retarded the development of a questioning discourse on heterosexuality. For it's difficult to critically analyze heterosexual discourse without using the word. To openly name heterosexuality, and to speak explicitly and at length about it, removes it from the realm of the taken-for-granted, subjecting it to the dangers of analysis—and the possibility of critique. A different-sex erotic ideal was slipped silently into modern consciousness, constructed as the dominant term of the dominant sexual ideology, the norm we all know without ever thinking much about it.

If the quantity of Freud's references is an accurate guide, homosexuality would seem to be much more interesting to him than heterosexuality.[35] Those disparate references *are* an accurate index of Freud's problematizing of the homosexual and assumption of the heterosexual. That assumption constructs heterosexuality as unproblematic. At the same time, "the problem of homosexuality" was an explicit phrase of Freud's and, later, a cliché of Freud's popularizers.[36]

Freud's implicit work as heterosexuality promoter, and the distorting effect of such privileging, is clear in his analysis of Dora's reaction to Herr K's first heterosexual advance. On this occasion, Herr K had arranged with his wife and the then thirteen-year-old Dora to visit his office—ironically, to view a religious procession. He'd then persuaded Frau K to stay home, sent away his clerks, and, Freud tells us, "was alone when the girl arrived." Having carefully premeditated his move, Herr K pulled down the outside shutters on the windows, and "suddenly clasped the girl to him and pressed a kiss upon her lips." Dora experienced "a violent feeling of disgust, tore herself free from the man, and hurried past him . . . to the street door."[37]

Telling Freud of this event five years afterward, Dora says she can "still feel upon the upper part of her body the pressure of Herr K's embrace."[38] After Herr K's kiss, Dora refused to join an expedition on which she was to have accompanied the Ks, and avoided being alone with Herr K. Later, the ambivalent Dora again began to meet Herr K alone for outings. Dora told no one of Herr K's first advance until she recounted it to Freud.

Analyzing Dora's response to that kiss, Freud assures his readers, "This was surely just the situation to call up a distinct feeling of sexual excitement in a girl of fourteen who had never before been approached" (Dora was actually thirteen).[39]

Because Dora did *not* consciously experience heteroerotic arousal, her response was "entirely and completely hysterical," claims Freud. An "occasion for sexual excitement," stresses the doctor, "elicited feelings that were preponderantly or exclusively unpleasurable." Freud emphasizes Dora's failure to feel the "genital sensation which would certainly have been felt by a healthy girl in such circumstances."[40]

Arguing the case for Dora's psychic illness, Freud invents an imaginative scenario to explain her supposedly inappropriate reaction. He speculates that when Herr K kissed Dora she felt his erect penis against her body and this caused her "disgust."

Once, not many years earlier, a woman's lack of erotic response had proved her purity. Now Freud's modern heterosexual presumption made Dora's lack of erotic response a mental illness. Freud has clearly moved far here from the nineteenth-century ideal of woman as "angel in the house."

Freud's presumption of female heterosexual response endorses female erotic desire in general only to discredit a particular young girl's actual response. He ignores the specifics of the emotionally complex and frightening situation confronting an inexperienced young girl alone with an older man.

Freud's bias in favor of heterosexual response also distorts his analysis of Dora's second encounter with Herr K. Two years after his initial advance, the fifteen-year-old Dora was visiting the Ks at their summer home. Dora recalls that the young governess of the Ks' children "behaved in the most extraordinary way to Herr K," never speaking to him, and treating him "like thin air."[41]

One day this young governess took Dora aside and told her that "Herr K had made advances to her at a time when his wife was away." Herr K had "implored her to yield to his entreaties, saying that he got nothing from his wife." The governess told Dora that she had " 'given way' " to her employer, " 'but after a while he had ceased to care for her, and since then she hated him.' " The young governess's "respectable" German parents, informed by their daughter of the situation, had ordered her immediately to leave Herr K's employ. When she failed to do so, hoping for a revival of Herr K's interest, her parents told her " 'never to come home again.' "[42]

Just a day or two after Dora heard this dramatic story, Herr K made his second overt move, beginning by telling Dora, " 'You know I get nothing out of my wife.' " As soon as those words were out of Herr K's mouth, Dora "slapped him in the face and hurried away."[43] Herr K begged Dora "not to mention the incident."[44]

This time, however, Dora told her mother that Herr K had had "the audacity to make her a proposal," and Dora's mother obligingly told her husband. On "the next occasion" that Dora's father met Herr K that gentleman was "called to account."

Herr K denied "in the most emphatic terms" having "made any advances," and then "proceeded to throw suspicion upon the girl." He had heard from Frau K that Dora had read books about sex while visiting at their house. Such reading had "over-excited" her and she "had merely 'fancied' " his advance.[45]

Freud presents Herr K in the best possible light. Referring to his second advance, Freud assures readers that Herr K "had not regarded his proposal to Dora as a mere frivolous attempt at seduction."[46] This is pure conjecture. Freud presents no evidence whatsoever of Herr K's feelings for Dora, or their seriousness. We do, however, know of Herr K's frivolous seduction and subsequent rejection of his children's governess.[47]

Dora's father is also presented by Freud in the best possible light. Freud reports Dora's understanding that she'd been "handed over" by her father to Herr K to further her father's purpose: to get K's assent to the affair with Frau K.

Freud affirms the accuracy of Dora's perception. But he then destructively qualifies his support. Dora "was quite well aware," says Freud, "that she had been guilty of exaggeration in talking like this."[48] Dora's father, explains Freud, had not literally sat down at a bargaining table and offered his daughter to Herr K in exchange for access to Herr K's wife. Freud's point is beside the point, and only serves, once again, to undermine the accuracy of Dora's perception.

Freud seriously suggests to Dora that Frau K's affair with Dora's father "made it certain" that Frau K would agree to divorce Herr K. Dora, Freud tells his client, would then be free to act upon her unconscious fantasy of marrying Herr K. Dora's marriage to Herr K, suggests Freud, is "the only possible solution for all the parties concerned." His scheme was not "impracticable," this matchmaker emphasizes.[49] In light of the particular emotional relationships involved, Freud's scheme strikes me as downright loony.

Freud's narrative of Dora is structured like a mystery story. The mystery, according to Freud, is why Dora responded with such vehement outrage to Herr K's last proposition when, according to the psychoanalyst, most young women would be glad to get such a proposal, and would even be aroused by it. If we don't agree with Freud's premise, that Dora *should* have responded positively to Herr K's advance, there's no mystery to be explained.

Freud's story of Dora ends with the answer to the mystery—the revelation that Dora knew of Herr K's seductive line to his children's governess: "You know I don't get anything from my wife"—the same line he used on Dora. The mystery, according to Freud, is solved: Dora was outraged that Herr K used the same line on her that he used on a mere governess.[50]

But the wife from whom Herr K was getting nothing was the same Frau K to whom Dora had been and was still deeply attached. Herr K's complaint about the wife with whom he wasn't sleeping may well have aroused a mix of deeply conflicting feelings in Dora.[51]

Freud's analysis of Dora's same-sex intimacy with Frau K is deeply distorted by his privileging of the heterosexual and denigrating of the homosexual. In his text, Freud consistently presents the Dora–Frau K intimacy as secondary to Dora's relations with Herr K and her father. Yet Freud himself admits in one footnoted afterthought that young Dora had "lived for years on a footing of the closest intimacy" with Frau K:

> When Dora stayed with the K.'s she used to share a bedroom with Frau K., and the husband used to be quartered elsewhere. She had been the wife's confidant and adviser in all the difficulties of her married life. There was nothing they had not talked about.[52]

Dora had worshiped Frau K, Dora's father told Freud.[53] "Dora talked about Frau K.," says Freud, in terms appropriate to a lover, praising Frau K's " 'adorable white body.' "[54]

Discussing Dora's intimacy with Frau K, Freud refers to the "homosexual current of feeling" found in many adolescent boys and girls: "A romantic and sentimental friendship with one of her schoolfriends," he says, "is the common precursor of a girl's first passion for a man." Dora's homoerotic feeling for Frau K, Freud suggests, is a passing pubescent phase—a stage on the road to heterosexuality.[55] In contrast, Dora's alleged heteroerotic feeling for Herr K is treated by Freud as the real thing.

In two other footnoted afterthoughts, Freud refers to "Dora's deep-rooted homosexual love for Frau K."[56] In yet another footnote, Freud admits that his faulty "technique" in Dora's analysis resulted in his failing to discover and to tell Dora that her "homosexual . . . love for Frau K. was the strongest unconscious current in her mental life."[57] Although Freud admits that he mishandled the "strongest unconscious current" in Dora's emotional life, he nowhere pinpoints the distorting effect of his heterosexual bias.

THE MAKING OF A HETEROSEXUAL

Freud's partiality to heterosexuality informs his theory of erotic development and the focusing of sexual "object choice." Though the outcome of any individual's early development is definitely in doubt, Freud leaves no doubt that the successful outcome is heterosexual. Nonheterosexual outcomes are less than optimal, as abundant references by Freud make clear.

Homosexuals, for example, are typically spoken of as "fixated" at an "immature" stage of development—inferior, because less evolved, less civilized, closer to the natural, roaming, "polymorphous perverse" sexuality of the unsocialized child and primitive savage. Freud's judgmental terms, "fixated" and "immature," conveyed stinging, even devastating, negative verdicts to generations of homosexuals drilled in the master psychoanalyst's master narrative.

Freud's theory of a negative, "fixated" homosexuality implies a positive, ideal, full-blooming heterosexuality. Freud casts his story of the individual's psychosexual development as an ethical journey, with the concepts of fixation and full unfolding, infantilism and maturity, homosexuality and heterosexuality, conveying emphatic judgments about the proper way to end up feeling erotic—that is, heteroerotic. But, as usual, his message is mixed.

On the one hand, Freud suggests that homosexuals, by definition, get stuck at an early phase of development.

On the other hand, he suggests, most heterosexuals are also fixated, though in a different sense. Most heteros, like most homos, are fixated on one particular, exclusive sex.

In a 1905 essay Freud says: "the exclusive interest of the man for the woman is also a problem requiring an explanation, and is not something that is self-evident."[58] (The exclusive interest of women in men is not mentioned.)

In a footnote added to an essay in 1915, Freud points out that "a restriction" of the individual's early childhood "freedom to range equally over male and female objects . . . is the

original basis from which . . . both the normal and the inverted types develop." Freud then reiterates:

> [the] exclusive sexual interest felt by men for women
> is also a problem that needs elucidating and is not a
> self-evident fact based upon an attraction that is ulti-
> mately of a chemical nature.[59]

And in an essay of 1920, on the psychological development of homosexuality in a young woman, Freud says again,
"One must remember that normal sexuality too depends
upon a restriction in the choice of object."[60]

Freud's repeated reminders are necessary to call our attention to a phenomenon repeatedly repressed. That is, that
exclusive homosexuals are not the only ones whose erotic objects are restricted to one sex. Heterosexuals are just as
limited.

His reiterated comments on the need to analyze the cir-
cumscribed character of exclusive heterosexuality is one of his
most subversive and least followed-up suggestions. Freud is
not the only one who failed to analyze the limitations of exclusive heterosexuality. That failure to analyze originates with
a dominant morality requiring heterosexuality (and only
heterosexuality) of the "normal" and "good." That moral ab-
solutism even burdens heterosexuals in a way it doesn't homosexuals: For a single brush with homosexual feeling or activity
implicates heterosexuals in the dread abnormal. In contrast, a
homosexual's brief brush with heterosexuality has a positive
moral connotation.

Freud perceives exclusive heterosexuality to be the socially restricted result of an original, roving sexual instinct.
His normal heterosexuality is by no means natural. It's the
limited social product of a difficult developmental process.

The child, in Freud's theory, moves into heterosexuality
through stages, from polymorphous to exclusive, from nature
to culture, from biological to social, from primitive to civilized, from infantile to mature. In Freud's scheme, maturing

is assigned ethical significance; maturity and immaturity take on deeply value-laden meanings. Heterosexuality is mature and good, homosexuality is immature and bad.[61] The influence of Darwinian evolutionary theory and the idea of progress are prominent in this assignment of values to the developmental process. Though Freud explicitly recognizes the fallacy of attributing human values to value-neutral developments, he's a prime victim of such teleological thinking.[62]

Though heterosexuality is Freud's operative ideal, that ideal, he admits, is hardly ever completely realized. The "normal sexuality of adults emerges from infantile sexuality by a series of developments, combinations, divisions, and suppressions, which are scarcely ever achieved with any ideal perfection."[63]

Heterosexuality, for Freud, is always a compromise formation, like all sexualities. Yet an ideal, fully developed heterosexual is the standard against which the homosexual is always judged and found fixated.

Freud's idea that *heterosexuals are made, not born,* is still one of his most provocative and, potentially, his most subversive theories. Even if we don't agree with the specific ways Freud developed this idea, the basic insight remains a rich starting point for analysis of the heterosexual's historically specific making.

Freud suggests that the child, starting off originally with a desire for pleasure unlinked to any particular sex or object, goes through a largely unconscious process of erotic object selection and sexual identification. In this process, its response to those caring for it, and their response to it, determines this archetypal child's later interest in particular pleasure-satisfying objects and sexes.

In the genesis of eroticism according to Freud, the evolving love life of the originally polymorphous child focuses on the satisfactions derived from its own body, on the oral enjoyments associated with mother, mouth, and breast, the charms of the anus, and, later, on the delights linked with father and phallus—a journey, usually, from oral to anal to genital, through the autoerotic, to the heterosexual or homosexual.

Freud does also speak occasionally of a same-sex or different-sex object as the original "bisexual" focus of a child's desire. But that idea of a given bisexual object contradicts his dominant theory of an originally uncommitted, polymorphous eros.

In its simplest, schematic version, Freud tells the story of mother and father, boy and girl, the generic characters in an archetypal family sex play, a melodrama located in a "civilization" requiring the "repression" of essential "sexual instincts"—or their "sublimation" into pleasure-producing and productive (though not necessarily procreative) ends.

Freud's narrative of young boy's progress stresses this paradigmatic male's first and forever sex-love for mother and the other sex. Freud emphasizes boy's identification with father and the same sex, and boy's competition to the death with father and the same sex for the exclusive possession of mother's erotic love. (Freud assumes an economy of sex-love ruled by scarcity and exclusive private property in parent figures.) In boy's titanic fight with father for mother, boy guiltily fears for his penis. (Actual, explicit castration threats were routine in Freud's Vienna—in Freud's case study of "Little Hans," for example, even this five-year-old's sophisticated mother threatens her son's "widdler.") [64] Despite his castration consternation, the generic boy conquers his castration fears, identifies with his father, and turns triumphantly to a different-sex erotic object in the person of a not-mother-woman-wife. Boy thereby "resolves" his incestuous sex-love for mother, his killer rivalry with father, and, *if* he's successful in his developmental work, goes on to heterosexuality.

For many years patriarchal Freud assumed the universality of boy's sexual development, describing generic girl's erotic making as paralleling symmetrically the path of generic boy's. Dora and her brother are, for example, each presented as pursuing a primary relationship with the parent of the "other" sex.[65]

Dora's relationship with her mother is also described by Freud in only the most negative and judgmental terms. Mother, diagnosed by Freud (sight unseen) as suffering from a typical "housewife psychosis," cleans constantly, making her family's home a hell in a heartless world. A completely nonempathetic Freud fails to note that Dora knows that her mother has been infected by her husband with a venereal disease (gonorrhea, which Dora seems to have mistaken for syphilis).[66] Both diseases were serious illnesses, and a serious violation of female purity, a major attribute of respectable womanhood.

Freud himself also admits paying little heed to Dora's intense same-sex feelings for Frau K. Women's intimacies with women are far less important to the male- and hetero-centered Freud than men and women's relations.

Not until about twenty years after analyzing Dora, and quite late in his theorizing, did Freud stop to consider carefully girl's development and to notice a startling implication of his own theory.[67] The plot of his sexual origins story stresses the determining power of the child's first love. Firsts, according to Freud, play an influential role. The making of the female heterosexual does not therefore simply replicate the manufacture of the hetero male. Girl's first intimate attachment is for *mother and the same sex*. The initial sex-love of the future female heterosexual is *homosexual*.

Girl's successful arrival at heterosexuality therefore requires, says Freud, two additional difficult "tasks" not necessary for boy.[68] (It's never exactly clear who assigns the "tasks" about which Freud often speaks—tasks assuming a hetero imperative.)

According to Freud, girl, realizing mother's castrated, inferior state, is deeply offended, angrily rejects her original homosexual love for mother, and develops a heteroerotic love for her proud-penis-possessing father. Girl then competes with mother for father, then resolves this rivalry by finding in a husband her own heteroerotic man-who-isn't-father.

Girl's move from her original homosexual mother-love to

a heterosexual father-love also includes, claims Freud, her re-
pudiation of her early employment and enjoyment of her
"active," "masculine" clitoris. (The attribution of gendered
personality traits to the private parts is a myth-making for
which Freud was later repeatedly criticized by feminists.)[69]

The future female heterosexual, says Freud, must subli-
mate her original wish for a penis and her envy of its proud
possessors, and adopt her "feminine," "passive" vagina as the
single proper site of erotic pleasure. (The "penetration" of a
"passive" vagina by an "active" penis remains Freud's normative sex act, a holdout from the old reproductive ethic.)

Freud's concept of clitoris as "masculine" and "active"
and vagina as "feminine" and "passive" assigns these parts an
innate, universal meaning. According to Freud's clitoral, vaginal, and penile determinism, these body parts possess an essential character, deriving, allegedly, from their physiological
structure and function—thus his now infamous "anatomy is
destiny."[70] According to this theory, girl's lack of penis automatically generates a realization of her castration and her subsequent "penis envy," just as boy's proud penis possession
mechanically generates a basic fear of losing his essential signifier. In Freud's theory, the wish-producing, fear-generating
power of these body parts lies within them, *not* with their stra-
tegic position within a historically specific, male-dominant,
phallus-favoring social organization of powers, bodies, and
symbols.

Freud presents the successful achievement of normal heterosexuality as the result of a titanic, deeply problematic, utterly ordinary nuclear-family war. According to Freud, the
normal road to heterosexual normality is paved with the incestuous lust of boy and girl for the parent of the other sex,
with boy's and girl's desire to murder their same-sex parent-
rival, and their wish to exterminate any little sibling-rivals.
The road to heterosexuality is paved with blood-lusts. The archetypal family sex play presented by Freud is high melodrama, a hotbed of blazing loves and boiling hates. The
traditional family, as painted by Freud, is not a pretty picture.

The invention of the heterosexual, in Freud's vision, is a deeply disturbed production.

Freud's analysis of Dora stresses "at what an early age sexual attraction makes itself felt between parents and children," and he goes on to explain: the "legend of Oedipus is probably to be regarded as a poetical rendering of what is typical in these relations."[71] Freud later became absolutely sure that the typical child in the typical family typically suffers the fate of poor old Oedipus, the boy destined, according to ancient Greek myth, to kill his father, marry his mother and, as punishment, gouge out his own eyes. Freud says that every single child, following Oedipus's bad example, falls in love with his or her different-sex parent, and wishes to kill his or her same-sex rival.[72]

Why this particular Greek myth should apply universally to every developing individual is not specified, and reference to Freud's alleged "Oedipus complex" has become, perhaps, the most common thought-stopping psycho-jargon of the late twentieth century. Yet the power of the heterosexual regime is such that we usually overlook the disturbing paradox at the troubled heart of Freud's Oedipal theory of heterosexuality. His Oedipus story provides heterosexuality with the most deeply disturbed of origins. That this particular Greek *tragedy* should become the accepted Freudian paradigm for the normal, superior heterosexual is one more grand irony of heterosexual history.

Freud does claim that only the "successful" resolution of the child's "Oedipus complex" allows the adult to move on to normal heterosexuality.[73] The successful working through of baby's early passionate loves and murderous hates evidently cancels any residual fallout left after junior's active participation in the nuclear family war. Only the homosexual remains forever fixated in an uncompleted Oedipal drama.

According to Freud, homosexual preference is founded on fixation. But heterosexual and homosexual preferences are both founded on profound trauma. Given the troubled origins of each, Freud provides no convincing reason why heterosexuals should be able to resolve their early troubles, and homosexuals should remain fixed forever in arrested development. Freud presents no plausible rationale for considering heterosexuality the preferable preference.

It's easy to mock the fabrication of Freud-facts, among them the rigid, schematic outline of the master's Oedipal explanation of heterosexual development, and its grandiose, universal claims. But Freud does usefully draw our attention to the particular ways that active, desiring children early relate to significant others, developing specific patterns of erotic response. He usefully points us to our influential, unconscious patterns of response that start in earliest childhood and that often reappear in various guises, constructing us as sexed and sexual.

Though Freud simply assumes that heterosexuality is the optimal development, he also theorizes an open-ended developmental process in which the heterosexual is contingent, not inevitable. At the end of the twentieth century, Freud's ambiguous modern legacy deeply influences our understanding of heterosexuality. His theories still provide subversive incitements to analyses of the role that specific, time-bound social systems play in the making of heterosexuals and homosexuals.

In Freud's diagnosis of Dora's "hysteria" and her "failure" of positive response to Herr K (an older man), Freud, as we've seen, privileges heterosexual response. Freud (another older man) fails to note his own hostility to young Dora, his own heterosexual attraction, and that attraction's effect on Dora's analysis. Freud was only then realizing the importance of psychoanalysts' analyzing their own emotional response to clients.[74]

Perhaps the strongest (and strangest) clue to the invasive character of Freud's hostile heterosexual response to Dora is his imagining himself as her "gynaecologist." That revealing metaphor appears in Dora's case history, in Freud's opening warning to readers that in his report on Dora, "sexual questions will be discussed with all possible frankness." Freud will

be revealed discussing sex openly "even with a young
woman." Must he "defend" this sex talk? asks the defensive
Freud. If so, "I will simply claim for myself the rights of
the gynaecologist"—the rights, he means, of full, frank
examination.[75]

Thirty-nine pages later, Freud is still defending his explicit sex talk with "girls and women"—and the repressed returns again in Freud's second, even more revealing
analogizing of himself to a "gynaecologist [who] . . . does not
hesitate to make them [his female clients] submit to uncovering every possible part of their body."[76] The male doctor
who *makes girls and women submit* is the perfect metaphor for
Freud's relationship to Dora.[77]

It's no wonder that Dora abruptly quit analysis with
Freud after only three months. But even with Freud's hostile
bumbling, his talking cure encouraged this young woman to
go and confront the Ks. She even had the satisfaction of
hearing the Ks finally admit that she had not fantasized their
sexual exploits—Herr K with Dora, Frau K with Dora's father.

Dora returned to see Freud a year after her initial analysis, this time on her own volition, asking for the doctor's further help. Freud, however, now acted like a jilted suitor,
spitefully refusing Dora his services, and sending her back
into the world with her tormenting psychosomatic symptoms
and psychic conflicts intact. A recent biography of Dora/Ida
indicates that she lived the rest of her deeply unhappy life
dedicated to illness—including the dubious distinction of being the sad, neurotic subject of one of Freud's famous case
histories.[78]

The harm that Freud's heterosexual assumption did to
Dora in 1900 is but one small sample of the damage the dominion of the heterosexual ideal would do throughout the
century.

THE INCANTATION OF THE NORMAL

Throughout his essays Freud proclaims the "normal" sexual intercourse of "normal" men and "normal" women as the "normal" object, the "normal" aim, and the "normal" end of these "normal" individuals' "normal" sexual development. Though the word *heterosexual* is not much employed by Freud, the term *normal* is repeated *over and over* in reference to the sex-love of women and men for each other. While rebel Freud often devastatingly questions the idea of normal sexuality, conformist Freud was normal sexuality's prime mover. In this age of science worship, the word "normal" replaced "natural" as the term with which to conjure up a new heterosexual ethic.

Freud comes right out and says that he's interested in "abnormal" sexuality for what it reveals about "normal sexual life"—his admitted primary concern.[79] This makes explicit what I have suggested is implicit in Krafft-Ebing and most other late-nineteenth- and early-twentieth-century medical theorists of perverse sexuality. These psychiatrists' focus on a few powerless perverts is best explained by their primary interest in "normal sexuality." Their special interest is in defining and defending their normal sexuality—heterosexuality.

These medical men's obsession with normal sex had a social origin. The official ideal of middle-class sexual propriety was in a state of flux. The old reproductive ethic had given up the ghost in practice before a new different-sex erotic norm had won the day in theory. Freud and other psychiatrists were anxious, therefore, to establish the conceptual basis for a new distinction between sexual good and sexual evil. These doctors' dilemma was how to publicly rationalize their own private nonreproductive heteropleasure practices.

Freud and other sexologists did so by affirming the difference of heterosexual and homosexual, and the heterosexual's superiority. Their model was heterosexual-supremacist from the day of the term's cooptation. The homosexual served as the doctors' totem of the monstrous abnormal, an assurance of the heterosexual's benign normality. Freud's homosexuals were guilty of fixated arrest at an immature stage of development. Those fixed, nonprocreating, pleasure-seeking homos assured nonprocreating, pleasure-seeking heteros of their difference—and their own mature, fully blossomed, normal sexuality. Throughout the twentieth century Freud and the Freudians remained the most influential hucksters of the heterosexual norm.

In the first years of the twentieth century, with Freud's and other medical men's help, the nineteenth century's tentative, ambiguous heterosexual concept was stabilized, fixed, and widely distributed as the ruling sexual orthodoxy—The Heterosexual Mystique—the idea of an essential, eternal, normal heterosexuality. As the term *heterosexual* moved out of the small world of medical discourse into the big world of the American mass media, the heterosexual idea moved from abnormal to normal, and from normal to normative.

5

THE HETEROSEXUAL COMES OUT

From Doctor Discourse to the Mass Media

In the twentieth century, creatures called heterosexuals emerged from the dark shadows of the nineteenth-century medical world to become common types acknowledged in the bright light of the modern day.

Heterosexuality began this century defensively, as the publicly unsanctioned private practice of the respectable middle class, and as the publicly put-down pleasure-affirming practice of urban working-class youths, southern blacks, and Greenwich Village bohemians. But by the end of the 1920s, heterosexuality had triumphed as dominant, sanctified culture.[1] In the first quarter of the twentieth century the heterosexual came out, a public, self-affirming debut the homosexual would duplicate near the century's end.[2]

The discourse on heterosexuality had a protracted coming out, not completed in American popular culture until the 1920s. Only slowly was heterosexuality established as a stable sign of normal sex. The association of heterosexuality with perversion continued well into the twentieth century.

In 1893, for example, Charles Hughes, a prominent St. Louis physician, assured his fellow doctors that, by medical treatment, the mind and feelings could be "turned back into normal channels, the homo and hetero sexual changed into beings of natural erotic inclination, with normal impulsions."[3]

As treatment for his abnormal heteros and homos Dr. Hughes suggested heroic measures—hypnosis and sometimes surgery. For Hughes, as for Dr. Kiernan in 1892, the heterosexual, as person of mixed procreative and nonprocreative disposition, still stood with the nonprocreative homo in the pantheon of sexual perverts.

Though the new heterosexual/homosexual terminology began to catch on quite quickly, it did not immediately distinguish good and bad. In 1895, an American medical journal published a translation from the French of an article by poet-essayist Marc-André Raffalovich, a Russian Jew who later converted to Catholicism.[4]

Standing morally upon the old procreative code, Raffalovich employs the new heterosexual/homosexual terms to criticize the rising different-sex pleasure ethic. His jaundiced valuation of heterosexuality provides a startling insight into the historical relativity of our own day's victorious heterosexual standard.

If "heterosexuality is not suppressed," he argues, "homosexuality ought to be equally favored." He does *not* plead here for homosexual or heterosexual expression. The "repression of heterosexuality," he stresses ominously, "is one of the problems for the future."[5]

Both eroticisms are suspect: "Sexuality cannot be the goal of existence for superior persons whether homosexual or heterosexual."[6] Sexually active heteros and homos are identical in vice: *"There is no line of demarcation between the heterosexual and the homosexual."*[7]

Finding heterosexuality treated with "indulgence and enthusiasm," the invert's "conscience does not trouble him," he

protests. He endorses troubled consciences and the despica-
bility of sex: "It is only in learning to ... despise or to sur-
mount sexuality and sensuality that the congenital invert can
turn away from homosexuality."[8]

Already, in Raffalovich's day, some homosexuals were
proselytizing for equal rights. Their demand for equality, he
says,

> has as its basis the theory that every man has a right
> to sexual satisfaction. If one grants the right to the
> heterosexual, I do not see how it can be refused to
> the inverts. ... But in my opinion every man has not
> the right to lay claim to the sexual satisfaction of his
> desires.[9]

This writer is determined that homosexuals should *not*
enjoy a sex-love that heterosexuals find it difficult to achieve.
For heteros, he stresses, it's not easy to locate a person who simultaneously satisfies "sex, the soul and society and the family." So, why, he rather spitefully asks,

> should the invert have that which the heterosexual
> finds with so great difficulty? How many heterosexu-
> als are unhappy by reason of their sexual life?[10]

Homosexuals, he suggests, should resign themselves to the
same unhappiness as heterosexuals.

Raffalovich is bucking the moral innovation that placed
eroticism at the core of modern personality, positioning a valued sexuality at the center of modern life. He opposes the
modernization of sex, mirrored in his own terms *heterosexual*
and *homosexual*—categories that helped make erotic satisfaction a central, official value. In his article we observe the first
bloom of the hetero and homo terms before the full flowering
of the pro-heterosexual mystique.

As Raffalovich points out, if nonprocreative heterosexuality is legitimate, it's difficult to understand why a nonprocre-

ative homosexuality should not also be approved. In the 1890s, the antihomosexualists had not yet moved beyond a procreative norm to uphold a nonreproductive heterosexuality. They'd not yet condemned homosexuality for some *other* fundamental failing.

This essay points to the convergence of nonprocreative heterosexuality and nonprocreative homosexuality, judged by a late-nineteenth-century reproductive standard. A similar convergence of heterosexual and homosexual may be noted in the late twentieth century, judged by today's pleasure standard. Now, the decreasing value of procreation, and increasing value of pleasure sex, make heterosexual and homosexual seem ever more similar. This undermines, as we'll see, old rationales for unequal treatment, and, finally, the very basis of the heterosexual/homosexual distinction.

In the first years of the twentieth century *heterosexual* and *homosexual* were still obscure medical terms, not yet standard English. In the first 1901 edition of the "H" volume of the comprehensive *Oxford English Dictionary, heterosexual* and *homosexual* had not yet made it.

Neither had heterosexuality yet attained the status of normal. In 1901, *Dorland's Medical Dictionary,* published in Philadelphia, continued to define "Heterosexuality" as "Abnormal or perverted appetite toward the opposite sex."[11] Dorland's heterosexuality, a new "appetite," was clearly identified with an "opposite sex" hunger. But that craving was still aberrant. Dorland's calling heterosexuality "abnormal or perverted" is, according to the *Oxford English Dictionary*'s first *Supplement* (1933), a "misapplied" definition.[12] But contrary to the *OED*, Dorland's is a perfectly legitimate understanding of heterosexuality according to a procreative norm.

The twentieth century witnessed the decreasing legitimacy of that procreative imperative, and the increasing public acceptance of a new hetero pleasure principle. Gradually, heterosexuality came to refer to a normal other-sex sensuality free of any essential tie to procreation. But only in the mid-1960s would heteroeroticism be distinguished completely from reproduction, and male-female pleasure sex justified for itself.

Because early-nineteenth-century true love had not been lust-linked, late-nineteenth- and early-twentieth-century reformers of eros and affection began to refer to a new "sex-love." (The hyphen often used in sex-love visually registered the new horizontal linking of sex and love in close, mutual embrace.) The coinage of *sex-love* was designed to distinguish the increasingly prevalent, publicly lauded middle-class hetero-erotic amour from that class's old, spiritual true love. With the inauguration of *sex-love,* the erotic attraction of men and women was now supposed to lead to love which led to marriage which led to sexual relations—which might, or might not, lead to reproduction.

In many of its early popular versions, the twentieth-century heterosexual imperative continued to associate different-sex eroticism with a supposed human "need," "drive," or "instinct" for propagation. This procreant urge was now linked inexorably with carnal lust—as it had not been earlier. Nineteenth-century women's desire for motherhood, for example, was not linked to eroticism. But early in the twentieth century the middle class's falling birth rate, rising divorce rate, and "war of the sexes" were matters of increasing public concern. Giving vent to heteroerotic emotions was thus praised as enhancing reproductive capacity, marital intimacy and family stability.

One influential advance man for the new heterosexuality was, as we've seen, Dr. Sigmund Freud, who traveled to Worcester, Massachusetts, and spoke about "sex-love" and the "sexual pleasure" of the sexes in 1909, and whose major essay, *Three Contributions to the Sexual Theory,* was first published in New York in English translation in 1910.[13] In the twentieth century, in the name of Freud and popular psychology, heterosexuality was proclaimed throughout the land of the free as, simply, perfection.

Another early, influential hetero-mystique maker was Havelock Ellis, whose multi-volume *Studies in the Psychology of*

Sex began to be published in Philadelphia in 1900.[14] Though trained in medicine, Ellis never actively practiced that profession, but used his doctor title to authorize his speaking publicly and approvingly of the "sexual love" of men and women.

In Ellis's 1910 volume, *Sex in Relation to Society,* he defends that "normal sexual love" against Christianity which, he says, has so "poisoned the springs of feeling" that "all our words of sex" are "bespattered with filth." We therefore "have no simple, precise, natural word for the love of the sexes."[15]

But by 1915, in that year's U.S. edition of Ellis's volume on *Sexual Inversion,* he is using "heterosexual" in the modern mode as a simple, precise, natural word for the sex-love of the sexes.[16]

In conscious opposition to Freud's originally uncommitted libido, Ellis claims that a different-sex and same-sex erotic are usually inborn, an aspect of the biologically determined mechanics of "tumescence" and "detumescence," his terms for the ups and downs of erotic feeling.[17] Ellis nervously rejects the idea that the species depends for its tumescence and, ultimately, its reproduction, on the open-ended intrafamily war and fallible developmental process proposed by Freud.

Despite Ellis and Freud's argument over the physiological versus familial origins of heterosexuality, both men were major publicists of the new different-sex erotic norm among a "progressive" public. By the twentieth century's end, however, Ellis's rather superficial sex modernism was forgotten, while Freud's depth probes of the middle-class family melodrama continue to provide an influential source of psychological analysis and contentious social debate.

The first part of the new sex norm—hetero—posited a basic sex divergence. The "oppositeness" of the sexes was alleged to be the basis for a universal, normal erotic attraction between males and females. That stress on the sexes' oppositeness, harking back to the early nineteenth century, by no means simply registered biological characteristics and functions unique to females and males, or socially determined gender distinctions unique to women and men. The early-twentieth-century focus on physiological and gender dimorphism reflected the deep anxieties of men about the shifting work, social roles, and power of men over women, and the changing ideals of womanhood and manhood.

In 1895, for example, Dr. James Weir, Jr., wrote in *The American Naturalist* on "The Effect of Female Suffrage on Posterity," warning that if women got the vote, they'd change physically and psychically and pass along pathologies to their children. This would cause "a social revolution, in which the present form of government will be overthrown and matriarchy established." Women, he declared, "have already too much liberty." He reiterated: "I see in the establishment of equal rights, the first step toward the abyss of immoral horrors so repugnant to our cultivated ethical tastes." Weir warned that "female psycho-sexual aberrants" increased when women stopped being housewives and mothers.[18]

In 1897, *The New York Times* published the Reverend Charles Parkhurst's diatribe against "andromania," a "disease" of women causing a "passionate aping" of "everything mannish." Women who tried to "minimize distinctions by which manhood and womanhood are differentiated" he designated "andromaniacs."[19]

In 1913 *The New York Times* review of *The Nature of Woman*, a book by biologist J. Lionel Taylor, praised it as a "careful scientific study" which argued that "the campaign for woman suffrage" was "an effort of certain women . . . to give woman a status that would fit . . . their conception of her as nothing more or less than a 'female man.'"[20]

Later in 1913 *The Times* reviewed a book by scientist Walter Heape which argued that "the present woman's movement has its origins in sex antagonism" and the desire to "alter the laws which regulate the relations and therefore the relative powers of the sexes." If power was granted to women it would fall into the hands of the "dissatisfied and we may assume unsatisfied class of women" called "spinsters."[21]

These men's anxiety about gender difference was a conservative response to the changing social-sexual division of activity and feeling which gave rise to the independent "new woman" of the 1880s and heteroeroticized "flapper" of the 1920s, archetype of the new pleasure woman, mate of the new pleasure man.[22]

The second part of the new hetero norm referred positively to "sexuality." That novel upbeat focus on the hedonistic possibilities of male-female bodily conjunctions also reflected a social transformation—a revaluing of pleasure and procreation, consumption and work in commercial, capitalist society. Numbers of historians have analyzed the fall of independent farm and crafts work, and the old work ethic, the rise of wage-work, "consumerism," and a new pleasure ethic.[23]

The democratic attribution of a normal lust to females (as well as to males) served to newly authorize women's enjoyment of their own bodies, a sex-affirmative action still part of women's struggle (as feminist sex radicals stress). The twentieth-century ideal of the heteroerotic woman also finally undermined the nineteenth-century ideal of the pure true woman. The new heterosexual woman also undercut nineteenth-century feminists' assertion of women's moral superiority, and cast suspicions of carnal lust on women's passionate romantic friendships with other women.

The newly heterosexualized woman made possible her opposite, a menacing female monster, "the lesbian."[24] In the perspective of heterosexual history, the early-twentieth-century emergence of the lesbian in popular culture derives from the interest in defining the lesbian's contrary—the new female heterosexual.

Between 1877 and 1920 Americans were embarked on *The Search for Order,* documented in historian Robert H. Wiebe's book of that title. Though Wiebe doesn't mention it, this hunt for regularity gave rise in the arena of sex to the new, standard model heterosexuality. This paralleled early-twentieth-century moves to standardize railroad track widths, time zones, business and manufacturing procedures (discussed by Wiebe), as well as to test and regularize intelligence and femininity and masculinity.[25]

A bit of striking evidence from across the Atlan gests that by the second decade of the twentieth cent..., ... terms *heterosexual* and *homosexual* were slowly making their way into England's standard discourse. Around 1918, J. R. Ackerley, an intelligent young Englishman in his early twenties, the son of a banana importer, "met in Switzerland a mocking and amusing fellow," Arnold Lund, with "a rasping demonic laugh" that made him "the vitality and the terror of the community."[26] Ackerley reports:

> Almost the first mischievous question he shot at me was "Are you homo or hetero?" I had never heard either term before; they were explained and there seemed only one answer. . . .

Ackerley identified as "homo." He had already privately acknowledged to himself his attraction to men. But it had not occurred to him to name himself after that attraction. The public language of heterosexual or homosexual, first communicated by his sexually "advanced" hetero friend, gave Ackerley a name for his previously private, uncategorized lust. Lund's question also gave Ackerley a name for an identity based on his desire.

At the time of his defining encounter with Lund, says Ackerley, apart from schoolboy fumblings, he had "had no physical contact with anyone, not even a kiss, and remained in this virginal state" until Cambridge, where his chastity was cured. Lund's question, "homo or hetero?" introduced Ackerley to the twentieth-century necessity of being either/or—or a "bisexual" combination.

Ackerley adds: "Lund lent or recommended me books to read, Otto Weininger, Edward Carpenter, Plutarch, and thus and with his malicious, debunking thought opened my mind." In encounters like this, heteros and homos entered twentieth-century consciousness, culture, and conversation.

In the U.S. throughout the 1920s a mixed bag of novelists, playwrights, sex educators, publishers, and theatrical producers struggled to establish the legal right to discuss and distribute a new commodity, the explicit (for its time) hetero- sexual drama, novel, and advice book. The writers included novelists like James Branch Cabell, Theodore Dreiser, F. Scott Fitzgerald, Elinor Glyn, James Joyce, D. H. Lawrence, and sex educators like Mary Ware Dennett.[27]

From the perspective of heterosexual history, this early- twentieth-century struggle for the more explicit depiction of a different-sex eros appears in a curious new light. Ironically, we find sex conservatives, the social-purity advocates of censor- ship and repression, fighting against the depiction not just of sexual perversity, but also of the new normal heterosexuality. That a more open depiction of normal sex had to be de- fended against forces of propriety confirms that hetero- sexuality's predecessor, nineteenth-century true love, had sanctioned love and reproduction but not a public, official, different-sex eros.

In 1923, "heterosexuality" made its debut in Merriam- Webster's authoritative *New International Dictionary*. "Homo- sexuality" had, surprisingly, made its debut fourteen years earlier, in 1909, defined as a medical term meaning "morbid sexual passion for one of the same sex." The advertising of a diseased homosexuality preceded the publicizing of a sick het- erosexuality. For in 1923 *Webster*'s defined "heterosexuality" as a "Med." term meaning "morbid sexual passion for one of the opposite sex." Only in 1934 does "heterosexuality" first appear in *Webster*'s hefty *Second Edition Unabridged* defined in what is still the dominant modern mode. There, heterosexu- ality is finally a "manifestation of sexual passion for one of the opposite sex; normal sexuality." Heterosexuality had finally at- tained the status of norm.

In the same 1934 *Webster's*, "homosexuality" had changed as well. It's simply "eroticism for one of the same sex."[28] Both terms' medical origins are no longer cited. Heterosexuality and homosexuality had settled into standard American.

In 1924, in *The New York Times*, heterosexuality first be- came a love that dared to speak its name. On September 7 of

that year the word "hetero-sexual" made its first known appearance in *The New York Times Book Review*, significantly, in a
comment on Sigmund Freud. There, in a long, turgid review
of Freud's *Group Psychology and the Analysis of the Ego*, one Mary
Keyt Isham spoke of "repressed hetero-sexuality" and "heterosexual love."[29]

Digging Isham's point out of her convoluted prose, it
seems she's concerned to affirm that even sublimated heterosexuality is good: It serves the "productive."[30] Her review also
links heterosexuality with "maturity"—deconstructing it as
morbidity, constructing it as the proper endpoint of human
development. The Americanization of Freud and of heterosexuality went hand in hand.

But before 1930 in the United States, heterosexuality was
still fighting an uphill battle. As late as 1929, a federal court
in Brooklyn found Mary Ware Dennett, author of a twenty-
one-page sex education pamphlet for young people, guilty of
mailing an obscene essay.[31] Dennett's pamphlet criticized
other sex-education materials for not including a "frank, un-
ashamed declaration that the climax of sex emotion is an un-
surpassed joy, something which rightly belongs to every
normal human being"—*after* they fall in love and marry. If it
seemed "distasteful" that the sex organs were "so near . . . our
'sewerage system,' " Dennett assured America's disgusted
youth that this nasty positioning of parts was probably protec-
tive. ("At any rate, there they are, and our duty is . . . to take
mighty good care of them. . . .") In her pamphlet the word
heterosexual did not appear.

But on April 30, 1930, in *The New York Times Book Review*,
a critic described the subject of André Gide's *The Immoralist*
proceeding "from a heterosexual liaison to a homosexual
one."[32] The ability to slip between these sexual categories was
referred to rather casually as one human possibility. This is
also the first known reference in *The Times* to the hetero/
homo duo. From there on out in the American mass media
the heterosexual was defined by the homo-Alien, the homosexual by the hetero-Other.

The following month, in May, a second reference to the hetero/homo dyad appeared in *The New York Times Book Review,* in a comment on Floyd Dell's *Love in the Machine Age.*[33] This work revealed a prominent antipuritan of the 1930s using the dire threat of homosexuality as his rationale for greater heterosexual freedom—a common ploy of that day's sex liberals.

The Times quotes Dell's warning that current, abnormal social conditions keep the young dependent on their parents, causing "infantilism, prostitution and homosexuality." Also quoted is Dell's attack on the "inculcation of purity" that "breeds distrust of the opposite sex." Young people, Dell says, should be "permitted to develop normally to heterosexual adulthood." "But," *The Times* reviewer emphasizes, "such a state already exists, here and now."

And so it did. Heterosexuality, a new sex and gender- distinguished erotic category, had been distributed from a narrow, rarefied realm of doctor discourse to become a nationally, even internationally cited aspect of middle-class life.

In 1933, the *Oxford English Dictionary* tells us, the colloquial abbreviation "hetero" made one of its earliest published appearances, in Eileen A. Robertson's *Ordinary Families,* a satirical English novel reprinted in the U.S.[34]

Here, Marnie Cottrell is a Cambridge student with a "vocation for medicine," whose adenoid problem "had made her nose so small and her mouth so apt to drop open that no one was likely to want to marry her."[35]

Marnie, who enjoys "gloomy conversation about herself,"[36] declares to Lallie, her female friend: "The odd thing about me is that as a 'pic' [picturesque] type I should be so purely 'hetero' in spite of lack of opportunity."[37] Quote marks around that " 'hetero' " suggest the newness of the colloquialism. But the slang usage suggests that the advanced middle class was now on quite familiar terms with the hetero on both sides of the Atlantic.

Marnie clearly "wanted a love affair," her friend Lallie

concludes, though Lallie is dubious about Marnie's prospects. Marnie's parents had "failed to realize that no amount of the freedom of mind which they had laboriously implanted in Marnie was ever going to help the poor girl to live a normal sex life while the slightest freedom of choice remained for men." (A normal hetero sex life was now something progressive parents "laboriously implanted," even in daughters.)

In a modern world of full of attractive and newly heterosex-seeking women, it's said, "Marnie would find herself more hopelessly handicapped . . . then she would have been in an Early Victorian household, where goodness or money or birth might possibly have offset that loud breathing and porridge-like complexion."[38]

At the expense of poor Marnie, novelist Robertson perfectly catches the historically particular predicament of the "plain" heterosexual woman after the twentieth-century rise and reign of heterosexuality.

By December 1940, when the risqué musical *Pal Joey* opened on Broadway, a tune titled "Zip" satirized the strip-tease artist Gypsy Rose Lee, by way of a character who, unzipping, sang of her dislike for a deep-voiced woman or high-pitched man and proclaimed her heterosexuality. That lyric registered the emergence in popular culture of a heterosexual identity.[39]

By 1941, the glossary of a book about "sex variants" said that "straight" is being employed by homosexuals

> as meaning not homosexual. *To go straight is to cease homosexual practices and to indulge—usually to re-indulge—in heterosexuality.*[40]

The "not homosexual," a new creature, defined by what he or she isn't, had emerged among the cast of erotic characters on the twentieth-century stage. Here, "straight" is a not-necessarily-permanent condition toward which one may venture or not, depending on one's "practices" (feeling is not the issue).[41] Now, the sex variants are doing the defining—categorizing is a game that two preferences can play.

The "cult of domesticity" following World War II—the reassociation of women with the home, motherhood, and child care, men with fatherhood and wage-work outside the home—was an era in which the predominance of the hetero norm went almost unchallenged. In the late 1940s and the 1950s, conservative mental-health professionals reasserted the old link between heterosexuality and procreation.[42] In opposition, sex-liberals strove to expand the heterosexual ideal to include within the boundaries of the normal a wider-than-ever range of gender ideals and nonprocreative, premarital, and extramarital behavior. But that sex-liberal reform actually helped to secure the dominance of the heterosexual idea, as we shall see when we get to Kinsey.

The sex-conservative tendency is illustrated in 1947, in Ferdinand Lundberg and Dr. Marynia Farnham's book, *Modern Woman: The Lost Sex.* Improper masculinity and femininity is exemplified, the authors decree, by "engagement in heterosexual relations . . . with the complete intent to see to it that they do not eventuate in reproduction."[43] This postwar ideology of fecundity gave rise to the era's boom in babies.

The idea of the feminine female and masculine male as prolific breeders was also reflected in the stress, beginning in the late 1940s, on the homosexual as sad symbol of "sterility"—that particular loaded term appears incessantly in the fecund forties and fertile fifties.[44]

In 1948, in *The New York Times Book Review,* sex-liberalism was in ascendancy. Dr. Howard A. Rusk declared that Alfred Kinsey's just published report on *Sexual Behavior in the Human Male* had found "wide variations in sex concepts and behavior." This raised the question: "What is 'normal' and 'abnormal' "? In particular, the report had found that "homosexual experience is much more common than previously thought," and "there is often a mixture of both homo and hetero experience."[45]

Kinsey's counting of orgasms indeed stressed the wide

range of behavior and feeling that fell between the boundaries of a quantitative, statistically accounted heterosexuality and homosexuality. Kinsey's liberal reform of the hetero/homo dualism widened the hetero category to accord better with the actual varieties of sexual experience.[46]

Though Kinsey explicitly questioned "whether the terms 'normal' and 'abnormal' belong in a scientific vocabulary," his counting of climaxes was generally understood to define normal sex as majority sex.[47] That quantified norm constituted an influential, society-wide break with the old qualitatively defined reproductive standard. Though conceived of as purely scientific, Kinsey's statistical focus helped to substitute a new, quantitative moral standard for the old, qualitative sex ethic—another triumph for the spirit of capitalism.

This sex scientist popularized the idea of a "continuum" of activity and feeling between hetero and homo poles:

> Only the human mind invents categories and tries to force facts into separated pigeon-holes. The living world is a continuum.[48]

His recasting of the hetero/homo polarity did suggest that there are degrees of heterosexual and homosexual behavior and emotion. But that famous continuum also emphatically reaffirmed the idea of a sexuality divided between the hetero and homo.

Kinsey's "heterosexual-homosexual rating scale," from zero to six, sounded precise, quantitative, and scientific, fixing the het/homo binary in the public mind with new certainty.[49] His science-dressed, influential sex-liberalism thus upheld the hetero/homo division, giving it new life and legitimacy.

Kinsey also explicitly contested the idea of an absolute either/or antithesis between hetero and homo *persons*. Stressing the variations between exclusive heterosexual and exclusive homosexual behavior and feeling, he denied that human beings "represent two discrete populations, heterosexual and homosexual." The world's population, he ordered, "is not to be divided into sheep and goats." (That revealing Biblical metaphor positions heterosexuals as sheep, coupled with conformity, and homosexuals as goats, linked with licentiousness).

The hetero/homo division of *persons* is not nature's doing, Kinsey stresses, but society's. As sex-liberal reformer, he challenged the social and historical division of *people* into heterosexuals and homosexuals because he saw this person-labeling used to denigrate homosexuals. Motivated by a reformist impulse, he rejected the social reality and profound subjective force of a historically constructed tradition which, since the early twentieth century in the U.S., had cut the sexual population in two—and helped to establish the social and personal reality of a heterosexual and homosexual identity.

The idea of hetero and homo identities—two discrete, essentially different types of people—is a deeply ambiguous political legacy.

On the one hand, the historical establishment of a *heterosexual identity* as universal, presumed, and normative has supported the formation of heterosexual supremacy.

On the other hand, the historical establishment of a *female heterosexual identity* has encouraged twentieth-century women to pursue erotic enjoyments unknown to many of their nineteenth-century foremothers. At the same time, modern women's pursuit of heterosexual happiness has often been degraded by sexism and co-opted by commerce ("You've come a long way, baby!") and made dangerous by men's sexual harassment and violence.

The historical emergence of a specifically *homosexual person* has, especially since 1969, led to the development of a powerful movement publicly and actively affirming a gay and lesbian "identity." Modeled after American movements affirming "racial" and "ethnic" identities, the mass coming out of gay and lesbian persons has freed thousands of women and men from a deep, painful, socially induced sense of inferiority and shame. This movement has helped to bring about a society-wide liberalization of responses to persons identified as homosexual.[50]

At the same time, Kinsey's contesting the notion of homosexual and heterosexual *identities* and *persons* was one early, partial form of resistance to the antihomosexual use of the hetero/homo distinction. Another sex reformer, Gore Vidal, has for years been joyfully proclaiming:

> there is no such thing as a homosexual or a heterosexual person. There are only homo- or heterosexual acts. Most people are a mixture of impulses if not practices, and what anyone does with a willing partner is of no social or cosmic significance.
>
> So why all the fuss? In order for a ruling class to rule, there must be arbitrary prohibitions. Of all prohibitions, sexual taboo is the most useful because sex involves everyone. . . . we have allowed our governors to divide the population into two teams. One team is good, godly, straight; the other is evil, sick, vicious.[51]

But can we not take Vidal's analysis of our "wacky division" one step further? Can we now question, not only the division into hetero and homo persons, but the hetero/homo division itself?

As early as 1949, the twenty-five-year-old James Baldwin was initiating an inquiry into his society's sacred sexual labels. In "Preservation of Innocence," published obscurely in Tangier, Baldwin innovatively warned that the tagging of homosexual persons denied human complexity—not only that of homosexuals but of everyone:[52]

> It is quite impossible to write a worth-while novel about a Jew or a Gentile or a Homosexual, for people refuse, unhappily, to function in so neat and one-dimensional a fashion. If the novelist considers that they are no more complex than their labels, he

must, of necessity, produce a catalogue, in which we will find, neatly listed, all those attributes with which the label is associated. . . .

Though Baldwin doesn't mention it, a worthy novel about a Heterosexual would also seem to be ruled out, for the reasons he discusses:

> A novel insistently demands the presence and passion of human beings, who cannot ever be labeled. Once the novelist has created a human being, he has shattered the label, and in transcending the subject matter, is able, for the first time, to tell us something about it. . . . Without this passion, we may all smother to death, locked in those airless, labeled cells, which isolate us from each other and separate us from ourselves.[53]

The differentiation of homosexual and heterosexual persons, the young Baldwin suggests, is linked inextricably to a system of moralizing judgments about men and women:

> Before we were banished from Eden and the curse was uttered, "I will put enmity between thee and the woman," the homosexual did not exist; nor, properly speaking, did the heterosexual. We were all in a state of nature.[54]

The homo/hetero distinction, Baldwin hints, is not natural but social and value-laden, and tied to a problematic cultural connection of men and women. The "present debasement" of the male homosexual, "and our obsession with him," Baldwin stresses, "corresponds to the debasement of the relationships between the sexes."[55]

The division between man and woman, Baldwin declares, "can only betray a division within the soul of each." The either/or, man/woman distinction is a problem for the psyche. It won't help our souls to declare "that men must recapture their status as men and that women must embrace their function as women." That "rigidity of attitude" puts to death "any possible communion." Anyway, "having once listed the bald physical facts," it's difficult to "decide, of our multiple human attributes, which are masculine and which are feminine."[56]

"The recognition of this complexity"—this ambiguity of the sexes and sexual divisions—"is the signal of maturity, it marks," says Baldwin, "the death of the child and the birth of the man."

But American men yearn, says Baldwin, to preserve their innocence, their dream of "the Rover Boys and their golden ideal of chastity."[57] In men's attempt to deny complexity and remain innocent, he declares, "that mindless monster, the tough guys have been created and perfected." The toughs' "masculinity is found in the most infantile and elemental externals." Their "attitude towards women is the wedding of the most abysmal romanticism and the most implacable distrust.[58]

"Men and women have all but disappeared from our popular culture," says Baldwin, leaving only a

> disturbing series of effigies with a motive power which we are told is sex, but which is actually a dream-like longing, an unfulfillment more wistful than that of the Sleeping Beauty awaiting the life-giving touch of the fated Prince. For the American dream of love insists that Boy gets the Girl. . . .[59]

The American dream of heterosexual bliss denies other, more complex, ambiguous desires, Baldwin suggests. For example, James M. Cain's novel *Serenade* "contains a curious admission on the part of the hero to the effect that there is always somewhere a homosexual who can wear down the resistance of the normal man by knowing which buttons to press."[60] Having pressed too many buttons, this novel's "unattractive invert" is "promptly stabbed to death by the hero's mistress, a lusty and unlikely señorita."[61]

"Thus is that immaculate manliness within us protected," Baldwin says, "thus summarily do we deal with any obstacle to the union of the Boy and the Girl."[62]

He alludes to the formulaic happy ending of popular heterosexual novels (and, we recall, of Krafft-Ebing's successful treatments). These draw the curtain when Boy and Girl "finally come together" in what readers are supposed to imagine is love forever after: "For the instant that Boy and Girl become the Bride and Groom we are forced to leave them; not really supposing that the drama is over or that we have witnessed the fulfillment of two human beings. . . ." It is "not for our eyes," says Baldwin, "to witness the pain and the tempest that will follow." These partners in heterosexuality are unfitted for experience, he argues, for "the boy cannot know a woman since he has never become a man."[63]

The innocent, perfectionist ideal of happy heterosexuality must fail, he says, and the "harvest of this unfulfillment" is masculine violence.

The impossible American dream of perfect loving bliss finds buyers in the same-sex crowd, Baldwin suggests, and with the same violent result. He cites Gore Vidal's novel *The City and the Pillar* in which the "avowed homosexual . . . murders his first and only perfect love when at length they meet again, for he cannot bear to kill instead that desolate and impossible dream of love."

Similarly, in Charles Jackson's *The Fall of Valor,* a

> god-like Marine defends his masculinity with a poker, leaving for dead the frightened professor who wanted him. These violent resolutions . . . are compelled by a panic which is close to madness. Those novels are not concerned with homosexuality but with the ever-present danger of sexual activity between men.[64]

The mad panic of the heterosexually identified male confronted by homosexual desire inspires a brutality common in America, Baldwin warns. It will be a long, "vengeful time," he concludes, before Americans recognize the link between the innocent "Boy Scout who smiles from the subway poster and that underworld to be found all over America"—the complex, subterranean world of erotic ambiguity.[65]

Twenty-two years after this prescient "Preservation of Innocence," Baldwin was still pondering the social and psychological reasons for sexual and racial labeling. In a 1971 discussion, he says:

> People invent categories in order to feel safe. White people invented black people to give white people identity.

He adds:

> Straight cats invent faggots so they can sleep with them without becoming faggots themselves.

But writers, he says, are "forced to look behind the word into the meaning of the word." They're responsible for finding "the way to use that word to liberate the energy in that word, so it has a positive effect on the lives of people."[66]

And in 1984, interviewed in *The Village Voice*, Baldwin again railed against misapprehensions caused by labels:[67]

> The so-called straight person is no safer than I am really. . . . Loving anybody and being loved by anybody is a tremendous danger, a tremendous responsibility. . . . The terrors homosexuals go through in this society would not be so great if society itself did not go through so many terrors it doesn't want to admit.

Baldwin names the great fear that he believes eats at the heart of homosexual-hating society: "Terror of the flesh. After all, we're supposed to mortify the flesh, a doctrine which has led to untold horrors."

One particular body terror is caused by the homosexual feeling of the childish heterosexual man fixated in denial:

> the macho men—truck drivers, cops, football play-
> ers—these people are far more complex than they
> want to realize. That's why I call them infantile. They
> have needs which, for them, are literally inexpress-
> ible. They don't dare look into the mirror. And that
> is why they need faggots. They've created faggots in
> order to act out a sexual fantasy on the body of an-
> other man and not take any responsibility for it . . .
> I think it's very important for the male homosexual
> to recognize that he is a sexual target for other men,
> and that is why he is despised, and why he is called
> a faggot. He is called a faggot because other males
> need him.

The state, the church, and the political right all care about "controlling people," declares Baldwin:

> They care that you should be frightened at what you
> do. As long as you feel guilty about it, the State can
> rule you. It's a way of exerting control over the uni-
> verse, by terrifying people.

Hetero/homo is "an artificial division," Baldwin says: "There's nothing in me that is not in everybody else, and nothing in everybody else which is not in me." We're "trapped in language, of course," he admits. But the complex-ities of human experience—Baldwin's own experience, for example—cast doubt on the language of heterosexual and homosexual, words that divide and try to conquer:

> I loved a few people and they loved me. It had noth-
> ing to do with these labels. Of course, the world had

all kinds of words for us. But that's the world's
problem.

Baldwin's response to the world's sex problem parallels
his response to the world's race problem:

> My own point of view, speaking out of black America,
> when I had to try to answer that stigma, that species
> of social curse, it seemed a great mistake to answer
> in the language of the oppressor. As long as I react
> as a "nigger," as long as I protest my case on evi-
> dence or assumptions held by others, I'm simply re-
> inforcing those assumptions.

Imagining a radically new future sex, Baldwin says:

> No one will have to call themselves gay. Maybe that's
> at the bottom of my impatience with the term. It an-
> swers a false argument, a false accusation. That is,
> that you have no right to be here, that you have to
> prove your right to be here. I'm saying I have noth-
> ing to prove. The world also belongs to me.

In a world in which no one identifies as gay, no one will
identify as straight. That world, Baldwin suggests, divested of
the homosexual/heterosexual division, will belong to all of us.

James Baldwin's category questioning goes back to the
years of his intellectual formation. Then every child was
taught to admire the great American "melting pot." Politically
progressive people worked for the "integration" of America's
"minorities" into a single, universal, human "majority." This
melting was to include the country's persecuted Negroes,
Jews, and (even, on rare occasions) its homosexuals. This as-
similationist ideal encouraged several extremely courageous
writers—Baldwin, Gore Vidal, the poet Robert Duncan, the
novelist Ruth Seid (as Jo Sinclair)—to affirm publicly the hu-

manity of the homosexually inclined, and to urge their integration.[68]

But those daring integrationists often displayed a basic uneasiness about difference—those historical and cultural characteristics of homosexuals which set them apart. In the 1940s progressives advocated assimilation. Only in the late 1960s did black-power advocates declare that African Americans could reclaim their discredited humanity by actively affirming their cultural difference. Gay liberationists and feminists borrowed that black-radical mode of affirmation, and their protest movements have enriched today's politics of difference.

Countering Baldwin's rejection of labels, the modern gay and lesbian liberation movement—reversing the negative uses of the old homosexual category—has encouraged many of us to openly identify ourselves as "gay," "lesbian," "bisexual," or, more recently, by the more inclusive "queer." In the last twenty years many of us have joined together under the flag of the gay and lesbian, the new, positive inversion of the old, negative homo category.

On the one hand, then, gay and lesbian activists have emphatically affirmed the idea of a world divided between homosexual and heterosexual persons. On the other hand, one of the least-expected outgrowths of gay and lesbian organizing has been to foster intellectual work that radically questions the necessity of hetero and homo identities, and even the hetero and homo categories themselves.[69]

Meanwhile, back in 1953, anthropologist Clyde Kluckhohn was reviewing the new Kinsey report on women in *The New York Times Book Review,* and the word *heterosexual* appeared once.[70] Kluckhohn complained that the report did *not* treat the "frequency of rectal heterosexual coitus"—no doubt the first overt mention of hetero sodomy in the decorous Sunday *Times.* This historic sodomitical occasion illustrates how the Kinsey reports and responses to them expanded the discus-

sion of heterosex to include a wider range of variations than
the respectable media had previously admitted.

This era's liberalization of the heterosexual ideal is also
illustrated by the play *Tea and Sympathy,* reviewed in *The Times*
in 1953—the "story of a schoolboy falsely suspected of homosexuality."[71] But the false homo turns out to be a true hetero.
Though our eighteen-year-old hero is sweet, gentle, quiet, shy,
intellectual, guitar-playing, and nonconforming (and has
prettied up his "Spartan" college room with "an Indian bed-
spread and Indian print curtains"), the playwright finally cer-
tifies him as straight. (As usual, it turns out the villain has
homo tendencies.)

More about heterosexuality than homosexuality, the play
decries that era's narrow, loutish genderism, advocating the
expansion of the heterosexual norm to include young men
lacking in the brutish manly virtues. A sensitive young man
could put curtains up and still be heterosexual. But the progressive expansion of heterosexuality to include a wider-than-
ever range of sex-appropriate behaviors and feelings served to
strengthen the dominance of the hetero ideal. The expanded
heterosexual net caught more fish.

In 1963, after the State Liquor Authority revoked the li-
censes of several "homosexual haunts" in New York City, *The
Times* surveyed the "problem of homosexuality" (a "problem"
from an assumed heterosexual viewpoint). Reporting on the
city's increasingly open, organized homosexuals, Robert C.
Doty's story reads like the report of an anthropologist on a
weird tribe of natives:

> There is a homosexual jargon, once intelligible
> only to the initiated, but now part of New York slang.
> The word "gay" has been appropriated as the adjec-
> tive for homosexual.

Homosexuals are stealing "our" language, implies Doty. He
elaborates:

> "Is he gay?" a homosexual might ask another of a mutual acquaintance. They would speak of a "gay bar" or a "gay party" and probably derive secret amusement from innocent employment of the word in its original meaning by "straight"—that is, heterosexual—speakers.[72]

The image of two gay people laughing together secretly over the unknowing language of straights marks the emergence in *The Times* of heterosexuals as a majority newly nervous about the critical gaze of The Homo-Other.[73]

By the late 1960s, anti-establishment counterculturalists, fledgling feminists, and homosexual-rights activists had begun to produce an unprecedented critique—of sexual repression in general, of women's sexual repression in particular, of marriage and the family, of homosexuals' oppression—and of some forms of heterosexuality. This critique even found its way into *The New York Times.*

In March 1968, in the theater section of that paper, freelancer Rosalyn Regelson cited a scene from a satirical revue brought to New York by a San Francisco troupe:

> a heterosexual man wanders inadvertently into a homosexual bar. Before he realizes his mistake, he becomes involved with an aggressive queen who orders a drink for him. Being a broadminded liberal and trying to play it cool until he can back out of the situation gracefully, he asks, "How do you like being a—ah—homosexual?" To which the queen drawls drily, "How do you like being—ah—whatever it is you are?"[74]

Regelson continued:

> The Two Cultures in confrontation. The middle-class liberal, challenged today on many fronts, finds his last remaining fixed value, his heterosexuality, called

into question. The theater . . . recalls the strategies he uses in dealing with this ultimate threat to his world view. . . .

A few weeks later, in March 1968, *Times* critic Clive Barnes reviewed Paddy Chayefsky's new play, *The Latent Heterosexual*.[75] In this, a middle-aged and extremely effeminate writer discovered that "his homosexuality was . . . merely a cover-up for his fears of impotence." The play, said the ever-earnest Barnes, "makes a serious point." He lavishly praised Zero Mostel's acting of the playwright's "fag poet": "It is the humor of the shriekingly heterosexual actor pretending camp, with grotesquely exaggerated mannerisms that are funny simply through their very distance from reality."

In the perspective of heterosexual history, Chayefsky's holding out hope of hetero happiness for even the most unlikely queen is a document of heterosexuality on the defensive. This portrayal of latent heterosexuality triumphing against all odds was nervous propaganda for a norm increasingly challenged by feminists, counterculturalists, and homosexualists.

The new hetero defensiveness was illustrated again six months later in *The New York Times*, in a classic document of heterosexual history. In September 1968, Judy Klemesrud's interview with actor Cliff Gorman, who portrayed "The Definitive Screaming Queen" in *The Boys in the Band*, was headlined "You Don't Have to Be One To Play One."[76] Klemesrud satirically skewered the macho excess of Gorman's nervous assertion of heterosexuality.

Klemesrud began: Gorman's "flitting and floating and fluttering" as Emory, "the pansy interior decorator," was "not exactly the kind of part you'd imagine for a nice Jewish boy from Jamaica, Queens." But Gorman had taken the part, and *Boys in the Band* had become a "smash hit." Gorman had recently signed for television to play a rapist, and, he asked defensively, "What can be more heterosexual than that?"

"With a can of Schlitz in his hand," said Klemesrud, Gorman "rapped" with the reporter

about what everyone's asking him these days: "How can a straight guy like you play a fag in a gay play?"

"It's simple—I needed the money," he says in his very butch real-life voice. "I really don't give a damn what people think. . . . There's no question in my mind of my gender. And there's no question in my wife's mind. . . . I'm buying my own beer now. . . . If I was playing a psychopath that doesn't mean I'm psychopathic. . . ."

His incredibly beautiful wife, Gayle, tiptoes across the room and pours Cliff's beer into a glass. . . .

Cliff is still seething. "People think it's so amazing that a guy can play a homosexual in such a flamboyant way and still be straight. I guess we publicize the point because it's a selling point and makes everybody want to come and see the show. . . ."

Cliff unties his bandanna, flings it on the coffee table and strolls across the room to flip on a recording of the only kind of music that really moves him—country and western. . . . Then he pops open his second Schlitz. "They told me they called a lot of gay actors, but nobody wanted to do Emory. I guess a real homosexual might be too inhibited. . . . I didn't do anything special to prepare for [the part], although the walk took a lot of practice. . . . But I already knew how to lisp because I'd been telling gay jokes since I was a kid. . . ."

After making it as an actor, said Gorman, "I want to have four kids and a stereo and a boat and move to Baja, California, and fish and skin dive and all that wholesome stuff."

Printed with this *Times* interview was a large photograph of Gorman, his arms clasped tightly around his wife, both sad-eyed and clinging, a picture of a heterosexual couple haunted by the specter of homosexuality—a classic image in the historical iconography of heterosexuality.

Near the end of the 1960s, the fear of propagating a pervert haunted the anxious moms and pops who bought Peter and Barbara Wyden's *Growing Up Straight: What Every Thoughtful Parent Should Know About Homosexuality.*[77] In 1968 this how-to-make-a-heterosexual handbook is positive and sunny: "The heterosexual way of life is not only normal and right," but also "productive and fun."[78]

Making a heterosexual means instilling a sure sense of masculinity and femininity, the Wydens tell parents anxious to prevent junior's growing up bent. Gender deviance is the path to erotic aberrancy. Parents should appreciate "that a mother's acceptance of her role as a truly feminine woman will communicate itself to a daughter at a remarkably early age." A "mother's respect for the father's role as head of the family will help a small boy grow up to be masculine." But "if parents are themselves unsure about what constitutes appropriate male and female behavior today . . . their children are bound to become confused about their own place in the scheme of things."[79] Death to sex role confusion!

On the other hand, sixties liberals had recognized belatedly the demise of the old, sure masculinity and femininity: "Several experts deplored the all too rigid division of male and female interests in too many families."[80] Progressive parents "share activities," thereby showing their "children how men and women behave in their own distinctive ways." In "sexually normal homes," say the authors, the basic difference between women and men

> is taught naturally and early. Girls are given dolls to play with. Boys are told, "Boys don't cry." Excessive fussiness in toilet training is avoided.[81]

"Most experts on sexual behavior," say the authority-obsessed Wydens, point out that "heterosexuality is (next to a

sound upbringing) the best weapon against homosexuality."[82]
The battle to the death against homosexuality called for inciting youths to heterosexual activity, perceived as sex-radical advice: "Many people find this is a novel and somewhat
frightening thought." The Kinsey Institute's Dr. Gebhard is
said to tell counselors concerned about young men's "homosexual tendencies":

> "The only way you can prevent it is to encourage
> heterosexuality. You have to fight fire with fire."[83]

This advice, Gebhard recalled, "shocked hell" out of some of
the counselors.[84] This volume, and the psych-help genre it
represents, documents the intellectual blight that withers
minds and still often devastates mass-media discussions of heterosexuality and homosexuality.[85]

The uncritical reiteration of such gender banalities was
interrupted in the 1960s by the mobilization of liberal feminists and, then, by the emergence of radical and lesbian
feminists, and their pathbreaking, critical analyses of heterosexuality.

Between the 1890s and the 1960s the terms *heterosexual*
and *homosexual* moved into American popular culture, constructing in time a sexual solid citizen and a perverted unstable alien, a sensual insider and a lascivious outlaw, a hetero
center and a homo margin, a hetero majority and a homo minority. The new, strict boundaries made the new gendered,
erotic world less polymorphous. The term *heterosexual* manufactured a new sex-differentiated ideal of the erotically correct, a norm that worked to affirm the superiority of men
over women and heterosexuals over homosexuals. Feminists
questioned those gender and pleasure hierarchies.

6

QUESTIONING THE HETEROSEXUAL MYSTIQUE

Some Liberal Feminist and Radical Feminist Verdicts

The movement of modern feminists, it turns out, opened a new era in the history of the heterosexual order, publicly marking it as problematic. A close look at several liberal feminist and radical feminist commentaries from the years 1963 to 1975 reveals that all of them critically probe not only male supremacy, but the social arrangement of heterosexuality.

The early years of American feminism's second wave include Betty Friedan's 1963 publication of *The Feminine Mystique,* analyzed here for its comment on heterosexuality. The 1966 founding by Friedan and others of the National Organization for Women initiated the liberal feminist movement.[1] These feminists, led by Friedan, pointed to white, middle-class, college-educated women's restriction to home, housework, and child-care, and struggled to integrate such women into the wider world of paid labor.[2]

Starting about 1967, radical feminists argued that women

constituted a class socially differentiated and disempowered on the basis of their "sex," analogous to the invidious treatment of African Americans on the basis of their "race." As radical feminists saw it, women's problem wasn't just due to prejudice or misunderstanding and so wasn't solved by reeducating the bigoted or misinformed. Woman trouble was built in socially, a culturally structured inequity.

Many radical feminists came to the women's movement from the 1960s New Left, and their analyses of women's social position stressed the need for substantial changes beyond even the equal pay and labor force integration advocated by liberal feminists. Radical feminists explicitly linked the personal and sexual with power and politics, initiating the first open feminist critique of the social structuring of heterosexuality.[3]

What exactly do these second-wave feminists say about the social ordering of heterosexuality? And what does their analysis contribute to our understanding of heterosexuality as a historically specific system?

In the works examined, Friedan's criticism of "The Sexual Sell" that fashions women into "Sex Seekers" can be seen as implicit censure of the twentieth-century American heterosexualizing of women.[4] Radical feminists began to make such criticism explicit, formulating new concepts for analyzing heterosexuality.[5] They consider sex-love not only as individual and emotional but as preeminently social. Ti-Grace Atkinson names and blames "The Institution of Sexual Intercourse." Kate Millett indicts an inequitable "heterosexual politic" within a more general "sexual politics." Gayle Rubin critically christens "compulsory heterosexuality" and the "sex/gender system." Those new concepts, produced in struggle, are still being explored.

Analysis of women's problematic tie to the social organization of human reproduction plays a major part in these modern feminist critiques of the heterosexual order. The distinction between a biologically determined "sex" and a socially determined and changeable "femininity" and "masculinity" is another central strategy of these feminists' assessments of men's and heterosexuals' dominance.[6] Some stress the negative effect on women of male privilege as manifested in heterosexual relationships.[7] These feminists begin to expose the existence of a reproductive politics, a gender politics, and a pleasure politics, all of which support male and heterosexual supremacy.

The liberal and radical feminist works discussed here (and many of the lesbian-feminist analyses considered in the next chapter) were quite influential in their time among feminists. They remain valuable for the different ways they go about questioning a heterosexual system deeply resistant to examination.

Many other authors could be analyzed in a comprehensive survey of modern feminists' critique of heterosexual society. All the texts discussed derive from a largely white, middle-class political context, and black feminists, third-world feminists, socialist feminists, and psychoanalytic feminists (among others) all offered critiques from their own standpoints. The four writers discussed deserve study for their innovative analyses, and for the ways they began to bring to light the now-you-see-it, now-you-don't heterosexual regime.[8] Though I raise some objections to these analyses, these bold, original, and provocative formulations contributed to a historic break with the entrenched, unthinking presumption of heterosexuality.

FRIEDAN'S *FEMININE MYSTIQUE*

In 1963 Betty Friedan named "The Problem That Has No Name," calling this particular predicament of women "The Feminine Mystique." She thereby coined a phase and titled a book that marked a new era in feminist politics.[9] *The Feminine Mystique* quickly became the best-selling bible of the pioneering equal-employment-opportunity feminists of the National Organization for Women.[10]

The feminine mystique, Friedan explains, is the historically specific norm that defined femininity from the late 1940s through the early 1960s. That ideal decreed that women's proper place is the home, her proper function is procreation, her proper duties are child care and housekeeping, and her proper relation to her husband-provider is support. The antidote to this fatal feminine prescription, she says, is a society in which women are free to do all the work men do and are treated as their equals. Friedan's feminism-as-fairness is designed to win as many friends as possible to the then far-out feminist cause.

In the early 1970s Friedan explicitly attacked the analysis of "sexual politics" offered by radical feminists. She charged that the radicals' stress on women's erotic liberation replicated the sex obsession of women conned by the feminine mystique. So it's surprising how often in *The Feminine Mystique* Friedan herself focuses on the inequitable power politics that order women's and men's heterosexual relations.

Friedan never openly fingers the heterosexual order, however—her carefully worded critique remains tactfully implicit. Her criticism of "sexuality" is therefore often a coded critique of "heterosexuality." The use of "sexual" when "heterosexual" is meant is not a strategy unique to Friedan. It's one of the major conceptual means by which modern critics of women's and men's erotic relations avoid confronting the full, disturbing, heterosexuality-questioning implications of their own reports.

So that you can appreciate Friedan's tactic, try adding "hetero" to her comments on the "sexual" below. This will reveal how often heterosexuality is actually her object of criticism.

Women, says Friedan, put into "their insatiable sexual search the aggressive energies which the feminine mystique forbids them to use for larger human purposes."[11] Women's every problem is blamed on a disordered sexuality: "If a woman feels a sense of personal 'emptiness,' if she is unfulfilled, the cause must be sexual." The solution to every woman's problem, the feminine mystique suggests, is a properly ordered sexuality. But even good sex with men can't compensate for women's dissatisfaction with their limited access to paid work outside the home. Contrary to that mystique, Friedan declares, women can't live by "sex alone."[12]

To compensate middle-class women for their housewife life, she says, the feminine mystique offers women the dream of satisfying erotic relation with men. This theory of compensatory heterosexuality appears in numbers of antihedonist critiques of modern western social life.[13] Friedan's antihedonism rejects the idea that women's heterosexualized libidos can ever energize action for feminist social change.

Women's looking to sex with men to solve all their problems is alienating American men, Friedan warns.[14] The failure of "the sexual fix" is also alienating American women, making them dissatisfied with men.[15] If women are allowed satisfying work, she claims, they'll fully enjoy erotic relationships with men.[16]

Friedan criticizes a historically particular, socially dominant organization of heterosexuality, but hardly ever names that object of criticism. When she does occasionally refer critically to "heterosexual" relations, her negative comments are balanced by equally critical comments on the "homosexual."[17]

She deploys a problematic *likeness* of heterosexual and homosexual to criticize the conflicted state of women's and men's relations. All of Friedan's paired references to heterosexuals and homosexuals emphasize their *similarity*. But Friedan must atone for likening heteros to homos, and she indulges, therefore, in a little hyperbolic homo bashing: "The homosexuality that is spreading like a murky smog over the American scene is no less ominous than the restless, immature sex-seeking of the young women. . . ."[18]

Friedan's references to a homosexuality that is male or sex-unspecified elides the cultural difference between male homosexuality and lesbianism. Lesbians are not once mentioned in *The Feminine Mystique*. She's troubled, it seems, that uppity women like herself have long been called sexual perverts.

"Perversion" is on this twentieth-century feminist's mind when she protests the stereotyped representation of nineteenth-century feminists:

> It is a strangely unquestioned perversion of history that the passion and the fire of the feminist move-ment came from man-hating, embittered, sex-starved spinsters, from castrating, unsexed non-women who burned with such envy for the male organ that they wanted to take it away from them, demanding rights only because they lacked the power to love [men] as women.

Friedan then lists early feminists who loved and married men.[19] She (falsely) assures readers that nineteenth-century feminists fostered the idea that "equality for women was necessary to free both man and woman for true sexual fulfillment."[20]

In fact, the majority of nineteenth-century feminists ar-gued that women's special "purity," their freedom from, or control over, sensuality, was one good reason they deserved civic equality. Only a small group of radical, free-love feminists argued in the nineteenth century for women's and men's sexual fulfillment—*and then only when sanctioned by love.* The erotic pleasure of women and men remained illegitimate as independent value until the twentieth-century invention of heterosexuality.

Also, and contrary to Friedan, many feminists of the first wave remained unmarried, and many shared intense, lifelong romantic and sometimes erotically charged relationships with other women.[21]

Friedan protests that the picture of nineteenth-century feminist women "as inhuman, fiery man-eaters, whether ex-pressed as an offense against God or in the modern terms of sexual perversion, is not unlike the stereotype of the Negro as a primitive animal. . . ."[22] That mention of (female) "sexual perversion" is the closest Friedan ever comes in *The Feminine*

Mystique to talking explicitly about lesbians. The l-word seems to be so emotionally loaded for her that it's literally unspeakable.

The cause of Friedan's problem is clarified by one of her comments on nineteenth-century American feminists: "Theirs was an act of rebellion, a violent denial of the identity of woman as it was then defined."[23] Friedan's own act of rebellion in publishing *The Feminine Mystique* in 1963 also forcefully denied the "identity of woman as it was then defined." But since Friedan completely accepted the demonized image of lesbians and male homosexuals, she's terrified of the antifeminist charge that all feminists are lesbians. She's determined to show she's as antihomo as the next guy (or gal), and she refuses to so much as mention lesbians. Terror of the word *lesbian* is mentioned repeatedly in radical and lesbian-feminist essays of the early 1970s.[24]

Oddly, Friedan's enthusiastic antihomosexuality is rationalized by the same Freudian pop-psych theories she vehemently criticizes for justifying the inferiority of women. Friedan introduced a staple of second-wave feminism—a critique of Freud and his followers. Almost every major American feminist takes a shot at the influential sexism of Freud and the Freudians.

Friedan implicitly criticizes the ill effects of Freud and his disciples' twentieth-century heterosexualizing of women. She distinguishes between early and late Freudianism. Early in the twentieth century, she maintains, "Freudian psychology, with its emphasis on freedom from a repressive morality," and its stress on "sexual fulfillment, was part of the ideology of women's emancipation." But in Friedan's day "Freudian thought has become the ideological bulwark of the sexual counter-revolution."[25]

The "new psychological religion" that makes "a virtue of sex" (heterosex, she means) has had a "more devastating personal effect on women than men," she argues.[26] The popularization of Freudian theory gave women "permission to suppress the troubling questions of the larger world and pursue our own personal pleasures."[27]

In her discussion of Freud, Friedan focuses on how his sexual theories blamed women for "penis envy." This psychological reductionism denies that women who envy men's socially given power have any just cause for complaint.[28] Against that "anatomy is destiny" insult, she repeatedly and eloquently dissents.

Friedan also charges Freud with chaining femininity to passivity, masculinity to activity.[29] A "mask of timeless truth" disguises the culturally relative character of Freud's analysis of women.[30] Her implicit call is for a historically specific analysis of the womanhood norm and women's situation—the kind of analysis offered here of the heterosexual norm and heterosexual order.

Friedan's criticism of the ideas of anthropologist Margaret Mead illuminates our understanding of heterosexuality as historically specific institution and culturally constructed category.[31]

Wearing her antifeminist hat, Mead is a chief architect of a modern motherhood mystique, Friedan charges. Every society, Mead says, distinguishes women and men on the basis of women's procreative "function"—and men's lack of any such biologically given "function." That functionalist analysis, says Friedan, locks women into motherhood.

On the other hand, Mead's cultural relativism is famous for stressing that, *apart* from women's baby-making, the content of each society's prescriptions for "womanhood" and "manhood" is determined entirely by culture. In the United States, for example, the feminine is linked with passivity, the masculine with activity—elsewhere, such gender prescriptions are reversed.

Friedan quotes Mead: "Beneath the superficial classifications of sex and race the same potentialities exist" in all human beings.[32] Mead's cultural relativism, says Friedan, unlinks the biological female from social femininity, bio male from cultural manhood. That unlinking undermines the foundation of the mystique binding women to motherhood, child care, and home.

"From such anthropological observations," says Friedan, Mead might

> have passed on to the popular culture a truly revolutionary vision of women finally free to realize their full capacities in a society which replaced arbitrary sexual definitions with a recognition of genuine individual gifts as they occur in either sex.[33]

But Mead propagated a biologically and functionally determined motherhood mystique that kept women in their place.[34]

We can say of Friedan what she says of Mead: She fails to trace out the radical implications of her critique of "arbitrary sexual definitions" as socially devised and limiting of human potential. Friedan demystifies the feminine mystique but falls prey to—even prays to—the heterosexual mystique. Friedan does not extend her and Mead's insight into a culturally relative gender to query society's blessing of heterosexuality, and its damnation of homosexuality.

ATKINSON'S *AMAZON ODYSSEY*

Ti-Grace Atkinson's *Amazon Odyssey* includes essays dating from 1967 to 1972, two of whose titles illustrate her provocative style: "Vaginal Orgasm as a Mass Hysterical Survival Response" and "The Institution of Sexual Intercourse."[35] Atkinson positions herself as supermilitant "Amazon": "I'm always being denounced, even within the Women's Movement, for being so 'warlike.' "[36]

Without often explicitly naming heterosexuality, Atkinson's analysis, offered from the position of a separatist feminist (not a lesbian), begins to pinpoint the making of heterosexual society as a culturally enforced, inequitable arrangement. "The institution of the male-female relationship," she says, "has a fairly simple formalized structure," including unequal, sex-defined classes that restrict women's development.[37]

She argues against the liberal feminists of the National Organization for Women, who are terrified, she says, of confronting controversial sexual issues, such as abortion and lesbianism. Sexual issues are central to women's oppression, declares Atkinson, and her examples are mostly heterosexual.

The "institution of sexual intercourse," she maintains, enforces women's reproductive work, limiting women's options.[38] Speaking of "intercourse" as a coercive "institution" asserted its socially structured character—a new idea.

This radical feminist criticizes lesbians for accepting "the very premise of male oppression; the dynamic of sexual intercourse." Lesbians accept the idea "that human beings are primarily sexual beings."[39] Atkinson here challenges a major tenet of the modern sexual ethic: the centrality and value of eroticism.

Female and male heterosexuality and lesbianism are all deeply problematic, she suggests: "Our society has never known a time when sex in all its aspects was not exploitative and relations based on sex, e.g., the male-female relationship, were not extremely hostile." It's therefore "difficult to understand how sexual intercourse can ever be salvaged as a *practice*," even if it was ever abolished as an *institution*.[40]

Women's liberation, as she sees it, is a struggle for a society "in which sex is pivotal neither personally, nor politically."[41] Then, "sexual relations would be individually determined and socially unpatterned."[42] Under present arrangements, she thinks, everyone's sexualities are subject to a "psychological draft system."[43]

Atkinson envisions a de-institutionalized sexuality that "has no social function," a society in which reproduction no longer requires women's and men's "cooperative effort." Then, the "physical possibilities" of the sexual sense could be fully realized on their own, completely apart from procreation. But in such a society, she asks, "could you have anything remotely like what we know today as 'sexual relations'?"[44] After such a revolution, she hints, we'd need a new vocabulary and new concepts to signify our new pleasures.

She points to the historical process by which (heterosexual) vaginal orgasm was held up to women as the one proper way to achieve pleasure. As marriage was threatened in the late nineteenth century by feminist criticism of its inequities, and by women's growing economic independence, the theory of vaginal orgasm was concocted by Freud to coerce women into continuing their participation in intercourse and reproduction.[45]

The division of human beings into females and males, she argues, is based on a fundamentally inequitable sexual division of labor: In this, women are those who reproduce the species, men are those who do everything else.

But why, she asks, must society continue to use the physical difference of female and male reproductive organs as the basis for distinctions between two sexes, two kinds of workers? This makes as much sense, she says, as dividing humans according to physical characteristics like skin color, hair color, or height.[46]

The classification into sexes, she contends, is asymmetrical: women are defined and confined by their sex classification; the "class of men floats free of the sex class."[47] So women must radically challenge their "political" classification by sex.[48] To "improve their condition," those "defined as women must eradicate their own definition"—that categorization is at odds with their humanity and individuality. "Women," she declares, "must, in a sense, commit suicide."[49]

Women, in this analysis, are an oppressed class who, to free themselves from their group persecution, must become the grave diggers, not only of the class of men, but of their own class. Women's liberation requires the abolition of women and men as socially meaningful categories, the end, not only of sex roles, but of sex distinctions.

If this sounds absurdly utopian, the society Atkinson envisions is one in which sex would no longer serve as a major criterion for particular kinds of labor—a sex-blind society now envisioned by both liberal and radical feminists. That ideal also implies the end of the heterosexual/homosexual difference, for those terms are founded, in part, on the male/female distinction. (She does *not* yet make a distinction between biologically determined "sex" and socially determined "gender.")

The deconstruction of sex as a socially salient category, Atkinson concedes, would be a revolutionary change, and she admits that "the journey from womanhood to a society of individuals is hazardous."[50] Similarly, I suggest, the voyage from the hetero/homo division is equally difficult, and as important for us to consider.

Why do women consort with the men who dominate them, asks Atkinson. Radical feminists need "a theory of 'attraction' " to explain why "women, even feminists, consort with the enemy." Do they consort for sex? She doubts it. "What nearly all women mutter in response to this is: 'for love.' "[51]

Because the love of women for men involves a relationship of social unequals it is deeply problematic for women, she stresses. "Perhaps the most damning characteristic of women is that, in the face of horrifying evidence of their situation, they stubbornly claim that, in spite of everything, they 'love' their Oppressor."[52]

Love, she suggests, "is the psychological pivot in the persecution of women," the chain that binds oppressed women with oppressor men, keeping women in their place.[53] Women's love for men is a typical reaction of the subordinated, a traditional "response to overwhelming oppression," reflecting women's identification with men, and women's relinquishing of their own autonomy.[54] Women's love for men is "woman's pitiful deluded attempt to attain the human." By "fusing" with a man a woman "hopes to blur the male/female role dichotomy" and merge into the universal.[55]

By not explicitly naming and specifying heterosexuality in her essays, Atkinson somewhat defuses her analysis. But her pointed problematizing of the erotic relations of women and men makes her text an innovative critique of heterosexual society.

MILLETT'S *SEXUAL POLITICS*

Throughout her book *Sexual Politics,* published in 1970, Kate Millett points to a close connection between male supremacy and a "heterosexual caste system." She also refers to a problematic "heterosexual orthodoxy," a "heterosexual posturing," and "a rabid sort of heterosexual activism."[56] *Sexual Politics* is one of the first influential modern feminist texts to include a completely explicit critique of heterosexuality. Millett's repeated use of the term is central to her uncovering of ties between male and heterosexual supremacy.

Her famous indictment is grounded with illustrations of male and heterosexual dominion from the fiction of four male authors, D. H. Lawrence, Henry Miller, Norman Mailer, and Jean Genet. Millett's quotes from these writers convey with startling clarity how the supremacy of men and heterosexuals permeates even the most intimate erotic encounters of the sexes, constituting a "politics" of the "sexual."

The idea of "sexual politics" was breathtaking in 1970, countering the dominant notion of politics as voting, the sexual as individual, psychological, or biological. Though the idea of a "personal politics" was part of New Left rhetoric, the idea of a "sexual politics" was astonishing.

The concept that sexual relations are socially organized, and so can be reorganized, and even of a "sex-pol" movement, had existed briefly in Germany among unionists, leftists, and feminists before the Nazis' rise to power. But after the fascists' 1933 burning of books about sex and their closing of Magnus Hirschfeld's Institute for Sexual Science, the idea of sexual politics and the history of the sex-pol movement had been forgotten, the sexual and the political divorced.[57] Millett's book brought "sexual politics" back with a bang.

Early on in *Sexual Politics* Millett quotes a startling description of forced "heterosexual sodomy" from Norman Mailer's *An American Dream* (1964):

> I jammed up her ass and came as if I'd been flung across the room. She let out a cry of rage.[58]

Millett ironically sets the scene: "Mailer's hero, Stephen Rojack, has just finished murdering his wife and is now relieving his feelings by [forcibly] buggering his maid." Mailer, claims Millett, "transparently identifies with his hero," a man motivated to kill by his inability.

> to "master" his mate by any means short of murder. The desire for such mastery is perfectly understandable to Mailer and even engages his sympathy.[59]

The earlier boast of Rojack's estranged wife that she has been enjoying sodomy with her new male lovers is, says Millett, "the final blow to his vanity, his sense of property, and . . . his fancied masculine birthright of superordination, so he promptly retaliates by strangling the upstart."[60]

Rojack's sodomitical rape of his maid is similarly motivated, says Millett, by his desire to embrace death and evil, symbolized for Mailer by the rectum. (Anuses and vaginas, Millett says, are assigned deep moral, even religious significance by Mailer.) Rojack desires, she says, to appropriate through anal entrance the "canny lower-class self-preservation" skill attributed to his proletarian maid—for this woman has the "knowledge of a city rat" (she quotes Mailer).[61]

"Sodomy," continues Millett,

> has a number of possible meanings in Rojack's mind: homosexuality (he confesses to Cherry [his mistress] that he has some doubts about his heterosexual vocation); a forbidden species of sexuality at which he is an expert and over which he holds copy-

right; or anal rape, which is his way of expressing contemptuous mastery.[62]

Millett's analysis of Mailer points repeatedly to a problematic link between masculinity, virile violence, and the uncertainty of male heterosexual identity. For Mailer's men, she says, the "real abyss" is

the fear of nonexistence. That, or the secret terror of homosexuality; a mixture of sin, fascination, and fear which drives Mailer to his heterosexual posturing. To be faggot, damned, leprous—to cease to be virile were either to cease to be—or to become the most grotesque form of feminine inferiority—queer.[63]

Millett's picture of men's "heterosexual posturing" remains a suggestive analysis of the macho hetero mind.

In Mailer's code of manliness, says Millett, heterosexual equals masculine equals brutal. "Mailer's definition of masculinity," she says, depends on

a rabid sort of heterosexual activism and the violence he imagines to be inherent in male nature. Should he slack in either, he ceases to exist.[64]

Mailer's writing, comments Millett, shows the old dualisms, "male and female, virility and effeminacy, confronted by the twin perils of waning masculine dominion and the dangerous fascination of homosexuality. . . ." In his uneasy time

Machismo stands at bay, cornered by the threat of a second sexual revolution, which, in obliterating the fear of homosexuality, could challenge the entire temperamental categories (masculine and feminine) of patriarchal culture. . . .[65]

Millett even tentatively initiates a historical approach to heterosexuality. She refers to a temporal link between masculinity, violence, and heterosexual society. "In a climate of sexual counterrevolution," an era of reaction against feminist advances that Millett places between 1950 and 1970,

> homosexuality constitutes the mortal offense against heterosexual orthodoxy, the unforgivable sin that sends one off irreparably in the vast gray fields of virility's damned. And this equation of homosexuality and non-violence as effeminacy is ... Mailer's own, or that of one time and place (America in the last two decades).[66]

Her specifying a particular time frame for heterosexuality is, I believe, right on target. The early American colonies, for example, provide a sharp contrast to the modern era she discusses; in those colonies the sodomitical act of man with man was not thought to demasculinize either party, but was condemned as waste of procreative seed.

This radical feminist even discusses the "invention" of a changing historical "attitude toward heterosexual love." She thus begins to specify a history of changing responses to an eternal heterosexual essence:

> If a positive attitude toward heterosexual love is not quite in Seignebos's famous dictum, an invention of the twelfth century, it can still claim to be a novelty. Most patriarchies go to great length to exclude love [between women and men] as a basis of mate selection. Modern patriarchies tend to do so through class, ethnic, and religious factors. Western classical thought was prone to see in heterosexual love either a fatal stroke of ill luck bound to end in tragedy, or a contemptible and brutish consorting with inferiors. Medieval opinion was firm in its conviction that love was sinful if sexual, and sex sinful if loving.[67]

The "tale of Adam and Eve is," Millett says, "among other things, a narrative of how humanity invented sexual intercourse." Folk narratives, like Adam and Eve's tale, "strike us now as delightfully funny stories of primal innocents who require a good deal of helpful instruction to figure it out."[68] An embryonic notion of heterosexuality's social and historical construction is stirring in this feminist's mind.

Millett's comments on heterosexual society are most fully developed in her analysis of homosexual society as portrayed by a homosexual. In the novels and plays of Jean Genet, this French writer's homosexual characters serve as critical mirrors of society's real-life heterosexuals: "Because of the perfection" with which Genet's male homosexuals "ape and exaggerate the 'masculine' and 'feminine' of heterosexual society, his characters represent the best contemporary insight into its constitution and beliefs."[69]

Analyzing homosexuals to understand heterosexuals is a tactic earlier adopted by Freud. But Freud's reading from homosexual to heterosexual often served the cause of heteroerotic normalization. Millett reads from homosexual to heterosexual to reveal the female subordination typical of the dominant "heterosexual society."[70]

Genet's male homosexual characters, stresses Millett, "have unerringly penetrated to the essence of what heterosexual society imagines to be the character of 'masculine' and 'feminine,' and which it mistakes for the nature of male and female, thereby preserving the traditional relation of the sexes."[71] Millett here protests the confusion of socially constructed, inequitable gender distinctions with biologically determined sex differences.[72]

Genet's fiction, she emphasizes, constitutes "a painstaking exegesis of the barbarian vassalage of the sexual orders, the power structure of 'masculine' and 'feminine' as revealed by a homosexual criminal world that mimics with brutal frankness the bourgeois heterosexual society." Genet's

explication of the homosexual code becomes a satire on the heterosexual one. By virtue of their earnestness, Genet's community of pimps and fairies call into ridicule the behavior they so fervently imitate. . . .[73]

Her comments link the social construction of gender (masculinity and femininity) with the social production of sex-differentiated eroticism (heterosexuality and homosexuality).

Millett's analysis of Genet suggests how society uses biological sex distinctions to create the civil inequality of men and women. She approves of Genet's understanding that society's male/female distinction itself is

> the very prototype of institutionalized inequality. He is convinced that by dividing humanity into two groups [males and females] and appointing one to rule over the other by virtue of birthright, the social order has already established and ratified a system of oppression which will underlie and corrupt all other human relationships as well as every area of thought and experience.[74]

Throughout Genet's play *The Balcony,* Millett concludes, he

> explores the pathology of virility, the chimera of sexual congress as a paradigm of power over other human beings. He appears to be the only living male writer of first-class literary gifts to have transcended the sexual myths of our era. His critique of the heterosexual politic points the way to a true sexual revolution, a path which must be explored if any radical social change is to come about.[75]

Millett ends her book with the hope for not only a "sexual revolution but a gathering impetus toward freedom from rank or prescriptive role, sexual or otherwise," led by "expropriated groups—blacks, youth, women, the poor." Lesbian and gay militants were still too unorganized and controversial for even this radical feminist to include in her list of potential revolutionaries.

Changing "the quality of life" and transforming "personality" cannot be accomplished, Millett insists, "without freeing humanity from the tyranny of sexual-social category and conformity to sexual stereotype—as well as abolishing race caste and economic class."[76]

Deconstructing the male/female, masculine/feminine, and hetero/homo binaries is a tall order, Millett suggests, a job linked to the abolition of the white/black, capitalist/wage worker distinctions, and other revolutionary transformations.

Heterosexual relationships are deeply problematic in Millett's analysis. And yet her critical analysis of the hetero order doesn't go all the way. She challenges the limitations of masculine and feminine psychologies, the rigidities of the male/female distinction, and the hierarchical character of the heterosexual/homosexual division. But she does not move one step further to radically challenge the heterosexual and homosexual categories themselves.

In *Time* magazine of December 8, 1970 an article headed "Women's Lib: A Second Look," reported recent criticism of the feminist movement. Can feminists "think clearly?" the article asked:

> Do they know anything about biology? What about their maturity, their morality, their sexuality? Ironically, Kate Millett herself contributed to the growing skepticism about the movement by acknowledging at a recent meeting that she is bisexual. The disclosure is bound to discredit her as a spokeswoman for her cause, cast further doubt on her theories, and reinforce the views of those skeptics who routinely dismiss all liberationists as Lesbians.[77]

In response to *Time*'s nasty national outing of Millett, radical and liberal feminists formed an unusual united front. At a well-attended press conference on December 18, 1970, numbers of prominent feminist writers joined the head of the National Organization for Women, and the head of its New York chapter, to support Millett as she read a statement criticizing the lesbian-baiting of feminists. The statement read in part:

> Women's liberation and homosexual liberation are both struggling towards a common goal. A society free from defining and categorizing people by virtue of gender and/or sexual preference.[78]

A gender-neutral, sexual preference–blind society was one publicly stated dream of radical feminists and gay and lesbian liberationists in the early 1970s.

RUBIN'S "THE TRAFFIC IN WOMEN"

In 1975 Gayle Rubin published her daringly ambitious essay, "The Traffic in Women: Notes on the 'Political Economy' of Sex," proposing a new way of thinking about the social organization of biological sex and the social making of femininity and masculinity—the "sex/gender system" Rubin innovatively named it.

Her essay also offered original thoughts on what she called "obligatory heterosexuality" and "compulsory heterosexuality." The production of heterosexuality opened up under Rubin's scrutiny.

Feminist liberals and feminist radicals had both earlier struggled to publicize the influential social configuring of sex-biology and gender. But when Rubin published her "Traffic in Women," sex, gender, and sexuality were still often assumed to be essentially biological.

When manhood and womanhood were thought about, they might be understood, vaguely, as socially defined, diverse, and relative. Cross-cultural variations in men's and women's personality traits had been widely publicized by the writings of Margaret Mead. But modern feminists drew new attention to the social use of visible, bodily markers, and of socially produced differences of the sexes. Rubin's reference to a sex/gender system discussed both sex and gender differences as products of a specific social arrangement. Her innovative naming of the sex-gender system helped to authorize a new thought tool.

Rubin was then a graduate student "working on her doctorate in anthropology and teaching in the Women's Studies program at the University of Michigan," where she'd experienced "many incarnations of feminist politics."[79] Her theoretical essay discusses three institutions implicit in anthropologist Claude Lévi-Strauss's analysis of the "social organization of sex." That order, she says, "rests upon gender, obligatory heterosexuality, and the constraint of female sexuality."[80]

Rubin explains those three foundations of the social sex system:

(1) "Gender is a socially imposed division of the sexes," the product of a cultural process in which biological males and females are transformed into "domesticated" men and women. (Her domestication metaphor suggests wild females and males broken into docile women and men.)

"Men and women are, of course, different," she says, but the "idea that men and women are two mutually exclusive categories" does not arise out of any "natural" difference. The sexes are not naturally "opposite."

Opposite sexes are constructed socially by "the suppression of natural similarities," Rubin claims. Men must repress "whatever is the local version of 'feminine' traits." Women must repress "the local definition of 'masculine' traits."[81]

The social division of labor by sex, she explains, is the source of the opposition between the sexes. The sexed division of work exacerbates the sexes' "biological differences," separating women and men into "two mutually exclusive categories." The sexual division of labor "thereby *creates* gender," a fundamental contrast between women and men.[82]

(2) "Obligatory heterosexuality" is enforced by several means, Rubin argues. Her term innovatively names the sys-

tematic, coercive production of a different-sex eros called heterosexuality.

The making of obligatory heterosexuality is tied to the earlier sex segregation of work, she argues. Inspired by the analysis of Lévi-Strauss, Rubin says that the social purpose of the sexual division of labor is "to insure the union of men and women by making the smallest viable economic unit contain at least one man and one woman." She quotes Lévi-Strauss: " 'the sexual division of labor is nothing else than a device to institute a reciprocal state of dependency between the sexes.' "[83]

Rubin questions the symmetry of each sex's dependence on the other, but their mutual dependence is a repeated theme. The sexed division of labor creates needs in each sex that can only be fulfilled by the other. This forges a strong social incentive for women and men to join forces in heterosexual relationships stabilized by legal marriage. Rubin warns ironically that Lévi-Strauss

> comes dangerously close to saying that heterosexuality is an instituted process. If biological and hormonal imperatives were as overwhelming as popular mythology would have them, it would hardly be necessary to insure heterosexual unions by means of economic interdependency.[84]

The production of heterosexuality as obligatory also produces a mandatory antihomosexuality, Rubin argues. For obligatory heterosexuality involves the "suppression of the homosexual component of human sexuality" and the concomitant "oppression of homosexuals."[85]

But the social system that places heterosexuals over homosexuals produces, she says, figures more complicated than is suggested by any simple superior/inferior ranking. A close look at "specific sexual systems" indicates that the rules of proper human relations "do not merely encourage heterosexuality to the detriment of homosexuality." The rules incite "specific forms of heterosexuality." For example,

> some marriage systems have a rule of obligatory cross-cousin marriage. A person in such a system is not only heterosexual, but "cross-cousin sexual."[86]

Similarly, "particular forms of institutionalized homosexuality" are produced by difference sexual systems.[87] Rubin cites a Mojave custom which "permitted a person to change from one sex to the other." In this society sex was not thought of as anatomically determined. One's sex was socially constituted by one's adoption of the other sex's work, behavior, and dress. In Mojave society, an "anatomical man" might "become a [social] woman by means of a special ceremony." An anatomical woman might become a (social) man. The changeling

> then took a wife or husband of her/his own anatomical sex and opposite social sex. These marriages, which we would label homosexual, were heterosexual ones by Mohave standards, unions of opposite socially defined sexes.[88]

Rubin questions the idea of an essential, always-the-same homosexuality and heterosexuality by stressing their substantially different social forms. She employs heterosexual and homosexual as transhistorical categories with particular historical manifestations.[89]

(3) The "constraint of female sexuality" results from a social organization in which women are, in effect, owned, controlled, and exchanged as gifts by men, a system with a profound effect on the social shaping of heterosexual relations.[90]

If Rubin's "traffic in women" by men sounds like some rare native rite, she suggests that readers recall the "curious custom by which a father gives away the bride."[91] Hollywood's

Father of the Bride, it seems, documents the weird ritual of white Anglo-Saxon Protestant Americans.

A father's giving away of the bride, his exchanging of *his* daughter for a son-in-law, presumes the father's original ownership. Even if dad's property right in his daughter is now a mere formality in the U.S., Rubin suggests, women still do not give away, exchange, and traffic in men. Even modern women are not encouraged to give themselves—to dispose of their own bodies and sexuality—as readily as do men. The relations of men and women are still asymmetrical.[92] The exchange of women is an important analytical concept, says Rubin, because it "places the oppression of women within social systems, rather than in biology."[93] Likewise, countering the dominant biological idea of heterosexuality helps us situate it within a particular historical system.

In a section on the psychological theories of Sigmund Freud and Jacques Lacan, Rubin comments on the construction of female heterosexual desire. Here, she describes how notions of sex and gender, formulated first as external social rules, come to take up tenacious, internal residence deep within our minds.

Freud's late recognition that the girl-child first loves a woman, her mother, challenges, says Rubin, "the idea of a primordial [female] heterosexuality." Since a girl's libido is first woman-directed, a girl's eventual assumption of heterosexuality is something "to be explained."[94] Freud and Lacan explain, she says, that a girl internalizes the genital and power ranking system of her culture, realizes that she lacks the most highly prized, power-conferring genital, rejects her original mother-love, and takes up lusting after her father and other penis possessors.[95]

The "rule of heterosexuality which dominates the scenario," says Rubin, makes a girl's position "excruciatingly untenable."[96] She is always dependent on a man for her own sense of power and worth. Rubin's account of the making of female heterosexuals stresses how destructive this process is to women's autonomous sense of themselves. She emphasizes, however, that this process is socially arranged and therefore changeable.

In a major essay published in 1984, Rubin revised and clarified her original concept of the sex/gender system. There she more emphatically distinguished between the social structuring of "gender" (masculinity and femininity) and the systematic ordering of eroticism (or "lust").[97] Distinguishing the different histories of womanhood and manhood and of sex-pleasure is central to the developing history of heterosexuality as a specific system.

Rubin's 1975 description of a sex/gender system hostile to women's development suggests that this order operates with a certain autonomy, apart from the economy and other major systems. Her sex/gender system can't be understood simply as determined by those other systems.[98] Each sex/gender system has its own internal structure and unique operational logic. We need "to isolate sex and gender," she says, from the economic "mode of production."

On the other hand, Rubin explicitly argues for "a political economy of sex" that will point us to the links between norms of intimate relations, marriage systems, and larger "economic and political arrangements."[99] For "sexual systems cannot . . . be understood in complete isolation." We require, she says,

> a political economy of sexual systems. We need to study each society to determine the exact mechanisms by which particular conventions of sexuality are produced and maintained.[100]

We need, she suggests, a "systematic historical account" that recognizes "the mutual interdependence of sexuality, economics, and politics without underestimating the full significance of each in human society."[101] Comprehending heterosexuality's history, I believe, requires a similar systems analysis.

The end of Rubin's 1975 essay discusses the social structural changes necessary to realize her vision of a "sexually egalitarian society," a "society without gender hierarchy."[102] Her dream of future sex includes "the elimination of obligatory sexualities and sex roles," and the creation of "an androgynous and genderless (though not sexless) society." Hers is clearly a pro-sex feminist vision. In her erotic utopia "one's sexual anatomy is irrelevant to who one is, what one does, and with whom one makes love."[103] Rubin's heterosexuality-questioning is still powerful.

Liberal and radical feminists of heterosexual, bisexual, and lesbian persuasion pioneered in developing a critique of heterosexual society. Even Friedan, opposed as she was to feminists focusing on eroticism, and as afraid as she was of explicitly criticizing the heterosexual order, called for a historically specific analysis of the sexes' intimacies. And even Friedan criticized invidious "sexual definitions" in the name of furthering human development. Without precisely naming heterosexuality, Atkinson's analysis newly located the sexual intercourse of women and men firmly within a social institution. Millett talked explicitly about heterosexuality as a social arrangement. Rubin, launching the idea of a "sex/gender system," implied that heterosexuality is a socially "instituted process." Then, writers speaking from an explicitly lesbian-feminist standpoint furthered our insight into the social and even the historical ordering of the heterosexual regime.

7

THE LESBIAN MENACE STRIKES BACK

Some Lavender Feminist Critiques

In March 1970 Betty Friedan was quoted in *The New York Times Magazine,* complaining about the "lavender menace," the lesbian feminists who, she thought, were giving mainstream feminists a bad name.[1] Friedan's anxious epithet played into the antifeminist charge that the women's movement was just a bunch of lesbians. But even then the lesbian menaces were beginning to strike back.

Starting about 1970 analyses from an openly lesbian-feminist perspective began to stress the overlap of male and heterosexual supremacy, some even emphasizing the *causal* contribution of heterosexual domination to male dominion. Lesbian feminists emphasized the subordinating effect of heterosexual rule on heterosexual women, as well as lesbians.

Lesbian feminists' explicit critiques of the heterosexual order furthered the feminist-inspired break with the usual, unthinking assumption of heterosexuality. Lesbians who were feminists helped to constitute a historic moment in which heterosexuality was bluntly, publicly questioned.

In retrospect, it's not surprising that lesbian feminists contributed prominently, from their own particular standpoint, to the feminist analysis of the social arrangement of heterosexuality. Without thinking much about it, both the antihomosexual bigot and the gay and lesbian defender may assume that *any* feminist criticism of the heterosexual order is likely to be a specifically lesbian production. I therefore note that the feminist critique of heterosexuality was not entirely the work of lesbians, and that even Friedan's antihomosexual feminism includes an implicit critique of the heterosexual order.

Women identified as heterosexual, bisexual, and lesbian contributed to the liberal feminist and radical feminist analyses, previously discussed. But even when produced by self-identified lesbians or bisexuals, these critiques did not speak openly from a lesbian-feminist standpoint. That open speaking permitted the development of a more detailed critique linking heterosexual supremacy and male domination.

This close look at a few influential lesbian-feminist commentaries on heterosexuality—a Radicalesbian communiqué, an anthology edited by Nancy Myron and Charlotte Bunch, analyses by Monique Wittig and by Adrienne Rich—highlights the special insights and problematic aspects of this particular feminism.[2]

THE RADICALESBIANS' "WOMAN-IDENTIFIED WOMAN"

On May 1, 1970, three hundred feminists from different cities and of diverse politics gathered in a New York City school for the opening of the second annual Conference to Unite Women. An account pieced together from alternative press reports describes the dramatic, unscheduled start of that historic evening:

> Suddenly, the auditorium lights went out. There were
> shouts and sounds of scuffling. In moments the lights

went up to reveal walls blossoming with posters:
TAKE A LESBIAN TO LUNCH; . . . THE WOMEN'S
MOVEMENT IS A LESBIAN PLOT. . . . Surrounding
the astonished audience were seventeen smiling
women in lavender T-shirts emblazoned in red with
"LAVENDER MENACE." At that moment the wom-
en's liberation movement found itself confronted
with the fear that had haunted it since its inception.[3]

Interrupting the conference schedule, the T-shirted menaces
satirically confronted Betty Friedan's reference to lesbians in
the feminist movement.

As part of this action a group of Radicalesbians handed
out their essay "The Woman-Identified Woman," and this
manifesto was published soon after in the lesbian and gay
newspaper *Come Out!,* then reprinted in the radical feminist
Notes from the Third Year—becoming a much-quoted classic of
modern feminism's morn.[4] The Radicalesbians contested the
heterosexual order by way of questioning the world's division
into women and men, lesbians and gays, homosexuals and
heterosexuals.

Socially defined "sex roles" and sexual "categories," say
the writers, are major ideological forces that channel women
into reproductive and erotic relations with men. "Heterosexuality" and "homosexuality" are prominent among those suspect categories. "Homosexuality," they explain,

> is a by-product of a particular way of setting up roles
> (or approved patterns of behavior) on the basis of
> sex; as such it is an inauthentic (not consonant with
> "reality") category. In a society in which men do not
> oppress women, and sexual expression is allowed to
> follow feelings, the categories of homosexuality and
> heterosexuality would disappear.[5]

The writers advocate the deconstruction of all labeled
and patterned, sexed and sexual behaviors, including hetero-

sexuality (male and female), male homosexuality and lesbianism—allowing for the free rein of uncategorized feeling. They imagine a liberation in which emotion, freed from social constraint and conditioning, will bloom in unsocialized, unlabeled abandon. The Radicalesbians reject sexual category *reform* in favor of sexual category *abolition.* As I've said, the idea of a society without homosexual and heterosexual categories was discussed often in the lesbian and gay movement in the early seventies.

The Radicalesbians challenge all women to direct their energies to women and their freedom movement:

> As long as women's liberation tries to free women without facing the basic heterosexual structure that binds us in one-to-one relationship with our oppressors, tremendous energies will continue to flow into trying to straighten up each particular relationship with a man, into finding how to get better sex, how to turn his head around—into trying to make the "new man" out of him, in the delusion that this will allow us to be the "new woman."[6]

The naming of a "basic heterosexual structure," a specific institutional ordering of different-sex eroticism, points to a developing social systems analysis of heterosexuality, a concept central to the exploration of heterosexuality as historical.

The Radicalesbians reject all male-made classifications. Even lesbian, they say, is "one of the sexual categories by which men have divided up humanity."[7] Lesbianism, the writers declare,

> is a category of behavior possible only in a sexist society characterized by rigid sex roles and dominated by male supremacy. Those sex roles dehumanize women by defining us as a supportive/serving caste *in relation to* the master caste of men. . . ."[8]

The Radicalesbians implicitly suggest the revolutionary decategorization of themselves—and of heterosexuals.

The dominant social usage, say the writers, distinguishes a "lesbian" from a "woman." This implies that a "real woman" is dependent on a man. A woman not dependent on a man is not a "real woman." She falls into another category, a "lesbian" or a "dyke," someone different from a "woman."

That distinction between lesbian and woman reveals the subordinate place of heterosexual women, the Radicalesbians note. In "popular thinking" the difference between a "real woman" and a "lesbian" is based on "sexual orientation." According to such thinking, "the essence of being a 'woman' is to get fucked by men."[9]

But, the writers ask, are women in the feminist movement "going to continue the male classification system" that defines "all females in sexual relation to some other category of people?"[10] Sexual categorization itself is man-made and suspect in the Radicalesbians' analysis.

Even the category "woman" is suspect. Like Atkinson earlier, the Radicalesbians urge women to reject that category. Jettisoning that term is necessary, they argue, if the group called women are to claim their authentic selves. "As long as we cling to the idea of 'being a woman,' " say the writers, women will experience a conflict with their own personhood. Being "feminine" and "being a whole person are irreconcilable," they say. Women must work with other women to "create a new sense of self."[11] That new identity will abandon "woman" as its basic organizing principle. The writers appeal throughout their essay to "authenticity," "personhood," the "self," and the "human," turning those values to the lesbian-feminist cause.[12]

Countering feminists' fears of lesbianism, this essay confronts the terrible scare power of the words *lesbian* and *dyke*, so often hurled at uppity women in twentieth-century America. The power of language and the politics of categorizing are a pointed part of this early seventies lesbian-feminist critique.

These writers analyze how language is used by men to uphold male and heterosexual supremacy: "Lesbian is a label invented by the Man to throw at any woman who dares to be his equal, who dares to challenge his prerogatives . . . , who dares to assert the primacy of her own needs."[13]

The political function of the word *lesbian* is to brand and divide:

> Affixing the label lesbian not only to a woman who aspires to be a person, but also to any situation of real love, real solidarity, real primacy among women, is a primary form of divisiveness among women: . . . it is the debunking/scare term that keeps women from forming primary attachments, groups, or association among ourselves.[14]

The negative power of the word *lesbian* must be actively challenged, not only by lesbian feminists, but by all feminists, the writers urge:

> Women in the movement have . . . gone to great lengths to avoid discussion and confrontation with the issue of lesbianism. It puts people uptight. They are hostile, evasive, or try to incorporate it into some "broader issue." They would rather not talk about it. If they have to, they dismiss it as a "lavender herring." But it is no side issue. It is absolutely essential to the success and fulfillment of the women's liberation movement that this issue be dealt with. As long as the label "dyke" can be used to frighten a woman into a less militant stand, keep her separate from her sisters, keep her from giving primacy to anything other than men and family—then to that extent she is controlled by the male culture.[15]

The Radicalesbians urge women in the feminist movement, not necessarily to become active lesbians, but "to see in each other the possibility of a primal commitment which includes sexual love." They warn: "As long as male acceptability is primary—both to individual women and to the movement as a whole—the term lesbian will be used effectively against women."[16]

The writers stress the importance to all feminists of women "disengaging from male-defined response patterns"—though not necessarily from all men: "For irrespective of where our love and sexual energies flow, if we are male-identified in our heads, we cannot realize our autonomy as human beings."[17]

In passing, the authors remark that the lesbian learns "usually much earlier than her 'straight' (heterosexual) sisters about the essential aloneness of life (which the myth of marriage obscures)."[18] The need for that parenthetical clarification that " 'straight' " means "heterosexual" sets this essay in the past, a society in which the critical public discussion of heterosexuality was just beginning to get under way, a discussion to which the Radicalesbians contributed their eloquent, provocative proclamation.

MYRON AND BUNCH'S *LESBIANISM*

The anthology *Lesbianism and the Women's Movement,* edited by Nancy Myron and Charlotte Bunch, includes articles first published in 1972–73 by a lesbian-feminist collective in Washington, D.C., in their movement newspaper *The Furies.*[19]

Much of the pioneering criticism of heterosexuality as "ideology" and "institution," these essays remind us, was first developed and saw publication in the popular lesbian, gay, and feminist movement press before it moved outward to influence wider circles through publications such as the feminist academic journal *Signs* and honored authors such as Adrienne Rich. The achievement of Rich and *Signs* is not diminished if we recognize that both were encouraged to a critique of heterosexual society by earlier debates in alternative, feminist, lesbian, and gay papers.

One woman's personal story concretizes criticism of the hetero order made more abstractly by other *Furies* writers:

"In the winter of 1969–70," says Coletta Reid, "I joined a consciousness raising group and a newly formed women's newspaper." She had "never been in a political movement before." At twenty-seven, married to a man she'd helped put through graduate school, "pregnant and with a toddler, I came to the women's movement"—and immediately began to get wild ideas:

> If "The Myth of the Vaginal Orgasm" was true, then intercourse was not necessary or even relevant to *my* sexual satisfaction.[20] If "Sexual Politics" was right that male sexuality was an expression of power and dominance, then I was choosing my own oppression to stay in a relationship with a man. If sex roles were an invention of society, then women—not just men—were possible people to love, in the fullest sense of that word.[21]

If "sex roles" were perceived as an "invention" it would not be long before "sexuality," and even "heterosexuality," would be seen as such.

Since the man she was married to "really thought men were superior," Reid soon "asked her husband to leave; he took our son and I kept our daughter."[22]

At the time she left her husband, Reid says, she never envisioned herself as a "lesbian/separatist."[23] While married, she'd "heard the term 'heterosexual privilege,'" but had "never really understood how it worked." As she began to come out as a lesbian, however, she viewed her former heterosexual entitlement from the standpoint of one newly dispossessed of it:

> When I was heterosexual I was accepted as normal by my family, friends, acquaintances, and contacts. But once I started putting myself and other women

first in my life I was variously seen as: unnatural, immoral, perverted, disgusting, sick or a sexual fascist.[24]

As Reid "tried to live as an open lesbian I began to see the privileges I had taken for granted when married."

Reid began to question the naturalness of the arrangements constructed around eroticism, gender, reproduction, and work:

> Men have taken the natural fact that woman reproduces the species and constructed an ideology that says that motherhood, heterosexuality, marriage, the family, housewifery and a secondary place in the job market are natural.[25]

The insight that *heterosexuality*, in particular, is constructed socially was a new idea, says Reid:

> In early feminist analysis, all of those "natural" constructs were challenged except heterosexuality. Early feminism took for granted that "natural sexuality" was heterosexuality; that "natural sexual relations" was vaginal intercourse; that female sexuality must be directed toward men.[26]

But Reid had learned that women's sexuality is "in no way naturally or necessarily connected to penises or penile penetration."[27] She came to understand that "heterosexuality as an institution operates for the benefit of men."[28] Given "the institutional nature of enforced heterosexuality," women only *seemed* to choose heterosexuality. They were actually pressured into it. Given such pressures, she realized, "lesbianism is an act of individual rebellion."[29]

The future world Reid imagines is a universe unconcerned about same-sex and different-sex erotic divisions:

In a world devoid of male power and, therefore, sex
roles, who you live with, loved, slept with and were
committed to would be irrelevant. All of us would be
equal and have equal determination over the society
and how it met our needs.

She ends: "Until this happens, how we use our sexuality and
our bodies is just as relevant to our liberation as how we use
our minds and time."[30]

In Reid's case, the nightmare of the ultraconservative
came true. The heterosexual housewife transmuted into an
angry, militant lesbian feminist.

Margaret Small's essay, condensed from a speech delivered in the early 1970s, discusses "heterosexual ideology" as
support to male supremacy.[31] Small points to the unnamed,
unpaid, undervalued work that women perform for men
within marriage. Women's work, she says, is specifically the
procreation and socialization of children, and the physical
and emotional care—the feeding and fucking—of husbands.

Men justify this male-beneficent organization of women's
labor through a creed, the "ideology of heterosexuality,"
which "says it is natural for women to . . . take care of men."
Heterosexuality is "not merely an act in relation to impregna-
tion, but the dominant ideology" which defines women as
"appendages of men." It is not "reproduction itself" which determines the social organization which places men above
women. "The ideology of heterosexuality" does that, "not the
simple act of intercourse."[32] Seeing heterosexuality as an
"ideology"—an influential, political idea—was important in
the move to question it. And distinguishing a socially defined
heterosexuality from women and men's acts of reproductive
intercourse is central to the analysis of heterosexual history.

Heterosexual ideology, Small elaborates,

is the basic framework which determines a woman's
life from the earliest moments she learns to perceive

the world. It tells her what is natural that she do and be.

She adds:

> Heterosexual hegemony insures that people think it natural that male and female form a life-long sexual/reproductive unit with the female belonging to the male. . . . Now you go and tell people that there could be another purpose to life, that sexuality can be totally divorced from reproduction, that reproduction could be organized in a totally different way and they'll just laugh and say you're talking about Martians. Heterosexual hegemony insures that people can't even perceive that there could be other possibilities.[33]

Lesbians, claims Small, are "outside of the reality which heterosexual ideology explains." Lesbians therefore "have the potential for developing an alternative ideology, not limited by heterosexuality."[34]

Heterosexual ideology limits our vision of any alternative sexed, erotic community, she stresses, just as "bourgeois ideology" naturalizes the social organization of capitalism, thwarting any sense of a possible, viable alternative to that system of production. And since the "assumptions of heterosexual ideology," she says, have "existed far longer than bourgeois ideology," hetero assumptions are even more difficult to question:

> You have to create the space that stands outside of all the assumptions of heterosexuality—assumptions about the family, about marriage, about motherhood, about housework, about childrearing, about rape, about illegitimacy, about spinsterhood—about everything that has to do with the relationships between men and women. To stand outside of hetero-

sexual ideology and to develop an alternative way
that male-female relationships could exist is an incredibly creative act.[35]

Revolutionary lesbians, she admits, had not yet created an alternate vision of men's and women's relations.

The change she desires does not require women to become lesbians:

> The question, I think, is rather how all women will
> understand themselves. If the ideology of heterosex-
> uality can be attacked and exposed and an alterna-
> tive ideology can be developed, I'm not sure how
> important it is that all women stop being heterosex-
> ual. Because the way a woman would understand
> what it would mean to be heterosexual, would be to-
> tally different.

A "critique of heterosexual ideology," she argues,

> ultimately reduces heterosexuality to an act at the
> moment of impregnation. If you're going to have a
> baby, there is a role for heterosexuality. If we develop
> other ways to have babies, then what heterosexuality
> is becomes irrelevant.[36]

Small is right, I think, about how difficult it is to challenge our ingrained sense of heterosexuality's inevitability.
But she's wrong, I believe, in her historical claim that the "assumptions of heterosexual ideology" have "existed far longer
than bourgeois ideology."[37] Our strong sense of heterosexuality's necessity owes its tenacious hold, *not* to the heterosexual
category's long life, or the heterosexual system's timelessness.
Our deep feeling of heterosexuality's required character is
due simply to the force of what is, the present heterosexual
social structure, and the power of its dogma to cloud our

minds to alternate arrangements of the sexes, and alternate erotic orders.

Small suggests that heterosexuality be divested of its claim as generic, all-purpose name for male-female intimacy. She wants, thereby, to reduce heterosexuality to a name for a historically limited arrangement of impregnating activity. Her idea is to deprive heterosexuality of its mysterious, timeless status by pinpointing it as signifier of one particular historical arrangement of human reproduction. The possibility doesn't occur to her that heterosexuality signifies a system distinct from the reproductive order—a historically specific arrangement of the sexes and their pleasures.

Small ends her essay by suggesting that new ideas about heterosexuality won't, by themselves, change our minds about heterosexuality's eternal staying power. Only collective struggle against male supremacy and heterosexual dominion will do the trick.[38]

"The Normative Status of Heterosexuality" is the bold title of an essay included in this anthology by a group of Dutch lesbian feminists who produce a newspaper called *Purple September*.[39]

In the 1970s the idea that heterosexuality possessed "normative status" was new. Just how new is indicated by the essayists' need to repeatedly assert the idea and repeatedly press lesbian and straight feminists to analyze it.

Since the first half of the seventies, it turns out, feminists (especially lesbian feminists) have been pressing eloquently for an analysis of heterosexuality as norm. We may usefully ask why, then, in the mid-1990s, is that analysis still so undeveloped? The operation of a powerful taboo, I later argue, keeps heterosexuality outside of analysis.

The Purple Septembers suggest one reason why society's normative heterosexuality is "systematically barred from feminist analyses of women's oppression." Feminists don't analyze this norm because the social pressure toward heterosexuality is not directed exclusively at women:

boys are conditioned toward heterosexuality as well as girls. A 'real' man is a straight man, a 'real' woman is a straight woman. A gay fellow is [supposedly] effeminate, a gay woman, [supposedly] masculine. The straight norm applies to both sexes and thus does not count as part of female conditioning as such.[40]

But the pressure to become heterosexual, the writers argue, is only superficially similar for men and women. Although both sexes are "exposed to straight conditioning," that "does not prevent the *concept* of heterosexuality" from having "opposite meanings" for women and for men. Male heterosexuality "is linked to the male prerogative of human identity." Female heterosexuality "is linked to the denial of that same identity."[41] Heterosexual women are trained to look to men for approval, and for a basic sense of themselves.

Our culture makes heterosexuality seem an inevitable fate, say the Dutch women. So you "cannot convince anyone that you are straight by choice."[42] But if heterosexuality is actually as fated as the dominant ideology maintains, "no one would take the trouble to condition her children toward heterosexuality and culture could dispense with its taboos on . . . homosexuality."[43]

"Being gay does not determine your view of heterosexuality as a norm," say the authors:

> rejecting straight relationships in your personal life is not the same as analyzing the norm that would make straight girls of us all. But as things stand now, not all the lavender girls nor their straight sisters seem ready even to discuss it [normative heterosexuality] critically. Instead, they join hands in the struggle against the consequences of a norm which by tacit agreement is itself left undiscussed.[44]

The Dutch women

> reject the normative status of heterosexuality but not
> heterosexuality as one type of relationship among
> other, possible types. We do not doubt that there are
> straight relationships that derive their meaning and
> content from the people involved and not from the
> norm alone.

But "even in those relationships the male partner always has
the option of falling back on 'masculine' behavior," thereby
forcing the female partner to fall back on "feminine" conditioning.[45] Male privilege is a tempting option even for
liberated men.

The authors conclude that "the straight norm is not really a sexual norm at all, but a powerful instrument in the
perpetuation of the power relationship between the sexes."[46]
They don't consider that heterosexuality functions *simultaneously* as heterosexual supremacy booster *and* male supremacy
promoter.

In their introduction to this anthology, its editors, Myron
and Bunch, stress that lesbians have pioneered the analysis of
heterosexual dominion:

> Lesbians have been the quickest to see the challenge
> to heterosexuality as necessary to feminists' survival.
> However straight feminists are not precluded from
> examining and fighting against heterosexuality as an
> ideology and institution that oppresses us all. The
> problem is that few have done so. This perpetuates
> lesbian fears that a woman remaining tied to men
> prevents them from seeing the function of hetero-
> sexuality and acting to end it.[47]

Myron and Bunch "are less concerned with whether each
woman personally becomes a lesbian than with the destruction of heterosexuality as a crucial part of male supremacy."[48]

Their suggestion that heterosexuality can be destroyed assumes its nonessential character.

The editors charge that "Women's Liberation lacks direction now because it has failed to understand the importance of heterosexuality in maintaining male supremacy."[49] In the 1990s, challenging the social organization of heterosexuality still remains, I believe, an important political task, as well as an intellectually challenging labor.

WITTIG'S "THE STRAIGHT MIND"

In 1975, Monique Wittig, the novelist and lesbian-feminist theorist, began a series of condensed, provocative essays on heterosexuality as "political regime." These intellectual teasers together constitute one of the most extended, explicit, critical commentaries on heterosexuality as an organized practice of unequal power in which men dominate women and heterosexuals dominate homosexuals. Her speculations on the heterosexual empire are designed to carry us outside it, to see it suddenly as strange and puzzling.

A close look at her essays clarifies this theorist's bold, counterintuitive contentions, and points to some problematic aspects of her analysis.[50] Her inspection of heterosexuality is complex and abstract, but her audacious speculations can help us see the heterosexual order as historical.

In the earliest of her essays, "The Category of Sex," Wittig is already explicitly naming "heterosexual society" and its "heterosexual economy," conceptualizing them as power-drenched, inequitable orderings of different sexes.[51] Those terms reject heterosexuality's given, unproblematic status, furthering the intellectual project of many feminists: to remove heterosexuality from the realm of the undiscussed, the arena of the exclusively individual and psychological, and the domain of the biological. She rejects the idea of heterosexuality as a thing-in-the-body to analyze it as trouble-making social system.

In Wittig's analysis, the distinction between female and

male sexes, although referring to biological markers, is fundamentally social. She questions the usual feminist distinction between biologically determined "sex" and socially determined "gender." Both anatomical sex *and* feminine and masculine gender, she suggests, are socially produced distinctions with negative effects for those called women. This challenges our usual, "common-sense" assumption that "the category of sex," and particular bodily features, constitute a necessary, natural distinction between human beings. We assume the sexes' difference as if it arises automatically out of bodies, biology, or nature, as if human practices and judgments do not found and ground our distinctions. We mistakenly presume that sex differences are simple, transparent, unambiguous.[52]

Our assumption of different sexes, Wittig stresses, precludes inquiry into the social foundation of that difference, and its eternal necessity. Presuming the existence of different sexes, we fail to question the variety of standards human beings have used to distinguish the sexes, for different purposes, in different social systems, at different times. We don't, for example, use sex difference as an operative distinction in the sex-blind hiring practices mandated by recent prohibitions against sex discrimination.

Our use of particular biological characteristics to mark particular sexes makes the difference between males and females *seem* natural and inevitable, she argues, and helps to maintain the unequal social power of men over women. In particular, the male/female distinction supports the human female's culturally assigned, restricted place in the sexual division of reproductive labor. Sex differences originate in "a political, economic, ideological order," says Wittig.[53]

The "category of sex," she concludes,

> grips our minds in such a way that we cannot think outside of it. This is why we must destroy it and start thinking beyond it if we want to start thinking at all, as we must destroy the sexes as a sociological reality.

The category of sex is the category that ordains slavery for women. . . .[54]

Wittig recognizes that abolishing the social salience of female and male would also do away with "woman" and "man." To feminists who want to retain the category "woman," she asks:

Can we redeem *slave?* Can we redeem *nigger, negress?* How is *woman* different?[55]

She argues that "woman,"

like "slave" is . . . an irretrievable concept. The reality "woman" must disappear just as the reality "slave" after the abolition of slavery. . . .[56]

"Man," she indicates, would have to go the way of "slave owner" and "master."[57] The man/woman, master/slave oppositions, she suggests, both result from and support social systems of domination.[58]

But what would happen to women's liberation if "women" and "woman" weren't available as rallying points for the feminist troops? Wittig answers by distinguishing "women fighting for women as a class" (a strategically useful feminist concept), and women fighting for " 'woman' as essentialist concept" (an antifeminist move because the eternal woman is an idea inseparable from women's subordination).[59]

Wittig also recognizes that the homosexual/heterosexual distinction depends on the prior distinction between women and men, females and males: The sex distinction "is at the base of (heterosexual) society."[60] The homo/hetero contrast assumes and "conceals" the opposition between socially inferior women and civilly superior men. So the abolition of sex differences would mean dissolving the homo/hetero binary.

But what about the fate of "lesbians" when sex distinctions and the het/homo opposition are abolished? Wittig explains that "women" are defined only in relation to "men." Lesbians are not defined in relation to men.[61] Her logical conclusion was announced dramatically in 1978, in the last sentence of a talk presented at the Modern Language Association: "Lesbians are not women."[62]

Lesbianism is something more than sex, she explains, "much more than homosexuality, much more than sexuality."[63] She adds, "Lesbianism opens into another dimension of the human."[64] Separating lesbians from sex and sexuality, she places them outside heterosexual society, in some other universe.[65]

The equation of heterosexuality with reproduction, Wittig says, is a major social and conceptual means of normalizing heterosexuality, making it seem inevitable. Identifying the heterosexual with the reproductive and the normal was, she argues, the particular work of a relatively recent, scientific, Freudian model of proper procreative sex. "The concept of heterosexuality was created in the French language in 1911" and, she claims, "admits as normal only that sexuality which has a reproductive purpose." She adds: "Everything else is a perversion. . . ."[66]

But Wittig's analysis itself falls prey to the equation of heterosexuality with reproduction. Heterosexual society is founded on women's "obligatory" procreation, she insists.[67] "Heterosexuality," she says, "is dominated by its final cause, reproduction."[68] That, I believe, is a fundamentally mistaken interpretation of heterosexual history. The rise of the hetero pleasure norm, I think, broke with the earlier rule of reproduction.

The heterosexual order enshrines not procreation but sex difference and eroticism. Wittig does analyze those sex and gender differences, the "hetero" half of heterosexuality. But she presents no adequate analysis of the "sexual," erotic half. Discussing heterosexuality "as a political regime," she asserts, "sexual pleasure" is "not the issue here."[69] It is, I think, half the issue.[70]

Pleasure, Wittig says, is essentially outside the heterosexual reproductive system, inside the homosexual erotic order. "Pleasure for pleasure's sake," she suggests, distinguishes the subjectivity of lesbians and male homosexuals from that of heterosexuals, enmeshed as they are in their reproductive system.[71] For homosexuals "sexuality has . . . no finality apart from its own exercise"; it's above all about "the search for pleasure and the creation of a unique being."[72] But sexuality as pleasure pursuit and subjectivity search provides no clear basis, I think, for distinguishing heterosexual from homosexual.

Wittig's essay "The Straight Mind," exposing and demystifying prominent heterosexual thought modes, was the talk with which she prodded the Modern Language Association in 1978. Her title comments ironically on *The Savage Mind* by anthropologist Claude Lévi-Strauss, but satirically reverses the usual association of civilized and heterosexual. The existence of such a thing as a straight mind—a mental "conglomerate of all kinds of disciplines, theories and current ideas"—was a new idea.[73]

This amazon of letters named the "battle" that needs to be waged against the "goes-without-saying" of the straight mind—the unquestioned assumption of heterosexuality.[74] Years after her original call, the continuing assumption of heterosexuality still illustrates straight thinking's power.

Influential "discourses of heterosexuality," she says, prevent lesbians, gay men, and feminists from speaking "unless we speak in their terms." This dominant discourse denies these groups "every possibility of creating our own categories." Everything which puts the ruling discourse "into question is at once disregarded as elementary." Questioners of heterosexual discourse, she suggests, are dismissed for their analytical crudity, and that charge of naïveté silences inquiry.[75]

Wittig begins to point to the particular ways specific ideologies work to protect heterosexuality from basic questions.[76]

She points to those "rules and conventions that have never been formally enunciated" but nevertheless constitute the terms of the "heterosexual contract." When we merely "live in heterosexuality," we accede to that contract and its rules.[77]

She begins to pinpoint the strange, now-you-see-it, now-you-don't quality of the heterosexual system. For example, American marriage codes did traditionally refer to a "husband" and "wife" (persons of different sexes). But only since the 1970s have numerous legal challenges by gay and lesbian rights advocates forced attention to the implicit privileging of heterosexual relations caused by the restriction of state-approved marriage to different sexes (and, ostensibly, those with heterosexual desires). Heterosexuality "as an institution" has little clear existence, yet functions powerfully and invisibly as any written law.[78] Wittig's heterosexual mimics the title character of the film *The Invisible Man*. When he removes the bandages that define his shape, he vanishes.

When we try to define "heterosexuality," Wittig says, we find it eludes us: "I confront . . . an ideological form which cannot be grasped in reality, except through its effect, whose existence lies in the mind of people, but in a way that affects their whole life, the way they act, the way they move, the way they think."[79]

We treat heterosexuality as axiomatic, she argues, and this assumption keeps it from being examined, a circular silencing continually reenacted in practice. She stresses: Heterosexuality is treated as "always already there within all mental categories"—so it never gets questioned.[80]

Naturalizing heterosexuality is another conceptual move that helps it avoid a specifically social study. The "heterosexual relationship," she protests, is always "excluded from the social in the analysis," treated as "a core of nature which resists examination."[81]

Universalizing heterosexuality is another common mental maneuver that prevents its critical analysis. The straight mind "cannot conceive of a . . . society where heterosexuality would not order not only all human relationships but also its very production of concepts and all the processes which escape consciousness."[82] Like the eternal feminine, the eternal heterosexual assumes "that what founds society, any society, is heterosexuality."[83] And if heterosexuality's inevitable, it's not worth thinking about, for nothing can be done about it.

The power of the universalizing tendency is illustrated by Wittig's herself succumbing to it when she equates "the heterosexual relationship" with that of "male and female."[84] With this equation the universal returns with the biological. Identifying male-female relationships with heterosexuality buys into one of the twentieth century's dominant, mystified notions. That equation ignores the specific historical system that shapes male and female relationships into the particular institution we call heterosexuality.

The universal also returns in Wittig's analysis when she equates "society" with "heterosexuality." Though she first rejects the assumption "that the basis of society or the beginning of society lies in heterosexuality," she later asserts that to "live in society is to live in heterosexuality."[85] But if a generic heterosexuality is equated with a generic society it's difficult to see the heterosexual as a specific historical construct, and hard to imagine an alternative order.

Wittig also protests the "totalizing interpretation of history, social reality, culture, language" which eternalizes heterosexuality—another common, thought-stopping conceptual stratagem.[86] But her own analysis falls under the clock-stopping hand of a timeless heterosexuality.[87] She writes sometimes as if the concept and social ordering of heterosexuality are antique, referring, for example, to Ovid bringing Sappho "into line by making her the heroine of a heterosexual romance."[88] She cites the existence of a "lesbian culture" in ancient Greece to demonstrate that an alternative then existed to what she calls "heterosexual society"—an apparently eternal order.[89]

Heterosexuality also escapes questioning, she points out, through a conceptual strategy that dematerializes it, reducing it to "Irreal Ideas." Such dematerializing is accomplished when heterosexuality is spoken of as only a matter of words and concepts, and not also as an institution in which men and heterosexuals exert power over women and homosexuals.

The "material oppression of individuals by discourses" is illustrated, for Wittig, by pornography, presented by her as a form of "violence" against women.[90] Pornography, she says, "has a meaning," one meaning. For women, she says, "pornographic discourse . . . humiliates, it degrades." Porn is "a harassing tactic," functioning as "warning," it "orders us to stay in line," it "calls upon fear."

When feminists "demonstrate against pornography," she says, they are reproached by academics for confusing "discourses with the reality," images with life. Academic critics of antiporn feminists, she declares, do not see that pornography "*is* reality for us."[91]

In 1978, when Wittig first publicly discussed pornography, the feminist antiporn movement was just getting under way. But in the 1980s and 1990s an analysis like hers became the standard argument of the antipornography feminists who joined with ultraconservatives and the Christian right to try to pass antiporn laws and actively engage the state (and its mostly male staff) in an antismut, social purity crusade.[92] More recently, prosex feminists, anti-censorship feminists, and free-speech advocates have pointed out that pornography, in its multiple varieties and complex effects (feminist and male chauvinist, gay and straight, sadomasochist and vanilla, educative and objectifying, for example), provides a most ambiguous example of the material, actual violence done by heterosexual discourse. Happy hetero homemakers, depicted as mindless in thousands of TV commercials, may be cited as more prevalent, insidious, and damaging.[93]

Wittig points out that "straight society is based on the necessity of the different/other."[94] For heterosexuals to regard themselves as normal, homosexuals must stay abnormal. Hetero society requires a variety of different others, she says—not only a different sexual desire, but a different sex, and a different race. But while women and people of color are constituted as different, "men are not different, whites are not different, nor are the masters." All these differences, Wittig argues, are premised on the original social relation of dominator and dominated.[95]

Wittig suggests that those who don't consent to the "heterosexual social contract" can break if off—wives can run away from husbands, women can become lesbians.[96] She urges women (and men?) to flee heterosexual society one by one, if necessary, like the fugitive slaves who fled from slavery.[97] But U.S. slaves had somewhere to run: free states and Canada, outside the slave system. Where is the liberated zone outside heterosexual supremacy?

The idea of "heterosexuality as a must-be" is affirmed by the whole world, says Wittig. Opposing that necessity "is only the dim, fugitive . . . vision of heterosexuality as a trap, as a forced political regime."[98] The power of that "must-be" is so strong that even this iconoclastic lesbian feminist does not completely escape it. A historically specific understanding of heterosexuality provides a sense of a possible alternative.

RICH'S "COMPULSORY HETEROSEXUALITY"

"Compulsory Heterosexuality and Lesbian Existence," by the poet and essayist Adrienne Rich, was published in 1980 in *Signs,* the feminist scholarly journal.[99] One of the first essays in so respectable an academic periodical, by so respected an author, to put "Heterosexuality" in its title and make it the explicit, central topic of critical analysis, Rich's "Heterosexuality" was a fighting word—quite apart from "Compulsory." Simply naming "Heterosexuality" her major object of analysis, Rich contested that norm's usual silent treatment.[100]

She speaks repeatedly of "the institution of heterosexuality" and of a power-saturated "ideology" of heterosexuality.[101] These, "like motherhood," need "to be . . . studied as a political institution," along with the "economics, as well as the cultural propaganda, of heterosexuality."[102]

As the "Compulsory" in Rich's title suggests, she focuses on the many kinds of intense pressure that society places on women to ensure that heterosexuality becomes their sex's usual fate.

For example, an ideal "heterosexual romance" is "represented as the great female adventure, duty, and fulfillment."[103] This means that the negative aspects of women's intimate relationships with men receive much less publicity. The "sexual revolution" and its erotic-woman ideal also bind women to their dominators.

Men also deny women their own unique, autonomous sexual pleasure, tying women to men. Rich cites the surgical removal of the clitoris and also its denial by Freudians; the death penalty for female adultery and lesbian sexuality; strictures against female masturbation; and the physical destruction of documentary evidence of lesbian history.[104]

Some men force on women acts pleasurable only to these men. Besides rape and incest, Rich cites "pornographic depictions of women responding pleasurably to sexual violence and humiliation."[105]

Under such coercion, Rich says, heterosexuality is not accurately called "choice" or "preference." Those terms suggest a free, unpressured access to alternative possibilities. The idea that heterosexuality is women's "choice" obscures the social forces converging on women to heterosexualize them.[106]

Rich specifically criticizes the Freudian social-constructionist model in which a girl becomes heterosexual as she freely interacts with significant others in her life. Because women are subjected to men's and heterosexuals' greater power, that process is actually coercive.

She also criticizes the biological model that posits heterosexuality as an innate, predetermined "orientation." This effectively denies the social pressures on women that impel them toward heterosexuality.[107]

In contrast to that coerced heterosexuality, she describes a resistant, self-chosen "woman-identified existence," characterized by various "forms of primary intensity between and among women."[108] She presents woman-identification as a choice for women, freely maintained against the dominant hetero compulsion. As oppositional, women's close alliances with women are based on women's own authentic feelings. But are not such resistant intimacies of women also shaped fundamentally by the compulsory heterosexual regime against which they strive?

Rich frames women's central problem as "compulsory heterosexuality," implying the possibility of a liberated hetero-sexuality.[109] But it seems to me that whenever "heterosexual" and "homosexual" operate as a dominant social distinction they force people into one or the other of those two sexed eroticisms—or a "bisexual" combination. Any society split be-tween heterosexual and homosexual is compulsory. Rich's "compulsory heterosexuality" is redundant.

Rich questions the idea that the male and female part-ners in an erotic relationship, although both called by the name heterosexual, are equal in social status and power. Countering that democratic presumption of heterosexual equivalence, she points to the many social inequities that make heterosexuality a socially asymmetrical association, with women in the inferior position. She pointedly criticizes sev-eral feminist analyses of women's social status that do not ex-amine the negative effect on *all* women of that standard inequality of the heterosexual arrangement.[110] Because the so-cial organization of heterosexuality reproduces the inequality of women and men, she argues, feminists should consider heterosexuality not a minor side issue for women, but a major problem.

The idea of "heterosexuality as the 'natural' emotional and sensual inclination for women," Rich says, makes wom-en's identification with women seem "deviant," "pathologi-cal," and "deprived," obstructing women's political alliance with women.[111] The system of mandatory man-identification, she charges, also produces a silence, a great gap in knowl-edge, about the wide variety of women's close, supportive relationships with women.

In a heterosexual-dominant society, an especially acute silence denies the intense intimacies between women called "lesbian."[112] Even "sadistic heterosexuality," she says, is presented as "more 'normal' than sensuality between women."[113]

Heterosexuality must be placed in time, Rich stresses: "Historians need to ask at every point how heterosexuality as institution has been organized and maintained."[114] But she equates heterosexuality with "the coupling of women with men," a relation found in every society. Similarly, "woman-identification" and "lesbianism" remain universal phenomena that appear, as Rich says, "throughout history."[115] She does list the multiple varieties of women's "woman-identified" relations through time and across cultures. But she abstracts women's intimacies, resistance, and woe from the particular historical systems in which they occur.

History and time exist in Rich's analysis as the medium which makes possible, generation after generation, an essential, compulsory heterosexuality and the occasional organized, active resistance of women-identified women. But time provides no way of sweeping away the compulsory in heterosexuality by sweeping away its institutionalization, and the heterosexual designation itself.

In a speech delivered at a feminist conference in 1979, the black lesbian poet Audre Lorde warned that "The Master's Tools Will Never Dismantle the Master's House."[116] Her phrase served as internal criticism of that meeting, yet another academic gathering at which blackness and lesbianism signified excluded differences.

The master's idea of difference as inferiority must be rejected, Lorde suggests:

> *For the master's tools will never dismantle the master's house.* They may allow us temporarily to beat him at his own game, but they will never enable us to bring about genuine change.[117]

Lorde celebrates as a valuable, creative force distinctions between black women and white, and between homosexual

and heterosexual feminists. She does not, however, fundamentally question the homosexual/heterosexual polarity.

But in the twentieth-century the heterosexual concept
has been deployed as one of the master's most influential
tools. The master's house was heterosexual, and homosexuals
inhabited it as second-class poor relations, with lesbians a second class of that second class. Lorde's warning about the
handicapping effect of the master's tools may be taken as incitement to question the limits of thinking and politicking
within the parameters of the hetero/homo divide. Her words
incite us to forge new analytical tools, and leave the master's
behind.

Daring lesbian feminist analyses of the heterosexual order, and passionate liberal feminist and radical feminist analyses, inspired gay and lesbian liberationists of the early 1970s
to dig for their own hidden history. And that excavation of
the gay and lesbian past has led, gradually, to a new look at
heterosexual history. Now it's leading us to imagine a new
pleasure system.

8

TOWARD A NEW PLEASURE SYSTEM

Looking Forward

Ninety years after heterosexuality's American debut, in 1982, *The New York Times* was regularly sending out distress signals about a different-sex erotic challenged from within and without its own ranks. In August, novelist Margaret Atwood reviewed Marge Piercy's poems, calling them the

> product of a mind rooted firmly in time and place and engaging itself with the central dilemmas of its situation. How, for instance, is a heterosexual feminist to respond to (a) men as they are and (b) more extreme feminists who want her to divest herself of them?[1]

In October, John Osborne's review of Noel Coward's *Diaries* reported that Coward "challenged heterosexuality as a failure of style." Coward's aesthetic critique (the resistance tactic of the cultured queen) has roots reaching back to Oscar Wilde.[2]

In December, *The Times* described *Tootsie* as a film about "the crucial importance of friendship as a prerequisite to love between a man and a woman."[3] *Tootsie*'s director, Sydney Pollack, was quoted: "Isn't it a sad comment on heterosexual relationships that it's so rare to see a man and a woman who are best friends?" Heterosexuality's problems had become a cliché. That year the challenge to the hetero norm was so acute that an embattled California psychologist felt compelled to publish the world's first book *In Defense of Heterosexuality.*[4]

Even before herpes and, then, AIDS became major focal points for the anxiety of the heterosexually inclined, their sex-love had begun to lose its old certainty, its unquestioned status. Masters and Johnson's *Crisis: Heterosexual Behavior in the Age of AIDS* (1988) in fact named an emergency predating AIDS.[5] Yet the media response to AIDS has created a major increase in explicit references to heterosexuality, a quantifying that has furthered a qualitative change in public perception. Though AIDS was first generally linked in the U.S. with men who had sex with men, reports of the virus's migration have now created a change in public perception: Heterosexual and other fluid-exchanging acts are one mode of virus transmission—heterosexual persons are one of the endangered erotic species. Denying the existence of any special heterosexual AIDS threat, Michael Fumento's *The Myth of Heterosexual AIDS* (1990) evangelized against the grain.[6]

That year Pete Hamill's "Confessions of a Heterosexual" gave *Esquire*'s seal of approval to this self-declared straight male's anger at gay and AIDS militants (pitting the bad homosexual against the good is a classic diversionary tactic).[7]

As a young sailor, Hamill reveals, he had bashed some homos: "We were all so young that we arrogantly assumed that all of us were straight and they were bent . . ."[8] But many years later, after the Stonewall uprising of 1969, he had met gay men as upstanding as heterosexuals:

> gay men living in monogamous relationships, gay
> men of austere moral codes, gay men with great

courage . . . I knew that there were thousands of gay
men living lives of bourgeois respectability.[9]

Respectability did not, however, provide a lasting cure for his
deep-seated antihomosexuality. For then, Hamill says, "came
AIDS"—"And for people like me, everything about homosexuals changed once more. . . ." Now, he says, "the gulf between
straight and gay seems to be widening instead of closing." For,
like others he knows, he can't help blaming gay men for the
epidemic (they apparently went out looking for a virus to kill
them).[10]

His confessions constitute an example of the now-
common heterosexual coming-out piece. In these sex-
troubled times, Hamill, and numbers of other men, often feel
the need, under a variety of circumstances, to establish their
heterosexuality.

The heterosexuality establishing shot appears in March
1989, on the front page of *New York Newsday,* which carries a
large photo of New York City's former mayor and the head-
line: *"Koch: 'I'm Heterosexual.' "*[11]

A month later, Bruce Weber, an editor of *The New York
Times Magazine,* writes an "About Men" column on "My Best
Friend's Girlfriend."[12] He begins by confessing his fear that
the new live-in female lover of his best male friend will disrupt
the two men-friends' long-standing intimacy. He then immediately (though sheepishly) establishes his sexual orientation:
"We are the oldest two heterosexual men I know who have
never lived with a woman." These public confessions of heterosexuality suggest a sex-love dispossessed of its former silent
certainty. In 1990, the title of an off-off Broadway revue, "Heterosexuals in Crisis," satirically sums up the general sense of
a different-sex erotic emergency.[13]

By 1992, a full century after the American discursive debut of heterosexuality, for the first time in history, the word
heterosexual was appearing almost daily in this nation's newspapers and other mass media, usually in the explicit company of
homosexual. The words surfaced most often in reports of the

mass movement for homosexual civil rights and the movement of AIDS activists protesting the state's inadequate response to the epidemic.

As gay and lesbian equality advocates struggled for their
group's right to equal employment opportunity (the U.S. mil-
itary was the most famous employer attacked), for the right to
legal marriage, and for the right to domestic partnership benefits for unmarried couples of all erotic persuasions, they appealed often to the social contrast between homosexual and
heterosexual—stressing the unfair assignment of gay men and
lesbians to second-class citizenship. The rising of gay and lesbian activists, and the media response to them, now makes homosexual and heterosexual utterly ordinary, utterly ossified
categories. At this century's end hetero and homo have settled into two fixed, concrete objects of everyday postmodern
life.

But at this same moment, the sexed, gendered, and erotic are in motion and up for question. Numbers of gay and
lesbian intellectuals, and queer and feminist scholars, are
vociferously doubting the eternal feminine and masculine,
the everlasting woman and man, the timeless female and
male, the perpetual lesbian and gay, and the essential homosexual and heterosexual.

As this century closes the world's in flux. Many things
once fixed eternally are now exposed as "social constructions"
and "inventions"—thus, changeable. These exposés are contributions to a political debate about the limits and possibilities of transformation in the social shaping of reproduction,
sex differences, gender, and eroticism. Furthering this constructive deconstruction, even a few historians pitch in.

MICHEL FOUCAULT'S CATEGORY QUESTIONING

In the late 1980s and early nineties, in preparation for this
book, I studied Michel Foucault's volumes on *The History of
Sexuality*, and many of his essays and interviews.[14] As one of
the leading sex skeptics of the twentieth century, this French

historian and philosopher questioned the received sexual wisdom of his society and ours.

In particular, this creative doubter cross-examined "the repressive hypothesis"—his name for the Freud-inspired, prevailing notion that capitalist society's characteristic social response to sexuality has been to deny it.[15] Rather than repressing eroticism, Foucault argued, this society has busily produced it—in lavish variety and luxuriant abundance. Among this society's multiple eroticisms, a repressed, censored eros is only one particular, nondominant type.

If "sexual repression" is not what's wrong, freeing an alleged natural sex from its social shackles is not the job that lies ahead. With an eye to the future, we need to focus instead on the ways eroticism is produced, now and in the past, noting how these social-sexual systems regulate and control individuals and populations.

He questions the popular twentieth-century idea that sexuality has an essential core that constitutes us, unambiguously, as sexed and sexual: female or male, homosexual, heterosexual, or bisexual. He queries the ways in which we are all now socially pressured to privately believe in and publicly proclaim our "sexual identities" as the defining truth of who we are. This problematic labeling of sexual selves is, he argues, one influential means by which we moderns are managed.

He explores the changing social rules by which statements about "homosexuality" and "sexuality" come to seem obvious, common-sense, axiomatic truths. He suggests that we trace the "genealogies" of such categories back to historically particular "discourses," and the powerful institutions linked with them.[16] Such ostensibly descriptive categories as *homosexuality* and *sexuality*, he hints, are just as value-laden, ethics-loaded, and power-serving as the moralizing sexual prescriptions of early puritanical preachers about *sodomy* and proper procreativity.[17]

This historian refuses to take for granted "the question of sexual perversion" or "the problem of homosexuality."[18] Instead he raises basic questions about whose sexuality is questioned, the issue of which pleasure is designated an issue. By what rules and mobilization of power does it come about that questions are asked about some pleasures and not others? Sexual problematizing has a politics and a history, he warns us. The politics of sexual problem solving, he suggests, is secondary to the politics of sexual problem-naming.

Just as other scholars have publicized a process of "modernization," this historian advertises the process of social-sexual "normalization." This produces our experience of some bodily pleasures as normal and good, others as abnormal and bad.[19] His *History of Sexuality* is filled with references to the "normalizing functions of psychoanalysis," and to "normalizing interventions" into sexuality by a variety of moralizing doctors.[20] The sexual "norm," "normativity," and "normalization" are, in fact, his ongoing obsession.

Questioning our traditional assumption that "sexuality" is biologically given and ahistorical, Foucault provocatively proposes that "sexuality" dates to the late eighteenth and early nineteenth centuries. He speaks of the "production of sexuality" as a "historical construct."[21] Our own day's scientized "sexuality," he points out, is substantially different for the ancient Greeks' "aphrodisia" (and, for that matter, different from the early-American Puritans' "carnal lust," and the Enlightenment's erotic "tastes").[22] Sexuality, he argues, is a uniquely modern phenomenon and idea, constituted by a historically specific, institutionalized practice and ideology.

Querying our usual idea of sexuality as a basically private thing residing in individuals, Foucault names an "economy of pleasures," placing enjoyment squarely within a changing social and historical arrangement of power.[23] Different human pleasure systems, he suggests, give our bodies' capacity for delight particular historical configurations, isolating eroticism from other joys.[24]

Foucault's analysis of pleasure's history challenges earlier work in the field of sexuality, querying by example the limitations of a history of "Victorian repression," a history of "attitudes toward homosexuality," a history of an essential "homosexuality," and even a history of a fundamental "sexuality." His own history of the social ordering of ancient Greek and Roman enjoyments (including "Dietetics," "Erotics," "The Body," "Marriage," and "Boys") compares pleasure systems past with pleasure systems present. His radical historicizing of carnal lust subverts the idea of any predetermined erotic destiny. He posits the possibility of a revolutionary new social organization of pleasure.

But what, exactly, does Foucault say about *heterosexuality?* This historian's most profound suggestions for analyzing heterosexuality are, significantly, implicit—contained within his analysis of homosexuality.

His most notorious comment on that subject appears in a chapter on "The Perverse Implantation" in which he speaks of a historically "new persecution" and "specification of individuals" as kinds of sexual perverts. He contrasts the late-nineteenth-century specification and disqualifying of "homosexual" persons with the early Christian prohibition of acts of "sodomy":

> Homosexuality appears as one of the forms of sexuality when it was transposed from the practice of sodomy onto a kind of interior androgyny, a hermaphroditism of the soul. The sodomite had been a temporary aberration; the homosexual was now a species.[25]

Inspired by Foucault's comments on "The Perverse Implantation," may we not now ask about "The Normal Implantation"? In the late nineteenth century was not heterosexuality also implanted as one form of sexuality? I suggest: The sodomite had been a temporary aberration from a procreative norm; the procreator his and her undeviating mate. The homosexual and heterosexual were now permanent, inferior and superior, species of sex-differentiated erotic types.

In another major comment on "homosexuality," Foucault talks of the specific historical moment in which, in the late nineteenth century, the homosexually inclined first began to speak out in defense of their maligned pleasure:

> the appearance in nineteenth-century psychiatry, jurisprudence, and literature of a whole series of discourses on the species and subspecies of homosexuality, inversion, pederasty, and "psychic hermaphroditism" made possible a strong advance of social controls into this area of "perversity"; but it also made possible the formation of a "reverse" discourse: homosexuality began to speak in its own behalf, to demand that its legitimacy or "naturality" be acknowledged, often in the same vocabulary, using the same categories by which it was medically disqualified.[26]

Foucault here questions the " 'reverse' discourse" that is still one of the basic political tactics of modern gay and lesbian liberationists.[27] Reversing the bigot's judgment that "homosexual is bad," the liberationist responds: "gay is good," and organizes thousands under the flag of that avowal.

But that reverse affirmation, Foucault suggests, is a mechanical inversion, limited by the oppressive terms set originally by the bigot. The liberationists' reverse discourse, he admits, has practical uses in the important struggle for homosexual rights and equality—the fight for a better deal within the dominant system. But reverse affirmation does not expressly challenge the deep social structure of homosexual oppression in which the heterosexual and homosexual categories are implicated as basic terms.

This historian points to that late-nineteenth-century moment in which speech for and against *homosexuality* was becoming increasingly public and common. But may we not also ask what was happening at that time to the talk of *heterosexuality?* Was not the heterosexual first being publicly, though more quietly, defined just then? Is not that more reticent late-nineteenth-century discussion of the heterosexual at least as

important as the talk about the homosexual and sexual pervert? Is not, in fact, the doctors' talk about the homosexual
and pervert an indirect way of talking about the heterosexual?
If so, why does Foucault focus his explicit comments on the
homosexual and pervert and almost completely ignore the
heterosexual?

Foucault's own way of talking, I suggest, uncritically mirrors something peculiar about the heterosexual idea as we've
known it. That notion was constituted from the start as, simultaneously, an influential presence and powerful absence.
Foucault begins to hint as much.

"The discursive explosion of the eighteenth and nineteenth centuries," he says, was linked with a modification in
the system of marriage (a social organization of kinship relations, of economic alliance, of property transfer, and of pleasure). In the 1700s and 1800s, he declares, the standard of
"heterosexual monogamy" was

> spoken of less and less, or in any case with a growing
> moderation. Efforts to find out its secrets were aban-
> doned; nothing further was demanded of it than to
> define itself from day to day [in social practice, he
> seems to mean, rather than in explicit discourse].
> The legitimate couple, with its regular sexuality, had
> a right to more discretion. It tended to function as a
> norm, one that was stricter, perhaps, but quieter. On
> the other hand, what came under scrutiny was the
> sexuality of children, mad men and women, and
> criminals; the sensuality of those who did not like
> the opposite sex; reveries, obsessions, petty manias,
> or great transports of rage. It was time for all these
> figures, scarcely noted in the past, to step forward
> and speak, to make the difficult confession of what
> they were.

He adds: "if regular sexuality happened to be questioned
once again, it was through a reflux movement, originating in

these peripheral sexualities."[28] (In our own day, the questioning of "regular sexuality" from the viewpoint of "peripheral sexualities" is exemplified by lesbian feminists' and gay liberationists' critiques of the heterosexual order.)

Speaking of what he anachronistically calls the norm of "heterosexual monogamy," Foucault directs our attention to a historic shift—from the rule of an external, community-enforced law of proper procreative deportment in marriage to the rule of an internal, self-policed norm defining the proper experience of eroticism.

The earlier system of sodomy law enforcement had publicly and dramatically employed the fear of death, physical punishment, or peer-group ostracism. The developing, middle-class rule by sexual norm quietly mobilized a self-administered guilt, a self-punishing shame, and the personal, private terror of being sexually abnormal. That middle-class rule of sexual regularity to which Foucault points is certainly the ancestor of our later, historically specific "heterosexual" standard.[29]

Foucault's analysis suggests that the explicit, critical talk in the late nineteenth century about the homosexual and sexual pervert was a way for respectable middle-class doctors to speak covertly in defense of the procreatively ambiguous and thus still controversial "heterosexual." Speaking of the sexual pervert, doctors did not have to risk talking up often, loudly, and explicitly for the heterosexual.

The new heterosexual norm, he suggests, began life as a mystified, infrequently named, hidden persuader. It continues its relatively secret operation today. Despite its wide influence, the heterosexual norm still generally works quietly, unspoken, behind the scenes. Though hundreds of handbooks on how to be a better heterosexual treat it as problematic achievement, that norm itself is usually unquestioned.

The operation of that implicit heterosexual norm may also be seen in the absence, until recently, of references to "heterosexuality" in many psychological, sociological, and historical texts where it's actually alive and kicking. The word *het-*

erosexual, for example, makes relatively infrequent appearances in Freud's works, though he admits he's only interested in homosexuals as clue to heterosexuals. *Heterosexuality* is also typically absent from the indexes of modern books in which that norm is dominant. In all these volumes the physical absence of the word *heterosexual* is by no means trivial—it's evidence of the heterosexual norm's operation as unquestioned, subliminal seducer.

Foucault's focus on normalization is, I've noted, one of his most original achievements as historian. How odd, then, that he never extends his explicit analysis of normalization to heterosexuality—the name, after all, of our society's dominant, gendered, erotic norm. Why did Foucault not talk in detail and in depth about heterosexuality, given the unflagging, subversive gusto with which he tore into other cherished sexual notions and institutions? *About heterosexuality, how could he, in fact, have said so little?*

What specific arrangements of power stopped Foucault from explicitly problematizing heterosexuality? Specifying those arrangements provides insight into the means by which the hetero norm continues to escape an explicit inquest.

First, the power for so many years arrayed against the serious study of gay and lesbian history has recently resulted in a reactive push by scholars outside and inside academia for such research. Since the 1970s, the development of a whole new intellectual field, "lesbian and gay studies," owes its ascension to the deep interest of the homosexually inclined for a sight of ourselves in the world, a revelation of our formerly obscured social lives. Lesbian and gay history and studies is emerging as a way of resisting that soul-destroying invisibility.

It's not surprising, then, that Foucault, and others of "homosexual" and "pervert" predilection, have pioneered in homosexual history and queer studies. A profound personal interest motivated his and our problematizing of the sex scientists' problematizing of homos and perverts.

What's not so obvious is that, by continuing to focus on homosexuals and queer sex marginals, the peculiar objects of the sex doctors, Foucault and the rest of us reproduced a traditional problematic. Starting as a compensatory, affirmative action, research in the history of homosexuals and other marginalized sexualities reversed the historical silence about these groups, countering their denigration. But, in focusing on the historical construction of the homosexual category and group, we did not question deeply enough the basic system of unequal alliance in which a specifically heterosexual term and practice was produced as dominant.[30]

A compensatory history of homosexuals fails to study heterosexuals in equal depth and so fails to interrogate half the "problem." By focusing on homosexuals and other sexual "minorities," we continue to let the sexual "majority" off the hook (and we fail to question the idea of erotic minorities and majorities).[31] So it is that heterosexualism continues to escape the status of enigmatic, peculiar institution.

A few bad-faith, reactionary groups calling recently for "heterosexual rights" and "heterosexual liberation" have no serious interest in the critical study of heterosexual history. So it is gay male liberationists, and lesbian and heterosexual feminists, and their allies, who are most likely to protest that the focus on homosexual history apart from heterosexual history replicates the idea of gay men and lesbians as Aberrant Others, Marginal Mutants. However eye-opening the view from the sexual margin, we also need works that question the idea of a sex margin and sex center, a queer eros and a standard brand.

By not studying the heterosexual word, idea, and social system, analysts of sex, gay and straight, continue to privilege the "normal" and "natural" at the expense of the "abnormal" and "unnatural." Such privileging of the norm accedes to its domination, protecting it from questions. By making the sex-normal the object of historical study, we simultaneously pursue truth and a subversive, sex-radical goal: We upset basic preconceptions. We discover that the sex-normal, the sex-natural, the different-sex erotic, and the specifically "heterosexual" have a history of changing, often opposed, contradictory, and socially contested definitions. The sexes and their eroticisms have been arranged, perceived, and named in a great variety of not-always-"heterosexual" ways.

Studying the sex norm, we learn that it is not always or necessarily taken for granted, despite casual comments to the contrary.[32] "Because 'heterosexual' is conceived to be the norm, it is unmarked and unnoticed," claims John Boswell. Though the hetero norm has been unmarked and unnoticed for a good part of its history, at other times it's been furiously marked and hotly contested—for example, by feminists. Conflict over sexual norms is in fact quite common in U.S. and in other nations' histories. But in some eras the power of the sex-norm police succeeds in naturalizing and normalizing the reigning standard, placing it beyond the pale of inquiry.

As long as we, like Foucault, do not focus specifically on heterosexual history (along with homosexual), gay men, lesbians, and assorted queer people will continue to seem uniquely contingent, problematic, and weird. Heterosexuals will continue to seem perfect specimens, and perfectly transparent.

Second, the power that deters us from directly confronting the inequalities of condition of men and women kept Foucault from making women or gender his own particular object of theoretical concern. His analysis of the history of sexuality and pleasure indicates his lack of interest in feminists' problematizing of sex differences and women's unequal power.

Heterosexuality escaped Foucault's unusually probing mind, I suggest, because investigation of the "hetero" (as opposed to the "sexual") held no pressing personal interest for him. This permitted him a major failure of empathy with women and with feminist concerns—and an atypical failure of intellectual curiosity. As long as women's, men's, and gender studies are not taken as seriously as other traditional academic fields, we won't be driven to deeply question the social use of sex differences, including the hetero and homo halves of the heterosexual/homosexual distinction. Foucault's making a generic "sexuality" and a general "pleasure" his object of research excluded our sex-distinguished, gender-divided heterosexuality from his field of vision.

On November 20, 1980, I went alone to the crowded auditorium of the New York University Law School to hear Michel Foucault speak on "Sexuality and Solitude."[33] Afterward, alone, I joined a demonstration, announced at the lecture, to protest the recent murder of two gay men, shot down randomly in front of The Ramrod, a bar on Washington Street in Greenwich Village. *(The New York Post* reported that the killer, a patron of male prostitutes, had "told his minister father before the murder the 'Homos are serpents' and said he hit the 'serpents' because they touched him.")[34]

Among the hundreds of people gathered in protest in that West Village street was Michel Foucault, standing alone in the crowd. I, too, was alone in the crowd, and an impulse told me to introduce myself to him as a fellow sex sleuth.

But Foucault's first volume on sexuality had deeply irked me with his constant references to "power" doing things—his blithe disregard, even obliteration of active, resisting subjects (among others, himself, the one writing; me, the one reading; and us, those protesting in that street). His highly abstract level of discourse, his elusive prose, and his unwillingness to clarify his meaning with sufficient concrete examples, had annoyed me as the high mandarin indulgence of one so safely ensconced in academe he felt no need to explain himself to ordinary folk. So I did not say hello.

Thirteen years later, in preparation for this book, rereading Foucault's first volume on sexuality and his other chronicles and interviews on pleasure's history, I am struck by the immense, rich suggestiveness of his analysis, by his provocations to new, counter-intuitive ways of seeing, even by the clarity of his almost jargon-free (though abstract) presentation. I am profoundly sorry now not to have said hello, never to have laughed at sexuality with this subverter, a sex-rebel so obviously delighted to disturb our intellectual peace, whose brilliant work for us was so prematurely terminated by the current plague. Now, I can only mourn the loss of this great man, and honor his work, by employing it as tool in this heterosexuality-questioning project.

Foucault's provocative talk of "sexuality" as "historical construct," other scholars' discussion of the "social construction" of "sexuality" and "homosexuality," and feminists' talk of the making of "gender" encouraged me to pursue the history of heterosexuality's "invention."[35] But exactly what do I mean by *The Invention of Heterosexuality?* In what sense do I think heterosexuality is invented?

When I started this research, I believed, like most of us, that heterosexual feelings, acts, and relationships exist completely apart from the word and concept. I perceived the word and concept to be reflections of a heterosexual thing-in-itself. That thing, I assumed, had long preceded the word and idea.

I've ended up thinking that this, our usual, commonsense assumption, significantly distorts and substantially simplifies the historical relationship of the word *heterosexual* and the concept, the feeling, activity, and system. I now believe that those relationships are much more active and complicated.

To be as clear as I can about this complexity: I *don't* think that the invention of the word *heterosexual,* and the concept, created a different-sex erotic.

I *do* think that the doctors' appropriation of the word and idea of heterosexuality newly and publicly legitimated the previously existing but officially condemned different-sex eroticism of the middle class. The word *heterosexual,* and the concept, then helped to re-create this sexed eroticism as, specifically, "heterosexual" within a new, specifically "heterosexual" society.

This radical social-contructionist analysis contradicts our hard-held contrary hypothesis, that heterosexuality *just is,* unmediated by language and ideas, or only superficially mediated. According to that just-is hypothesis, heterosexuality is a

thing apart from the word and concept, an objectively existing fact of male and female flesh.

The idea that a heterosexual thing exists apart from discourse is itself a powerful conceptual ploy that keeps the
historical discourse about heterosexuality from being examined closely. For the just-is idea makes a history of the word
heterosexual, and the concept, a paltry trifle. If heterosex just
is, the history of the word and the concept is superstructual,
an overlay on top of the real, essential, authentic heterosexual
thing. It's not, as I've written this book to show.

Heterosexuality, I now think, is invented in discourse as
that which is outside discourse. It's manufactured in a particular discourse as that which is universal. It's constructed in a
historically specific discourse as that which is outside time. It
was constructed quite recently as that which is very old: Heterosexuality is an invented tradition.[36]

Heterosexuality, claims our dominant hypothesis, is emphatically not just a norm, not just one possible vision of the
place of eros in the intimacies of different sexes, not just one
ideal that should or should not continue to rule in practice.
It's not just one particular historical sex-differentiated erotic
system. The discourse that heterosexuality just is denies the
politics and history of this truth's production. Finally, this discourse asserts that, because heterosexuality just is, there's
nothing we can do about it.

But if a specifically heterosexual system didn't exist in the
past—in Walt Whitman's New York, for example—it doesn't
have to exist in the future—though a powerful hierarchial system of heterosexual inequality certainly exists in the present.
But how, then, can we possibly go about abolishing that system, and how to institute a new, more equitable organization
of pleasure?

Today's political struggles over the proper forms of sex
and gender, reproduction and eroticism, are even now constructing the shape of sex to come.

Unprecedented numbers of women in wage-work fosters
insubordinate impulses in women not necessarily identified as

feminists. These many newly uppity women demand sex-blind hiring practices and the equal employment opportunity of the sexes, helping to destabilize the old sex verities. Before the nation's fascinated eyes, one of the new women, Anita Hill, charges Supreme Court nominee Clarence Thomas with (hetero)sexual harassment, creating a novel national consciousness of the issue. Soon other new women are publicly protesting the Navy's annual condoning of (hetero)sexual harassment at the Tailhook convention, and exposing Senator Bob Packwood's years of unwanted (hetero)sexualizing. Next, Lorena, a battered wife, takes direct action to Bobbitt (her husband John Wayne). Taking the patriarchy into her own hands, she challenges, in her own, literal way the rule of the phallus.

The many wage-working women finally put to rest nineteenth-century associations of their sex with passivity and domesticity. Despite less than equal wages for equal work, lower-level jobs, and men's domination of the workplace, wage-earning makes women more independent of men, fostering new relations between the sexes, and a new idea of womanhood fully equal to manhood. Disposing of their bodies on the labor market, these new women assert their right to dispose of their bodies' eroticism, earlier the sole prerogative of men. The "high proportion" of women working for a wage, say historians of American sexuality John D'Emilio and Estelle B. Freedman, is linked to "upheavals . . . in heterosexual relations."[37]

During the 1980 presidential campaign, the New Right makes sexuality and femininity and masculinity national political issues. The following year Republican conservatives in Congress try to prohibit funds to schools which "deny the role differences between the sexes as they have been historically understood in the United States." The same politicians try to deny government benefits to anyone presenting homosexuality "as an acceptable alternative lifestyle."[38] But even these traditionalists keep sex differences and sexuality at the center of public consciousness.

During the 1992 presidential campaign, Republican Party conservatives make candidate Bill Clinton's (hetero) sexual adventures a national issue, along with gay rights, "traditional family values," and the politics of hate. Earlier, Senator Gary Hart was eliminated from the presidential race because of a (hetero)sexual indiscretion. Later, the (heterosexual) adultery of Long Island family man Joey Buttafuoco with teenager Amy Fisher is reenacted in three nationally televised dramas. The public airing of heterosexual scandals now makes it difficult to claim the moral high ground for this particular sex-love.

The fall of the old reproductive ethic also eliminates one rationale of the distinction between homosexual and heterosexual. With most of the western world, Christian fundamentalists and the great majority of Catholics regularly employ pleasure enhancers (euphemistically, "birth control"). Few people now, except the Pope, judge the quality of heterosexual relationships by their fecundity.

As D'Emilio and Freedman describe it, "since the early nineteenth century, when the reproductive moorings of sexual relations came loose for the urban middle class, many Americans have had to grapple, in a self-conscious way, with the meaning and purpose of sexual relations."[39] Now, the "near universality of birth control" highlights the separation of the procreative from the erotic.[40]

Today, the meaning of sexuality no longer seems to reside, self-evidently, within our bodies or in nature, but depends on how we use it. Striking discoveries by biologists of reproduction, and the development of new reproductive technologies, upset "age-old certainties about the natural connection between sex and procreation." Whatever ideas about sexuality most Americans hold in theory, the majority now commonly act as if there's no necessary link between "making love and making babies."[41]

At the same time, conservative legislators and right-wing activists battle to maintain the old link between sexual intercourse and reproduction. They deny federal funds for abortions for poor women, and anti-abortion fanatics try to deny all women the option of terminating a pregnancy. They prevent the dissemination of birth control information and devices to the many girls and boys having sex, and deny heterosexuals and homosexuals the sex education information that can save their lives.

Today's public destabilizing of heterosexual tradition is also clear in the rise of divorce and the creation of new families. "Between 1960 and 1980," say D'Emilio and Freedman, "the number of divorced men and women rose by almost two hundred percent; the divorce rate itself jumped ninety percent." Second marriages "had even less chance of surviving."[42] By the 1980s the "traditional two-parent family with children accounted for only three-fifths of all living arrangements."[43] The idea and reality of "the family" is pluralizing before Americans' astonished eyes. Lesbian couples and gay male partners bring up their children from former marriages, or adopt children; single heterosexual women impregnate themselves with the help of an obliging male and a turkey baster, as do numbers of lesbians.

As the "gender gap" between women and men narrows, so does the sexual orientation gap. The convergence of heterosexuality and homosexuality becomes ever more apparent. The instability of homosexual relationships (unsupported by law and the dominant culture) no longer serves to distinguish them essentially from the many heterosexual relationships destabilized by divorce.

Starting in the 1970s, the cohabitation of increasing numbers of unmarried, young, different-sex couples became "highly visible," making the cohabitation of same-sex couples seem quite ordinary. "As Americans married later, postponed childbearing, and divorced more often, and as feminists and gay liberationists questioned heterosexual orthodoxy," say D'Emilio and Freedman, "non-marital sexuality became commonplace and open." Another traditional distinction between hetero- and homosexuals vanishes.[44]

Particular sexual acts once imagined to distinguish het-

erosexuals and homosexuals no longer clearly serve that function. Though "Kinsey had found few heterosexuals who had
tried fellatio or cunnilingus," say the historians, "by the 1970s
it was a commonplace experience among those in their twenties."[45] In the 1970s, they add, "even the supposedly immutable 'sex act' underwent redefinition in ways that weakened a
male monopoly over the nature of sex."[46] The variety of erotic
acts hailed in today's heterosexual handbooks also weakens
the old heterosexual monopoly over the definition of sex.

The convergence of hetero and homo lifestyles is furthered by the ascendance of the consumer economy and its
pleasure ethic. ("Double your pleasure, double your
fun. . . .") This challenges the old work ethic, helping to usher
in a major transformation of sexual values. While the Victorian work ethic touted the value of economic production, that
era's procreation ethic extolled the virtues of human reproduction. In contrast, the modern economic ethic hawks the
pleasures of consuming, while the modern sex ethic praises
an erotic pleasure principle for men and even for women.

As D'Emilio and Freedman put it, "the dynamics of a
consumer-oriented economy" retails pleasure to those with
cash. It won't be long before condoms are sold casually in
every supermarket. The "commercialization of sex and the
sexualization of commerce places the weight of capitalist institutions on the side of a visible public presence for the erotic."[47] By the late twentieth century, "much of mainstream
culture was promoting the erotic."[48]

The commodification of pleasure further breaks down
old distinctions between hetero and homo. "As the dominant
middle-class culture has come to attach more value to sexual
fulfillment and pleasure," say the historians, it becomes difficult to preserve heterosexual marriage as the only legitimate
site for sexual expression.[49]

The commercial stimulation of eroticism lifts the veil off
the old sex mysteries. The marketing of pleasure-sex to all
comers with cash helps to demolish old rationales for heterosexual supremacy—even old rationales for the hetero-homo

difference. For, as pleasure pursuits, heterosexuality and ho-mosexuality have little to distinguish them. Heterosexuals are more and more like homosexuals, except for the sex of their sexual partners. Political scientist of sex Dennis Altman calls the growing legitimacy of recreational heterosexuality the "homosexualization of America." Heterosexual ways of life, he suggests, no longer differ essentially from gay and lesbian life modes.[50] The homogenization of heterosexual and homosexual heralds a paradoxical emerging trend: the declining signi-ficance of "sexual orientation."

In the mid-twentieth century, say D'Emilio and Freed-man, sexual liberals had "celebrated the erotic, but tried to keep it within a heterosexual framework of long-term, monog-amous relations that retained marriage as its final goal."[51] Now, that liberal consensus about the erotic has collapsed.

Today, thousands of homosexuals and their supporters take active part in an organized, national, mass movement for civil equality with heterosexuals. And this, surprisingly, fur-thers a radical leveling of the old homo/hetero distinction. For the open assertion of homosexual equality—the mass coming out of homosexuals—fundamentally threatens hetero-sexual supremacy, and the het/homo division itself.

The homosexual and heterosexual were first named in the fledgling attempt of reformers of the German "unnatural fornication" law to counter that act's lowly position in the social-sexual hierarchy. The homo/hetero division was then coopted by doctors as a means of asserting heterosexuals' supremacy. Historically, the reason to name and distinguish heterosexual and homosexual was either to refute the homosexual's inferiority or to affirm the heterosexual's supe-riority.

There'd be no reason for the hetero/homo division if heteros did not stand above homos in a social hierarchy of su-perior and inferior pleasures. If homosexuals were to win society-wide equality with heterosexuals, there'd be no reason to distinguish them. The homosexual/heterosexual distinction would be retired from use, just as it was once invented.

In one sense, the right is right. Religious fundamentalists and ultraconservatives are correct to accuse the gay and lesbian rights movement of a threatening homogenization. Homosexuals' political assertion of equality may be conceived by gay and straight liberals as a strategy for equalizing the civil status of heteros and homos. That equalizing may even be understood as fortifying the hetero/homo difference. But whatever their conscious goals, if gay and lesbian liberationists ever achieve full equality, they will do away with the social need for the hetero/homo division. The secret of the most moderate, mainstream gay and lesbian civil rights movement is its radically transformative promise (or threat, depending on your values).

The world of sex now turns upside down. Influenced by many social movements, heterosexual and homosexual grow ever more similar. Hence the mass media's mad dash to publicize every new "scientific" study demonstrating that homosexual desire, and heterosexual, is in the genes, hypothalamus, hormones, or whatever, and never shall the orientations meet. Once again the sure physiological line is drawn. Homosexuals and heterosexuals of biological determinist persuasion sigh with relief: heterosexuals because their feelings are not homosexual, and therefore good, homosexuals because their feelings are natural, and therefore good.

But then the hetero/homo difference slips again, and anxious lovers of a different sex and nervous lovers of their own sex are forced to affirm their desire with no helping hand from science, no backup from biology.

Biological determinists and their critics struggle today over values, politics, and the possibility of making a radically new sexual world. But exactly what kind of new sex world do we hope for?

Though a specifying of future sex is appealing, I decline the role of pleasure prophet.

For one thing, we need to look less to oracles, and trust more in our own desires, visions, and political organizing.

For another thing, the shape of future sex cannot now be known, for it remains for all of us to determine. That is, we construct the shape of future sex as we act up in the present in response to AIDS, gay and lesbian rights, domestic partnership benefits, sex education, abortion, birth control, universal health insurance, equal employment opportunity, and the definitions of queer and normal, lesbian and gay, homosexual and heterosexual. As we struggle to create a society less productive of pain, more productive of pleasure, we invent the sexuality of tomorrow.

But will that system distinguish between heterosexual and homosexual? If heterosexuality was constructed in the past, and continues to be constructed in the present, it can also be deconstructed in the future. What are its prospects?

Heterosexual and *homosexual* refer to a historically specific system of domination—of socially unequal sexes and eroticisms.[52] It makes as much sense, then, to look for the cause of heterosexual or homosexual feeling in biology as it does to look for the physiological determinants of the slave's mentality or the master's. Biological determinism is misconceived intellectually, as well as politically loathsome. For it places our problem in our bodies, not in our society. We now commonly think, "Well, of course, biology and society together determine our destinies." But that simply reinstates the old bio fatalism within a "sociobiological" framework.

Only the supreme arrogance of the heterosexualizing gaze allows us to view the hetero/homo division of modern Western society as rooted in biology, nature, or evolution, and other ages' different categories, sexes, and pleasures as superficial constructions. That biology has determined our historically particular heterosexuality and homosexuality is a vain, difference-denying conceit.

Contrary to today's bio-belief, the heterosexual/homosexual binary is not in nature, but is socially constructed, therefore deconstructable. With the abolition of the slave system, the relations of domination signified by the terms *master* and *slave* lost their immediate salience and gradually became archaic, though racism continues on. With the abolition of the heterosexual system, the terms *heterosexual* and *homosexual* can become obsolete.

Then what? Then, after all the put-down peoples unite to enhance the pleasure of their short shift on earth, we will finally become a nation, not only founded, but actually operating according to the principles of "life, liberty, and the pursuit of happiness." Of those three "traditional values," the happiness pursuit is "the real joker in the deck"—in the words of Gore Vidal. The pursuit of happiness, Vidal adds, "was a revolutionary concept in 1776. It still is."[53] For the pursuit of happiness, and the achievement of a few earthly joys, require the end of the mean society and the private greed principle, the making of a new pleasure system.

I take my stand here with the pleasure party. But the happiness pursuit is a "traditional value" not limited in appeal to the party of eros.

Feminists have recently shown us that sexual anatomy does not determine our gender destinies, our femininities and masculinities. Now, analysis of heterosexual and homosexual history suggests a further liberation: neither does biology determine our erotic fates. The social organization of erotic interactions is not fixed, the political economy of pleasure has changed substantially over time—and can change again. We can struggle together to make relationships and a social world more welcoming to erotic diversity and carnal joy. Within the limits and possibilities of our social situation, we can be the agents of our own happiness. We can unmake heterosexual supremacy and the hetero/homo distinction.

In other words, human beings make their own different arrangements of reproduction and production, of sex differences and eroticism, their own history of pleasure and happiness. But they do not make that history just as they please; they do not make it under circumstances chosen by themselves, but under circumstances directly encountered, given and transmitted from the past.

With that qualification, the future pleasure system is a matter of political debate and activist organizing. The pursuit of happiness in the twenty-first century is up to you.

AFTERWORD

by Lisa Duggan

Jonathan Ned Katz's mission in this volume—to present "heterosexuality" as a historical social convention, rather than as a natural and eternal given—is bound to make many readers uncomfortable, if not downright hostile. To some liberals, ready to tolerate "homosexuality" in others as long as their own "heterosexuality" remains undisturbed, this book may seem absurd in its attacks on such self-evident categories of identity. To some conservatives, Katz's claims may seem an immoral threat leading to the breakdown of civilization's core institution, the family. Even to some lesbian- and gay-rights advocates, these arguments may seem to unsettle familiar political strategies based on notions of fixed identity.

But Katz's arguments are not as outrageous and unprecedented as they may at first seem to many readers. He is following a long line of argument advanced by social and political movements trying to destabilize hierarchies, correct injustices, and end inequalities in social, cultural, and political life.

When feminists in the United States began to challenge widespread beliefs that women are "naturally" different from men in ways that justify systematic inequalities, they were met with ridicule, guffaws, and disbelief. Nineteenth-century suffragists, for example, were represented by their opponents as advocating an attack on nature itself, as well as on the family, the church, and the state. When African Americans challenged slavery, then worked for political equality at the end of the last century, they were attacked with "scientific" evidence that black people are biologically and culturally different from whites in ways that justify unequal treatment.

Over the decades, however, it has become possible to argue that most, if not all, of what were thought to be "differences" between the sexes and the races are historical and political, without being laughed out of the "mainstream" and into the margins of thought and belief. Of course, there is still plenty of debate. And it isn't only the opponents of progressive change who argue for fixed categories of identity. Some feminists and some Afro-centrists, for instance, would argue that gender and race do constitute significant, fixed lines of difference, though they would reverse the relative evaluations of such categories proposed by conservatives. An "essentialist" feminist might argue that women are naturally more peaceful and nurturant than men, and would do a better job of running the world; some Afro-centrists believe that people of African descent are better equipped to promote democracy and cultural vitality than Caucasians descended from cold, vicious "ice" people. In response, antiessentialists acknowledge that differences exist (though they often disagree about their content and meaning), but argue that they are cultural, historical, and political, not natural or fixed.

Jonathan Ned Katz enters the fray here with the argument that the categories "heterosexual" and "homosexual" are historical, and thus changeable. He will meet with opposition from conservatives, who might believe that *homo*sexuality can and should be changed, but are wedded to the natural and eternal nature of *hetero*sexuality. Homosexuals, to such bigots, are not only inferior but should be wiped out through scorn and punishment. But Katz will also be challenged by lesbian and gay "essentialists" who believe that sexual identity is fixed, perhaps inborn. Understandably, these advocates of equality believe that their kind of argument works better against the conservatives who would banish them from the earth. If lesbians, gay men, and bisexuals are born, not made, then the wish to ban or punish them is itself *against nature* and thus wrong as well as mean.

But such arguments are short-sighted as well as ahistorical. All they can win is tolerance for a supposedly fixed minority called "lesbian" and "gay." What they can't do is change the notion that "heterosexuality" is "normal" for the vast majority of people, and shift social, cultural, and political practices based on that assumption. Nor can they destabilize the rigid notions of gender that underlie sexual identity categories.

Far-sighted arguments like Katz's are difficult to make in the present cultural and political climate. As anthropologist Carole S. Vance has pointed out, we see headlines announcing the existence of a "gay brain," but no such reporting on the multiplying historical studies that show sexual identity to be cross-culturally and historically variable. We wait to open a copy of *USA Today* to read, "Heterosexuality Not 'Natural,' Not 'Normal,' Study Finds." Chances are, we'll be waiting a long time.

That's why this book is so important. In putting the arguments of historians of sexuality, that the categories heterosexual/homosexual are historical and changeable, into public discourse, Katz has done us a very significant service. If such arguments remain confined to the university classroom and academic conference, they won't push public debate and policy the way we need them to.

Katz will no doubt face attack and ridicule for his arguments here, but in doing so he joins a long and distinguished line of thinkers who have challenged the "common sense" of their contemporaries and paid for it. Others of us will be grateful for his pioneering spirit.

Let the debate begin!

ACKNOWLEDGMENTS

Those to whom I'm grateful may agree or disagree, of course, with some or many of my formulations.

This book is dedicated to David Barton Gibson, whose steady affection since June 1976 has enabled this independent scholar to write and think outside the academic system that usually supports intellectual work.

My aunt, Cecily Brownstone, provided professional editorial comment on parts of the manuscript, as well as delectable alimentary sustenance.

For Gore Vidal's encouragement over the years, and for his agreeing, before this book was written, to write a Foreword, I am most grateful. To Lisa Duggan, also, I'm grateful for the Afterword, for her friendship, and for a critical reading of the whole manuscript.

My friends John D'Emilio, Jeffrey Escoffier, Ed Jackson, and Carole S. Vance read the whole manuscript, and their constructive criticisms were most useful and are much appreciated.

For their critical readings of particular chapters, and for their friendship, I'm also grateful to: Robert Benton, Allan Bérubé, Mark J. Blechner, Judith Levine, David Schwartz, Ann Snitow, Sharon Thompson, Jeff Weinstein, and Gil Zicklin.

For bravely supporting my applications for major grants to research heterosexual history, I am grateful to John D'Emilio, Martin Bauml Duberman, Laura Engelstein, Estelle Freedman, John Gagnon, Mary P. Ryan, Joan Wallach Scott, Christine Stansell, and Catharine R. Stimpson. Thanks also to David Geffen for a contribution.

Elizabeth Lobofsky Kennedy has also supported my work in many ways and her friendship and her own research is much appreciated. For their support I thank some new and old friends: Ian Birnie, Alan Bray, Madeline Davis, Neil Derrick, Frances Doughty, Allen Ellensweig, Edward Field, Richard Fung, Eric Garber, Myra Goldberg, Greg Gunter, Edna Haber, Bert Hansen, Amber Hollibaugh, Tom Holt, Becky Johnston, Bob and Carol Joyce, Suzanne Kessler, Gary Kinsman, Tim McCaskell, Wendy McKenna, Joan Nestle, Esther Newton, Marc Ostfield, John Perreault, David Roggensack, Michael Savino, Judith Schwarz, Ed and Eudice Segal, Barbara Smith, Herb Spiers, Jim Steakley, Ed Strug, David Thomas, Vince Vitali, Tom Waugh, Paula Webster, Jeffrey Weeks, Harold Wells, Albert Wolsky, and Mary Wright. For their inspiration I thank Harry Hay, Jim Kepner, and Richard Plant.

To Herb Freudenberger, for his good humor and help, I am most thankful.

I am grateful to my editor at Dutton, Arnold Dolin, who, with John Paine, provided many suggestions and skillful line edits, to Miranda Spencer for copy editing, and to my agent, Diane Cleaver, for her advice and encouragement.

For computer counsel, thank you Beth Haskell and Eric Jennings. For translations and copies, I am grateful to Michael Lombardi-Nash and Paul Nash.

To the many campus groups which, since the early 1980s,

have invited me to speak on "The Invention of Heterosexuality," your enthusiasm and support helped to keep me at work on this. The many readers who have written to me since 1976 have certainly helped me to keep going.

In Memoriam

By way of holding in memory some dear friends and relatives and a great many acquaintances taken by AIDS, cancer, diabetes and other illnesses, and to protest our ridiculously inadequate health care system, I recall Lois Adler, Robert Adler, Dan Allen, Allen Barnett, Vincent Beck, Mike Belt, Bill Bogan, Robert Chesley, Winston Davidson, Ken Dawson, Mike Folsom, James Frazer, Ray Gray, Richard Hall, Mable Hampton, Ben Katz, Phyllis Brownstone Katz, Gary Knobloch, Gregory Kolovacos, Reed Lenti, Michael Lynch, Keith McKinney, Lawrence Murphy, Gerard Mutsaers, Bill Neitzel, Jim Owls, Marty Robinson, Craig Rodwell, Vito Russo, Neil Sandstad, Richard Schmiechen, Michael Sherker, Gregory Sprague, George Whitmore, and Connie Zoff.

NOTES

Chapter 1
The Genealogy of a Sex Concept
From Homosexual History to Heterosexual History

1. Joseph Epstein, "Homo/Hetero: The Struggle for Sexual Identity," *Harper's Magazine* 241:144 (Sept. 1970), 37–51.
2. Epstein 46.
3. Epstein 43.
4. Epstein 43.
5. Epstein 51.
6. Jonathan [Ned] Katz, *Gay American History: Lesbians and Gay Men in the U.S.A.* (NY: T. Y. Crowell, 1976) 1; hereafter, Katz, *GAH.*
7. Katz, *GAH* 1–2.
8. I suspect that the concept of an "identity" based on one's erotic and affectional feelings, and a politics affirming that "identity," does not explain the activism of many of those whose energies have fueled the gay, lesbian, and, more recently, the queer movements, and AIDS organizing. The concepts of gay and lesbian "identities," and of "identity pol-

itics," have been the major terms we've used to explain the open, mass affirmation of erotic and affectional feeling that fuels the modern gay and lesbian movement. We need a variety of other analytical terms.

9. Earlier, Martin Duberman had compiled a successful theater piece, *In White America,* from historical documents of the conflict between African Americans and whites. I probably had that model in mind, though I'd not seen Duberman's play. Inspired by my father's long interest in African-American history, I had in the late 1960s researched two documentary radio plays, and would in 1973 and '74 publish two books on resistant black people of the slavery era. With my father, Bernard Katz, I wrote *Black Woman: A Fictionalized Biography of Lucy Terry Prince* (NY: Pantheon, 1973). Also see my *Resistance at Christiana: The Fugitive Slave Rebellion, Christiana, Pennsylvania, September 11, 1851* (NY: T. Y. Crowell, 1974).

10. Katz, *GAH* 8.

11. Jonathan [Ned] Katz, *Coming Out!: A Documentary Play About Gay and Lesbian Life and Liberation* (NY: Arno Press, 1975). This includes facsimile reprints of most of the reviews in the mainstream and gay press.

12. Katz, *GAH* 6.

13. See, for example, Marty Anderson, "Is Heterosexuality 'Natural'?" *The Ladder,* June/July 1969, 4–7; reprinted in Barbara Grier and Coletta Reid, eds., *The Lavender Herring: Lesbian Essays from The Ladder* (Baltimore, MD: Diana Press, 1976), 55–60, attributed to Martha Shelley. Also reprinted is Rita Laporte's "The Causes and Cures of Heterosexuality," 43–49.

14. Radicalesbians, "The Woman-Identified Woman" (1970), in Anne Koedt, Ellen Levine, and Anita Rapone, eds., *Radical Feminism* (NY: Quadrangle Books/New York Times, 1973), 241. See the discussion of this essay in my chapter "The Lesbian Menace Strikes Back."

15. Dennis Altman, *Homosexual Oppression and Liberation* (NY: Outerbridge & Dienstfrey, 1971), espec. ch. 7, "The End of the Homosexual?": 216–28. In 1972, the gay writer Allen Young declared: "The artificial categories 'heterosexual' and 'homosexual' have been laid on us by a sexist society." Allen Young, "Out of the Closets, Into the Streets," in Karla Jay and Allen Young, eds., *Out of the Closets: Voices of Gay Liberation* (NY: Douglas Book Corp., 1972), 29.

16. Katz, *GAH* 6. In *GAH* my scattershot snipping at "the heterosexual dictatorship" represents a first embryonic comprehension of heterosexuality as a coercive social institution, but one not yet fully understood as historical (6). A comment on same-sex "love" argues that different-sex relations "also should be studied," a first vague call for heterosexual

studies (446). "The study of homosexual history," I also say, "raises questions about . . . relations between the sexes. . . ." (8).

17. Carroll Smith-Rosenberg, "The Female World of Love and Ritual," *Signs* 1:1 (1975), 28–29; reprinted in her *Disorderly Conduct: Visions of Gender in Victorian America* (NY: Alfred A. Knopf, 1985), 53–76.

18. Katz, *GAH* 446.

19. *Gay American History* rejects the idea of homosexuals as individuals apart from a particular historical "context," as the psychological model envisioned them. The importance of situating same-sexers in time is strongly emphasized as antidote to the idea of the homosexual "divorced from any temporal-social context" (6). See, also, 4, 7, 130.

20. See David F. Greenberg, *The Construction of Homosexuality* (Chicago: The University of Chicago Press, 1988). John Boswell pointed to this contradiction in a devastating review of Greenberg's book, "Gay History," *The Atlantic*, Feb. 1989, 74–78; see especially 75. Examples of such complacent essentializing continue to be common, even among self-declared anti-essentialists. Most researchers still conceive of a timeless essence of homosexuality and heterosexuality marching unchanged through the ages, though they now stress the radically different historical attitudes, responses, and political power arrangements that essence encounters.

21. Jeffrey Weeks, *Coming Out: Homosexual Politics in Britain, from the Nineteenth Century to the Present* (London: Quartet Books, 1977; revised and updated London: Quartet Books, 1990). I also eagerly read and learned from Weeks's *Sex, Politics and Society: The Regulation of Sexuality Since 1800* (London: Longman, 1981); *Sexuality and Its Discontents: Meanings, Myths & Modern Sexualities* (London: Routledge & Kegan Paul, 1985); *Sexuality* (London: Tavistock Publications, 1986); and *Against Nature: Essays on History, Sexuality and Identity* (London: Rivers Oram Press, 1991).

22. For a list of this pioneering work, see Lisa Duggan, "Lesbianism and American History: A Brief Source Review," *Frontiers* 4:3 (Fall 1979), 80–85; and Randolph Trumbach, "London's Sodomites: Homosexual Behavior and Western Culture in the 18th Century," *Journal of Social History* 11 (Fall 1977), 1–33.

23. John Boswell, *Christianity, Social Tolerance, and Homosexuality: Gay People in West Europe from the Beginning of the Christian Era to the Fourteenth Century* (Chicago: University of Chicago Press, 1980).

24. Lillian Faderman, *Surpassing the Love of Men: Romantic Friendship and Love Between Women from the Renaissance to the Present* (NY: William Morrow, 1981).

25. Mary P. Ryan, *Womanhood in America: From Colonial Times to the Present* (NY: New Viewpoints/Franklin Watts, 1975).

26. Jonathan [Ned] Katz, "Womanhood in America," *The Body Politic* (Toronto), Dec./Jan. 1977/78, 19, 21. I was also much interested by Ryan's tying changing womanhood ideals to the changing organization of women's work. I had a contract for a second book on gay and lesbian American history, and I wondered whether I could not similarly correlate different historical concepts of homosexuality and heterosexuality with changes in the ordering of production. I undertook such analyses in *Gay/Lesbian Almanac: A New Documentary* (NY: Harper and Row, 1983); hereafter, Katz, *G/LA*.

27. This conference, "Constructing a History of Power and Sexuality," was organized by members of the Graduate History Society and the school's Women's Center, and took place on March 31, 1978. My talk, "Homosexual History: Its Import and Implications," was later revised and published as "Why Gay History?" *The Body Politic* (Toronto), Aug. 1979, 19–20.

28. James A. H. Murray, Henry Bradley, W. A. Craigie, C. T. Onions, eds., *Oxford English Dictionary Supplement* (Oxford: Clarendon Press, 1933), 460; and R. W. Burchfield, ed., *A Supplement to the Oxford English Dictionary*, Volume II, H-N (Oxford: Clarendon Press, 1976), 85.

29. Katz, "Homosexual History," 12–13. In 1993, reading over this 1978 talk for the first time in 15 years, I'm astounded at the length of time I've been pondering the heterosexual history problem.

30. Michel Foucault, *The History of Sexuality, Volume I, An Introduction,* trans. by Robert Hurley (NY: Pantheon, 1978).

31. Jeffrey Weeks's pioneering history of British homosexuality, *Coming Out* (1977) quotes once and briefly from Michel Foucault's *Madness and Civilization;* see Weeks, *Coming Out,* 23. I believe I first read the first volume of Foucault's *History of Sexuality* early in 1978.

32. Robert A. Padgug, "Sexual Matters: On Conceptualizing Sexuality in History," *Radical History Review,* No. 20 (Spring/Summer 1979), 3–4; reprinted in Kathy Peiss and Christina Symonds, with Robert A. Padgug, eds., *Passion and Power: Sexuality in History* (Philadelphia: Temple University Press, 1989), 14–31. In the same sexuality issue of *Radical History Review* I also remarked the thoughtful analysis of "The Historical Construction of Homosexuality" by Bert Hansen (a review of Jeffrey Weeks's *Coming Out*), 66–73.

33. Padgug 12–13.

34. Padgug 12–13. The difficulty we all have in thinking ourselves out of our ahistorical sexual concepts is indicated by the ambiguities and

contradictions in Padgug's statements. The struggle to historicize a sexuality conceived originally as fundamentally ahistorical results in some mixed messages.

35. My manuscript copy of Duggan's paper is dated Spring 1981. It was published as "The Social Enforcement of Heterosexuality and Lesbian Resistance in the 1920s," in Amy Swerdlow and Hannah Lessinger, eds., *Class, Race, and Sex: The Dynamics of Control* (Boston: G. K. Hall, 1983), 76–92.

36. I read that paper, "The Invention of Heterosexuality," to Duggan, John D'Emilio, Carole Vance, and Paula Webster, the members of the study group whose presence I now recall. I wanted, I told the group, to see how far I could plausibly push the idea of a historically specific, socially constructed heterosexuality. In the next dozen-plus years I talked on "The Invention of Heterosexuality" before dozens of East Coast gay and lesbian campus groups.

37. Katz, *G/LA* 13, 16, 147–50, 152–53.

38. Many of these medical texts discussing heterosexuality are reproduced in *G/LA*.

39. Despite my focus on words, ideas, and ideals, this history of heterosexual discourse intends finally to carry us beyond discourse to raise difficult questions about the historical invention of heterosexuality as feeling, act, relationship, and identity, and as a social system intimately entwined with language and ideas, ethics, power, and hierarchy—the supremacy of heterosexuals and men, the subordination of homosexuals and women.

40. Though the "invention of heterosexuality" puts my case bluntly, a number of scholars are now speaking of the "invention" (or the "construction," "production," or "making") of the body, class, emotions, gender, madness, race, reality, sex, sexuality, tradition, homosexuality, and even heterosexuality, as a glance at the bibliography will show.

41. "Primordial heterosexuality" is borrowed with gratitude from Gayle Rubin, "The Traffic in Women: Notes on the 'Political Economy' of Sex," in Rayna R[app] Reiter, ed., *Toward an Anthropology of Women* (NY: Monthly Review Press, 1975), 186.

42. We might, following the medical model, call this syndrome "homovestism," a term I thought of some years ago. Louise J. Kaplan, in *Female Perversions: The Temptations of Emma Bovary* (NY: Doubleday, 1991), also speaks of "homovestism."

43. "Whiteness" is now beginning to be problematized; see, for example, David R. Roediger, *The Wages of Whiteness: Race and the Making of the American Working Class* (NY: Verso, 1991).

"Race" has also recently been problematized (again) from a critical perspective; see Henry Louis Gates, Jr., "Editor's Introduction: Writing 'Race' and the Difference It Makes," in the anthology he edited, *"Race," Writing and Difference* (Chicago: University of Chicago Press, 1986), 1–20; and Anthony Appiah, "The Uncompleted Argument: Du Bois and the Illusion of Race," in the same volume, 21–37. This volume was originally published in slightly different form as two issues of *Critical Inquiry,* 12:1 (Autumn 1985) and 13:1 (Autumn 1986).

44. See, for example, E. Anthony Rotundo, *American Manhood: Transformations in Masculinity from the Revolution to the Modern* (NY: Basic Books, 1993); J. A. Mangan and James Walvin, eds., *Manliness and Morality: Middle Class Masculinity in Britain and America, 1800–1940* (NY: St. Martin's Press, 1987); and Michael Roper and John Tosh, eds., *Manful Assertions: Masculinities in Britain Since 1800* (NY: Routledge, 1991).

45. The problematizing of the norm, the normal, and normalization is also beginning. See Foucault, *The History of Sexuality, Volume I,* espec. 89, 105, and *The Use of Pleasure, Volume 2 of The History of Sexuality* (NY: Pantheon, 1985), especially 12. See also Georges Canguilhem, *The Normal and Pathological,* Introduction by Michel Foucault (NY: Zone Books, 1989), and Ed Cohen, *Talk on the Wilde Side: Toward a Genealogy of a Discourse on Male Sexualities* (NY: Routledge, 1993), especially his historical analysis of "normative masculinity," the "normalizing" of male sexuality, and his chapter "Legislating the Norm: From 'Sodomy' to 'Gross Indecency.' "

46. The distinct histories of heterosexual women and men remain subjects for future, detailed explorations.

47. See Sander L. Gilman, *Difference and Pathology: Stereotypes of Sexuality, Race, and Madness* (Ithaca: Cornell University Press, 1985), and Gilman's *The Case of Sigmund Freud: Medicine and Identity at the Fin de Siècle* (Baltimore: Johns Hopkins University Press, 1993). The intersections of "race" and "heterosexuality" remain a task for future researchers.

48. A number of books and articles have begun in recent years to trace the twentieth century "sexualization" of American society—the historic behavioral and emotional changes that might also be called the "heterosexualization" of America. For a good summary of these see John D'Emilio and Estelle Freedman's *Intimate Matters: A History of Sexuality in America* (NY: Harper & Row, 1988).

A few innovative writers, based mostly in English departments, have also recently begun to again question the social uses of the heterosexual/homosexual divide. I refer, primarily, to Eve Kosofsky Sedgwick's *Between Men: English Literature and Male Homosexual Desire*

(NY: Columbia University Press, 1985) and, especially, her *Epistemology of the Closet* (Berkeley: University of California Press, 1990); Judith Butler, *Gender Trouble: Feminism and the Subversion of Identity* (NY: Routledge, 1990); Diana Fuss, ed., *Inside/Out: Lesbian and Gay Theories* (NY: Routledge, 1990); and Ed Cohen, *Talk on the Wilde Side* (NY: Routledge, 1993). But the present book is the first empirically grounded, historical survey and analysis of the discourse on heterosexuality.

Chapter 2
The Debut of the Heterosexual
Richard von Krafft-Ebing and the Mind Doctors

1. Dr. James. G. Kiernan, "Responsibility in Sexual Perversion," *Chicago Medical Recorder* 3 (May 1892), 185–210; "Read before the Chicago Medical Society, March 7, 1892," but it's difficult to imagine him reading his footnote on Krafft-Ebing. Kiernan's note on 197–98 cites Krafft-Ebing's classifications in *Psychopathia Sexualis*, "Chaddock's translation" (no date). The U.S. publication in 1893 of C. G. Chaddock's translation of Krafft-Ebing's *Psychopathia Sexualis followed* Kiernan's article (see backnote 4 below). So there's some confusion about the exact source of Kiernan's brief note on Krafft-Ebing's terms "hetero-sexual" and "homo-sexual." Perhaps Kiernan saw a prepublication version of Chaddock's translation. It's also possible that Kiernan had seen some earlier article by Krafft-Ebing or the English translation by F. J. Rebman of the 10th German edition of Krafft-Ebing's *Psychopathia Sexualis*, published in London in 1889 (I have not inspected that edition). Kiernan seems to have based his brief gloss on Krafft-Ebing's definition of the heterosexual and homosexual on a superficial reading of pages 222–23 of the 1893 edition of Chaddock's translation of *Psychopathia Sexualis*, paragraphs numbered 1–4.

2. Mental hermaphrodites experienced, sometimes, the "wrong" feelings for their biological sex; their erotic desire was improperly inverted. A moral judgment founded the ostensibly objective, scientific concept of psychical hermaphroditism.

Kiernan's idea of "psychical hermaphroditism" is not exactly the same as the attraction we now label "bisexual," referring as we do to the sex of the subject and the two different sexes to which he or she is attracted. Psychical hermaphroditism referred to mental gender, while our bisexuality refers to the sex of a sex partner. Mental hermaphroditism might lead to both sexes as erotic partners, but the term laid the cause in the mental gender of the subject (like the concept of inversion). Our bisexuality does not involve any necessary link to mental gender. I am grateful to Lisa Duggan for this clarification.

3. But heterosexuals' appearance of triple the abnormality of homosexuals was deceiving. For Kiernan, the gender deviance of homosexuals *implied* that they were also, simultaneously, rebels from a procreative norm and an erotic norm. But it's significant that Kiernan explicitly stresses homosexuals' gender rebellion, not their erotic or reproductive deviancy. George Chauncey, Jr., discusses the late-nineteenth-century stress on gender inversion in "From Sexual Inversion to Homosexuality: Medicine and the Changing Conceptualization of Female Deviance," *Salmagundi* 56–59 (Fall-Winter 1983), 114–46.

4. R. von Krafft-Ebing, *Psychopathia Sexualis, with Especial Reference to Contrary Sexual Instinct: A Medico-Legal Study*, trans. Charles Gilbert Chaddock (Philadelphia: F. A. Davis, 1893), from the 7th and revised German ed.; preface dated November 1892. Hereafter cited as Krafft-Ebing. The U.S. Copyright Office received and registered this edition on February 16, 1893 (Copyright Office to Katz, May 25, 1990).

This book's year of publication is confused, because its copyright page and its preface are dated 1892, while its title page lists the year of publication as 1893. *The National Union Catalogue of Pre-1956 Publications* says this edition was first published in 1892, and the first citation of "hetero-sexual" listed in the *Oxford English Dictionary* (1976 Supplement, p. 85) is to this edition of Krafft-Ebing, attributed to 1892. That year is incorrect. Although it was evidently prepared by November 1892, the date of its preface, it was not officially published until 1893.

For Krafft-Ebing and his *Psychopathia* see Peter Gay, *The Bourgeois Experience: Victoria to Freud, Volume II, The Tender Passion* (NY: Oxford University Press, 1986), 221, 223–24, 226, 229, 230–32, 286, 338, 350; Gert Hekma, "A History of Sexology: Social and Historical Aspects of Sexuality," in Jan Bremmer, ed., *From Sappho to De Sade: Moments in the History of Sexuality* (first published 1989; NY: Routledge, 1991), 173–93; and Arnold I. Davidson, "Closing Up the Corpses: Diseases of Sexuality and the Emergence of the Psychiatric Style of Reasoning," in George Boolos, ed., *Meaning and Method: Essays in Honor of Hilary Putnam* (NY: Cambridge University Press, 1990), 295–325. I am also greatly indebted to talks with Harry Oosterhuis and an advance copy of his paper "Richard von Krafft-Ebing's Step-Children of Nature: Psychiatry and the Making of Modern Sexual Identity," presented as a talk at the Second Carleton Conference on the History of the Family, May 12, 1994, in Ottawa, Canada.

5. Krafft-Ebing's focus, as a psychiatrist, on disturbed mental states con-

trasts with the earlier nineteenth-century focus of neurologists on disturbed brains. I thank Lisa Duggan for this comment.

6. In this text the doctor's descriptions of sex sickness and sex health replaced the old, overtly moral judgments about bad sex and good sex, introducing the modern medical model of sexuality to numbers of Americans.

7. See, for example, L. F. E. Bergeret, *The Prevention Obstacle, or Conjugal Onanism. The Dangers and Inconveniences to the Individual, to the Family, and to Society, of Frauds in the Accomplishment of the Generative Functions,* trans. from the third French edition by P. De Marmon (NY: 1870; photographic reprint NY: Arno Press, 1974).

8. Krafft-Ebing 9.

9. Krafft-Ebing 169.

10. Krafft-Ebing 174.

11. Krafft-Ebing 234–36.

12. Krafft-Ebing 234–36.

13. Krafft-Ebing 230–55.

14. Krafft-Ebing 341.

15. Krafft-Ebing 342.

16. Krafft-Ebing 344–47.

17. Krafft-Ebing 346.

18. Krafft-Ebing 347; a typo in the original was silently corrected.

19. Krafft-Ebing 346.

20. Krafft-Ebing 346.

21. Krafft-Ebing 347.

22. Krafft-Ebing 351–57.

23. Krafft-Ebing 351.

24. Krafft-Ebing 354.

25. His uses of "hetero-sexual" link it specifically with "attempts," 346; "desires," 323; "feeling," 231, 250, 251, 321, 324, 333, 340–41 (two uses); "instinct," 222, 231, 319, 320 (two uses), 356; "individuals," 174; "intercourse," 234, 256, 338, 347; "love," 255, 280. Krafft-Ebing once uses "hetero- and homo-sexuality" (sex-differentiated erotic entities), 169.

26. Krafft-Ebing 1.

27. Krafft-Ebing 9. A positive link is even suggested between sexual and religious feelings (9–10). And a positive "sexual factor" is said to prove
     influential in awakening aesthetic feelings. What would poetry
     and art be without a sexual foundation? In (sensual) love is
     gained the warmth of fancy without which a true creation of

art is impossible. . . . It may thus be understood why great poets and artists have sensual natures (10).

A lack of sufficient sensuality is problematic, suggests this doctor: when
"the sensual element is weak," love is "sentimental" and "in danger of
becoming a caricature." Such sentimental "love is flat and soft, and can
even be silly" (11).

28. Krafft-Ebbing 1.

29. I am indebted for this point to Lisa Duggan, who discusses it in her
study "The Social Enforcement of Heterosexuality and Lesbian Resistance in the 1920s," in Amy Swerdlow and Hannah Lessinger, eds., *Class,
Race, and Sex: The Dynamics of Control* (Boston: G. K. Hall, 1983), 75–92.

30. Krafft-Ebing 4.

31. Krafft-Ebing's lecture in favor of women's equality employs evolutionary theory (see 2, 3, 4).

32. Krafft-Ebing 13.

33. Krafft-Ebing 13.

34. Krafft-Ebing 14.

35. Krafft-Ebing 13.

Chapter 3
Before Heterosexuality
Looking Backward

1. Michel Foucault's comments are scattered throughout the second
and third volumes of his *History of Sexuality*. See *The Use of Pleasure: Volume 2 of The History of Sexuality,* trans. by Robert Hurley (NY: Pantheon,
1985); and *The Care of the Self: Volume 3 of The History of Sexuality,* trans.
by Robert Hurley (NY: Pantheon, 1986).

Foucault's basic approach to ancient Greece and Rome is sup-
ported eloquently by David M. Halperin in *One Hundred Years of Homo-
sexuality and Other Essays on Greek Love* (NY: Routledge, 1990); John J.
Winkler, *The Constraints of Desire: The Anthropology of Sex and Gender in
Ancient Greece* (NY: Routledge, 1990); and in David M. Halperin, John J.
Winkler, and Froma I. Zeitlin, eds., *Before Sexuality: The Construction of
Erotic Experience in the Ancient Greek World* (Princeton: Princeton Univer-
sity Press, 1990).

Foucault's and the social constructionist interpretation of ancient
Greek and Roman society is contested in John Boswell's "Revolutions,
Universals, and Sexual Categories," in Martin Duberman, Martha
Vicinus, and George Chauncey, eds., *Hidden from History: Reclaiming the
Gay and Lesbian Past* (NY: New American Library, 1989), 17–36. Social

constructionism is also contested in numbers of the essays in Edward Stein, ed., *Forms of Desire: Sexual Orientation and the Social Constructionist Controversy* (NY: Garland, 1990).

2. Foucault, *The Use of Pleasure* II, 188–89.

3. Foucault, *The Use of Pleasure* II, 187.

4. Foucault, *The Use of Pleasure* II, 188.

5. This historian suggests that we may legitimately use our own society's term and concept "bisexuality" (or, implicitly, "homosexuality" or "heterosexuality") when we want to translate and describe for ourselves, in *our* terms, the emotions of individuals apart from their particular historical structure, their concepts, and their language (Foucault, *The Use of Pleasure* II, 188).

6. The first volume of Foucault's *History of Sexuality* was first published in France in 1976, and the second and third volumes in 1984.

7. See Jonathan Ned Katz, "The Age of Sodomitical Sin, 1607–1740," an essay in *Gay/Lesbian Almanac: A New Documentary* (NY: Harper & Row, 1983), 23–65; and documents, 66–136. Also see Michael Warner, "New English Sodom," in Jonathan Goldberg, ed., *Queering the Renaissance* (Durham, N.C.: Duke University Press, 1994), 330–58; Goldberg's "Sodomy in the New World: Anthropologies Old and New," in Michael Warner, ed., *Fear of a Queer Planet: Queer Politics and Social Theory* (Minneapolis: University of Minnesota Press, 1993), 3–18; Goldberg's, "Part Three: 'They Are All Sodomites': The New World," in his *Sodometries: Renaissance Texts, Modern Sexualities* (Stanford, CA: Stanford University Press, 1992), 179–249; and John D'Emilio and Estelle B. Freedman, "Part I. The Reproductive Matrix, 1600–1800," in their *Intimate Matters: A History of Sexuality in America* (NY: Harper & Row, 1988), 3–54. And note the sources cited in all these tests.

8. See Lyle Koehler, *A Search for Power: The "Weaker Sex" in Seventeenth-Century New England* (Urbana: University of Illinois Press, 1980), 146–52.

9. Katz, *G/LA* 31.

10. The term "Sodomite" was used in these colonies, but it referred directly to persons from Sodom and their whole array of sins, not to a person defined essentially by the act of sodomy. My interpretation of the uses of the term "Sodomite" in these colonies differs with the analysis of Michael Warner in his "New English Sodom."

11. On the making of the American middle class, for starters see: Mary P. Ryan, *Cradle of the Middle Class: The Family in Oneida County, New York, 1790–1865* (Cambridge, MA: Harvard University Press, 1981); Karen Halttunen, *Confidence Men and Painted Women: A Study of Middle-Class Cul-*

ture in America, 1830–1870 (New Haven: Yale University Pres, 1982); Stuart M. Blumin, "The Hypothesis of Middle-Class Formation in Nineteenth-Century America: A Critique and Some Proposals," *American Historical Review* 90 (1985), 299–338; and Blumin's *The Emergence of the Middle Class: Social Experience in the American City, 1760–1900* (NY: Cambridge University Press, 1989). Also see Paul Boyer, *Urban Masses and Moral Order in America: 1820–1920* (Cambridge, MA: Harvard University Press, 1978).

12. Ellen K. Rothman, *Hands and Hearts: A History of Courtship in America* (NY: Basic Books, 1984).

13. Rothman 54.

14. Rothman 51.

15. Karen Lystra, *Searching the Heart: Women, Men, and Romantic Love in Nineteenth-Century America* (NY: Oxford University Press, 1989).

16. Lystra 85.

17. Lystra 85.

18. Lystra 84.

19. Lystra 59.

20. Lystra 101–02, 113, 117, 118.

21. D'Emilio and Freedman xviii, 111–16, 120, 138, 156–57.

22. Rothman's, Lystra's, D'Emilio and Freedman's, and Peter Gay's work (discussed later) points to the absence in the nineteenth-century U.S. of any public ideology that naturalized, medicalized, and justified different-sex eroticism in and of itself, apart from different-sex love. A normal, official, medically modeled, physiological heterosexuality had not yet been declared.

23. Steven Seidman, *Romantic Longings: Love in America, 1830–1980* (NY: Routledge, 1991), 208–09.

24. Seidman 208–09.

25. Lystra 84.

26. Lystra never adequately explores this nasty underside of nineteenth-century true love—the idea (and the strong feeling) that sensuality divorced from true love was deeply, fundamentally problematic. Because Lystra separates her chapters on sexuality from her chapters on the tensions experienced by couples in love, her couples appear to enjoy eros without suffering any substantial, prolonged anguish, guilt, shame, or conflict about their erotic feelings or activities. A few pages by Lystra on tensions in the sexual relations of women and men fail to balance her stress on couples' ability to unambiguously justify sexual expression by love (see 69–76). In contrast, Rothman suggests throughout her book that the task of vindicating an otherwise unjustified carnal lust did

cause deep anxiety about love's sufficiency and intense consternation about love's faltering (see Rothman 52–53, 130, 135–37, 230, 233–41).

27. Seidman 22–23.

28. Seidman 8.

29. Seidman 189. But, then, Seidman uses the heterosexual term as if it *did* have a functional, operative life in mid-nineteenth-century society (see 22–23).

30. Barbara Welter, "The Cult of True Womanhood: 1820–1860," *American Quarterly* 18 (Summer 1966), 151–74; Welter's analysis is extended here to include True Men and True Love.

31. True women and men were distinguished from false women and men, called by a variety of derogatory names. Those who failed to live up to true woman's and true man's character and calling, or who deviated from these strict sex standards, were castigated as false-sexed creatures. For criticizing the traditional female role, Mary Wollstonecraft, Frances Wright, and Harriet Martineau were condemned by a minister in 1838 as "only semi-women, mental hermaphrodites" (see Katz, *G/LA*, 140). In 1852 the *New York Herald* referred to "mannish women," and a Mr. Mandeville referred to women activists as a "hybrid species, half man and half woman, belonging to neither sex." The following year the *Herald* referred to "unsexed women," and such epithets were hurled at feminists and other nonconforming women and men well into the twentieth century (see Peter Gay, *The Bourgeois Experience: Victoria to Freud, Volume I, Education of the Senses* [NY: Oxford University Press, 1984], 190, 191).

32. For the middle class's relation to the working class, see D'Emilio and Freedman, xvi, 46, 57, 130, 142, 152, 167, 183–84. Also see Seidman, 59–60, 117–118.

33. The term "true love" simultaneously asserted love's *existence* and love's *value*. True love and false love signified an essential contrast between an authentic and unauthentic affection. True love made no reference to any distinction between different-sex and same-sex eroticism.

34. Seidman 23, 37; D'Emilio and Freedman 68–69, 71, 72.

35. D'Emilio and Freedman 130–38. The term "male prostitute" seems to have referred in the nineteenth century to the man who employed women prostitutes, not specifically and only to the man who prostituted himself to men for money. I am grateful to Timothy Gilfoyle for this information.

36. Michael Lynch, "New York Sodomy, 1796–1873," paper presented at the New York Institute for the Humanities, February 1, 1985.

37. "Passionlessness" is one historian's confused and confusing name

for the emotions that nineteenth-century women and men referred to constantly as "passion"—and honored for their depth and intensity. See Nancy F. Cott, "Passionlessness: An Interpretation of Victorian Sexual Ideology, 1790–1850," *Signs* 4 (1978), 219–36.

38. D'Emilio and Freedman 121.

39. For the decline of fertility see D'Emilio and Freedman 57–59, 66, 146, 151, 172, 173–74, 189, 201, 247, 251–52, 330–31.

40. Rothman 120–22, 128.

41. Rothman 128–29.

42. Rothman 129.

43. Walt Whitman, *Leaves of Grass, Facsimile Edition of the 1860 Text* (Ithaca, NY: Cornell University Press, 1961).

44. Michael Lynch, " 'Here is Adhesiveness': From Friendship to Homosexuality," *Victorian Studies* 29:1 (Autumn 1985), 67–96. Although Whitman never refers to erotic acts between women, he had apparently heard of a problematic intimacy between women which he compared to his own tense relationships with Peter Doyle and Fred Vaughan. See Edward F. Grier, ed., *Walt Whitman, Notebooks and Unpublished Prose Manuscripts,* II (NY: New York University Press, 1984), 890, n. 77. The reference is to Jenny Bullard, of New Ipswich, New Hampshire, described as "handsome, bountiful, generous, cordial, strong, careless, laughing, large, regardless of dress or personal appearance and [who] appreciates and likes Leaves of Grass." Bullard is said to have lived with two women and never to have married.

45. Although Gay doesn't mention Emily Dickinson's letters to Sue Gilbert, these document Emily's own earlier, intense, passionate relationship with the female friend who was to become her brother Austin's unhappy wife. See Lillian Faderman, "Emily Dickinson's Letters to Sue Gilbert," *Massachusetts Review* 18:2 (Summer 1977), 197–225.

46. Gay 89.

47. Kathy Peiss's *Cheap Amusements: Working Women and Leisure in Turn-of-the-Century New York* (Philadelphia: Temple University Press, 1986), Peiss's " 'Charity Girls' and City Pleasures: Historical Notes on Working Class Sexuality, 1880–1920," in Ann Snitow, Christine Stansell, and Sharon Thompson, eds., *Powers of Desire: The Politics of Sexuality* (NY: Monthly Review Press, 1983), 74–87; and Joanne J. Meyerowitz's *Women Adrift: Independent Wage Earners in Chicago, 1880–1930* (Chicago: University of Chicago Press, 1988), argue that "heterosexuality" had its roots in working-class leisure practices in urban areas. I do not disagree. I am arguing that the middle class reevaluated working-class, "foreign," and African-American sexual culture when it publicly adopted the term and

idea of heterosexuality to justify its own class practices. Also see Christine Stansell, *City of Women: Sex and Class in New York, 1789–1860* (NY: Alfred A. Knopf, 1986).

48. Gay 77.

49. My understanding of the historical specifics of normalization is modeled on Foucault's analytical investigations, discussed in Chapter 8.

The "sexualization" of late-nineteenth- and twentieth-century U.S. culture is a theme of numbers of books and articles; see, for example, D'Emilio and Freedman, "Part III: Toward a New Sexual Order, 1880–1930" and "Part IV: The Rise and Fall of Sexual Liberalism, 1920 to the Present," 171–343; Rothman, "Part III: 1870–1920," 179–284; Seidman, "Part Two: Modern Times (1890–1960)," 65–120; Kevin White, ch. 4, "Male Ideology and the Roots of the Sexualized Society, 1910–1930," in *The First Sexual Revolution: The Emergence of Male Heterosexuality in Modern America* (NY: New York University Press, 1993), 57–79; and Peter Gardella, *Innocent Ecstasy: How Christianity Gave America an Ethic of Sexual Pleasure* (NY: Oxford University Press, 1985).

50. Hubert Kennedy, *Ulrichs: The Life and Works of Karl Heinrich Ulrichs, Pioneer of the Modern Gay Movement* (Boston: Alyson, 1988), 50, 56–58, 155. On Ulrichs also see Manfred Herzer, "Kertbeny and the Nameless Love," *Journal of Homosexuality* 12:1 (1985), 16. In general, see Gert Hekma, " 'A Female Soul in a Male Body': Sexual Inversion as Gender Inversion in Nineteenth-Century Sexology," in Gilbert Herdt, ed., *Third Sex, Third Gender: Beyond Sexual Dimorphism in Culture and History* (NY: Zone Books, 1994), 213–39.

51.The original German text of Kertbeny's letter to Ulrichs of May 6, 1868, is printed in facsimile and in typed transcription with a brief introduction in German and a bibliography by Manfred Herzer in the periodical *Capri: Zeitschrift für schwule Geschichte* 1 (1987), 25–35. I am grateful to Herzer for sending me a copy and to Michael Lombardi-Nash for translating this letter for me and for sending me copies of his translation of works by Karl Heinrich Ulrichs, and to Paul Nash for sponsoring those copies. Copies of these and other translations may be bought from Urania Manuscripts, 6858 Arthur Court, Jacksonville, FL 32211. Kertbeny and his work are discussed in Manfred Herzer, "Kertbeny and the Nameless Love," and Jean-Claude Féray and Manfred Herzer, "Homosexual Studies and Politics in the Nineteenth Century: Karl Maria Kertbeny," trans. by Glen W. Peppel, *Journal of Homosexuality* 19:1 (1990), 23–47. The meaning of Kertbeny's terms is also discussed in Manfred Herzer to Katz, April 16, 1989. I stress my gratitude for the letters and wonderful research of Manfred Herzer. I am also indebted to the pioneering work of John Lauritsen and David Thorstad on the history of the homosexual emancipation movement in nineteenth-century Germany—see their pamphlet *The Early Homosexual Rights Movement (1864–1935)* (NY: Times Change Press, 1974)—and to James D. Steakley's *The Homosexual Emancipation Movement in Germany* (NY: Arno Press, 1975).

52. Féray and Herzer 34–35.

53. Féray and Herzer 36.

54. Féray and Herzer 25, 34–35.

55. Féray and Herzer 25, 37; and Herzer to Katz, April 16, 1989.

56. Herzer, "Kertbeny and the Nameless Love," 6, 21 n. 6. The term "heterosexual" appears in the 4th edition of R. von Krafft-Ebing, *Psychopathia sexualis* . . . (Stuttgart: Ferdinand Enke, 1889), 96, 99. "Heterosexual" appears four times in three different phrases: *"heterosexuale Empfindung"* (heterosexual sensation); *"heterosexuale Gefühle"* (heterosexual feeling); and *"heterosexualer Verkehr"* (heterosexual intercourse): Herzer to Katz, July 6, 1983, and April 16, 1989. I thank James Steakley for help with the German.

57. See my discussion of Kiernan's article in Chapter 2.

58. Havelock Ellis, *Studies in the Psychology of Sex,* Volume II, Part II, *Sexual Inversion* (NY: Random House, 1936), 2–4.

59. Dr. Karl Friedrich Otto Westphal, *"Die conträre Sexualempfindung,"* *Archiv für Psychiatrie und Nervenkrankheiten* 2:1 (Aug. 1869), 73–108. I am indebted to James D. Steakley for the correct date of this major article. I comment on Westphal in *Gay/Lesbian Almanac: A New Documentary* (NY: Harper & Row, 1983), 147, 183, 188–90, 682 n. 14. Also see Vern Bullough, *Sexual Variance in Society and History* (NY: John Wiley and Sons, 1976), 639, 670 n. 12. Additional comment on Westphal and the psychiatric terms and concepts appears in Arnold I. Davidson, "Closing Up the Corpses: Diseases of Sexuality and the Emergence of the Psychiatric Style of Reasoning," in George Boolos, ed., *Meaning and Method: Essays in Honor of Hilary Putnam* (NY: Cambridge University Press, 1990), 295–325; in Féray and Herzer; Gert Hekma, "A History of Sexology: Social and Historical Aspects of Sexuality," in Jan Bremmer, ed., *From Sappho to De Sade: Moments in the History of Sexuality* (NY: Routledge, 1989), 173–93; also see Hekman's bibliography, 196–211; Herzer, "Kertbeny and the Nameless Love"; and Kennedy, *Ulrichs.* Peter Gay, *The Bourgeois Experience, Victoria to Freud, Volume II, The Tender Passion* (NY: Oxford University Press, 1986), 223–30, refers to Havelock Ellis's mini-history of these terms, first published in his *Sexual Inversion* in the English edition of 1897 and U.S. edition of 1900 (I believe Gay means

1901, the date of the first American edition of the *Sexual Inversion* volume); see Ellis, *Sexual Inversion*, 2–4. Also see Michel Foucault, *The History of Sexuality, Volume I, An Introduction* (NY: Pantheon, 1978), 43.

60. Ellis, *Sexual Inversion*, 3.

61. In 1879, Dr. Allen W. Hagenbach's American medical journal discussion of masturbation first referred to the case of an effeminate young man with a "morbid" attraction to persons of his own sex (though that attraction was not yet given a proper name; see Vern Bullough, "Homosexuality and the Secret Sin in Nineteenth Century America," *Journal of the History of Medicine* 28 [1973], 143–54). The first British medical journal article on the subject of same-sex attraction was published in 1881 (though the subject was German, the doctor Viennese). In 1883, the sexual emancipationist John Addington Symonds used "sexual inversion" in his *privately printed* publication, *A Problem in Greek Ethics* (see Ellis, *Sexual Inversion*, 3).

62. Ellis, *Sexual Inversion*, 3.

Chapter 4
Making the Heterosexual Mystique
Sigmund Freud's Seminal Conceptions

1. Citations to Freud's writings in this section refer to *The Standard Edition of the Complete Psychological Works of Sigmund Freud*, 24 volumes edited by James Strachey, published in London by Hogarth Press, starting in 1953. I list here only the first word of the title, followed, in parentheses, by the original year of publication (usually in German), followed by a small letter that identifies the text in the *Standard Edition*. For example, "Fragment" (1905e), *SE* 7: 3–122 is Freud's history of "Dora"/Ida Bauer, detailed in his "Fragment of an Analysis of a Case of Hysteria," written in 1901 and first published in German in 1905, in the 7th volume of the *Standard Edition*. Full citations are included under Freud in the Bibliography at the back of *Invention*.

For a wonderful biography of Dora/Ida see Hannah S. Decker, *Freud, Dora, and Vienna* (NY: The Free Press/Macmillan, 1991). For a number of major essays on Freud and Dora, see Charles Bernheimer and Claire Kahane, eds., *In Dora's Case: Freud—Hysteria—Feminism* (NY: Columbia University Press, 1985).

2. "Fragment" (1905e), *SE* 7: 23. I have not checked to see if Freud starts with a physical description in his other case histories, especially those of men.

3. "Fragment" (1905e), *SE* 7: 21, 56–58.

4. "Fragment" (1905e), *SE* 7: 32, 36, 48, 56.

5. "Fragment" (1905e), *SE* 7: 25, 27, 37, 38, 40, 46, 95, 105.

6. "Fragment" (1905e), *SE* 7: 32, 60–62, 107.

7. "Fragment" (1905e), *SE* 7: 105.

8. "Fragment" (1905e), *SE* 7: 84.

9. "Fragment" (1905e), *SE* 7: 19, 20.

10. Dora's negative feelings for Freud I infer from her quitting analysis after three months. Her positive feeling for him I infer from her asking to continue analysis with him a year later. Freud's active hostility to Dora is indicated by his acting like a proud, jilted suitor and refusing to take her on again as a client. His hostility is also evident in his "assuring her" (as he says) that a vaginal discharge was not evidence of VD inherited from her father, but "pointed primarily to masturbation" ("Fragment" [1905e], *SE* 7: 76). Freud's imagining himself Dora's gynecologist is evidence of an unconscious, invasive, heteroerotic impulse toward Dora (see "Fragment" [1905e], *SE* 7: 9, 48, and see my comments in the text). Freud also speaks of wanting to "penetrate" Dora's dreams ("Fragment" [1905e], *SE* 7: 92). Freud's aggressive hostility toward Dora is also revealed in his talk of her analysis "forcing through the limitations imposed by medical discretion" ("Fragment" [1905e], *SE* 7: 9). Freud defensively denies his own emotional investment in Dora's "successful termination" of her analysis, and his own fury at being spurned ("Fragment" [1905e], *SE* 7: 109).

11. On Dora's symptoms, "Fragment" (1905e), *SE* 7: 28.

12. Freud's term "libido" is discussed in a note in "Formulations" (1911b), *SE* 12: 219 n. 1; "Introductory" (1916–17), *SE* 15: 75 n. 2; Freud's term "pleasure principle" is discussed in notes in "Extracts" (1950a), *SE*: 1: 192 n. 4; "Grounds" (1895b), *SE* 3: 102 n. 1; "Encyclopedia" (1923a), *SE* 18: 255 n. 1.

13. "Leonardo" (1910c), *SE* 11: 96.

14. " 'Civilized' " (1908d), *SE* 9: 188, 204.

15. "Three" (1905d) *SE* 7: 199, 207; "Introductory" (1916–17) *SE* 16: 328; "Instincts" (1915c) *SE* 14: 138.

16. "Introductory" (1916–17), *SE* 16: 306.

17. "Three" (1905d), *SE* 7: 178. In other texts Freud explicitly criticizes the old procreative ethic from the standpoint of his pleasure principle. He points to the limiting judgment by which we "describe a sexual activity as perverse if it has given up the aim of reproduction and pursues the attainment of pleasure as an aim independent of it." Under that conventional reproductive standard any sexuality "that aims solely at

obtaining pleasure is given the uncomplimentary name of 'perverse' and as such is proscribed." See: "Introductory" (1916), *SE* 16: 316.

18. "Introductory" (1916), *SE* 16: 322.

19. "Introductory" (1916), *SE* 16: 316.

20. "Three" (1905d), *SE* 7: 191, 234.

21. " 'Civilized' " (1908d), *SE* 9: 204.

22. "Three" (1905d), *SE* 7: 177, 178.

23. "Civilization" (1930a), *SE 21:* 104. On "excess of sexual repression" see "Five" (1910a), *SE* 11: 54 and "Three" (1905d), *SE* 7: 172.

24. "Five" (1910a), *SE* 11: 54.

25. "Analysis" (1909b), *SE* 10: 145.

26. "Fragment" (1905e), *SE* 7: 47–48.

27. "Fragment" (1905e), *SE:* 49.

28. "Fragment" (1905e), *SE* 7: 50.

29. "Fragment" (1905e), *SE* 7: 52.

30. "Three" (1905d), *SE* 7: 140.

31. Re early uses of the word "heterosexual" in the medical literature, Freud refers to " 'heterosexual individuals,' " quoting Dr. Arduin (1900); see "Three" (1905d), *SE* 7: 143. Krafft-Ebing quotes Moll referring to "hetero-sexual individuals"; see Krafft-Ebing (1893), 174. The *Oxford English Dictionary* tells us that Charles Samson Féré (in *The Sexual Instinct: Its Evolution and Dissolution . . .* , trans. H. Blachamp [London: The University Press, 1900], viii, 183) refers to "Psycho-sexual hermaphroditism in which there are traces of hetero-sexuality, though homosexuality predominates." (See *OED Supplement* [1976], II, 85.) Also see my discussion of the history of the term "heterosexual' in Chapter 3.

32. See my comments on Floyd Dell in the next chapter.

33. Freud uses the term "heterosexuality" in "Hysterical" (1909a), *SE* 9: 165.

34. Samuel A. Guttman, Randall L. Jones, Stephen M. Parrish, *The Concordance to The Standard Edition of The Complete Psychological Works of Sigmund Freud,* 6 vols., v. III (Boston: G. K. Hall, 1960): 194, 227–29.

35. The *Index* to *The Standard Edition* of Freud's works (volume 24) includes an empty main entry for "Heterosexuality" that sends us off to "Object-choice, heterosexual"—the only indexed entry for heterosexuality—including a paltry eight references. See: "General Subject Index" *SE* 24: "Heterosexual attraction (*see* Object-choice, heterosexual," 295); and "Object-choice, heterosexual," 334. In contrast, the main entry of "Homosexuality" includes a full, fat column-plus of references. See: "General Subject Index," *SE* 24: "Homosexuality," 295. Another entry

for "Object-choice, homosexual" includes 19 references. See: "General Subject Index," *SE* 24: 334.

36. Freud uses the phrase "the problem of homosexuality"; see Kenneth Lewes, *The Psychoanalytic Theory of Male Homosexuality* (NY: Simon and Schuster, 1988), 35 n. 48, citing Freud's "The Psychogenesis" (1920a), *SE* 18.

37. "Fragment" (1905e), *SE* 7: 27–28.

38. "Fragment" (1905e), *SE* 7: 29.

39. Decker xi. Dora was actually thirteen: throughout Freud's account he mistakenly adds a year to Dora's actual age, an addition that obscures a little the age and power asymmetry between the adult man and teenage girl, helping to play down the incident's threatening character.

40. "Fragment" (1905e), *SE* 7: 29.

41. "Fragment" (1905e), *SE* 7: 105.

42. "Fragment" (1905e), *SE* 7: 105–06.

43. "Fragment" (1905e), *SE* 7: 98–99.

44. "Fragment" (1905e), *SE* 7: 98–99.

45. "Fragment" (1905e), *SE* 7: 25–26.

46. "Fragment" (1905e), *SE* 7: 95.

47. "Fragment" (1905e), *SE* 7: 105–06.

48. "Fragment" (1905e), *SE* 7: 34.

49. "Fragment" (1905e), *SE* 7: 108. There is now a large literature on homophobic bias in American psychotherapy and, in particular, psychoanalysis. See, for example, Lewes (1988).

50. "Fragment" (1905e), *SE* 7: 106.

51. See my comment on Kertbeny in Chapter 3.

52. "Fragment" (1905e), *SE* 7: 61.

53. "Fragment" (1905e), *SE* 7: 26.

54. "Fragment" (1905e), *SE* 7: 61.

55. "Fragment" (1905e), *SE* 7: 60.

56. "Fragment" (1905e), *SE* 7: 105. In another footnote Freud speaks of Dora's "most deeply buried group of thoughts—those relating to her love for Frau K" ("Fragment" [1905e], *SE* 7: 110–11).

57. "Fragment" (1905e), *SE* 7: 120.

58. Lewes, 35 n. 49, citing Freud's "On Psychotherapy" (1905a), *SE:* 7: 255–68. Unfortunately, Lewes includes no page references.

59. "Three" (1905d), *SE* 7: 146.

60. Freud, "The Psychogenesis of a Case of Homosexuality in a Woman" (1920a) *SE* 18: 153.

61. For Freud's moral assessment of maturity and immaturity, see Tim-

othy Murphy, "Freud Reconsidered, Bisexuality, Homosexuality, and Moral Judgment," *Journal of Homosexuality* 9:2/3, espec. 73–75.
62. For Freud's discussion of teleology see "Three" (1905d), *SE* 7: 156, 184n, 188n; and "Contributions" (1912f), *SE* 12: 247–48.
63. "Claims" (1913j), *SE* 13: 180.
64. See Freud, "Analysis of a Phobia in a Five-Year-Old Boy" (1909b), *SE* 10: 7–8, 35, 106, 120. Mom also threatens to beat her five-year-old with a carpet beater, 87.
65. "Fragment" (1905e), *SE* 7: 20–21.
66. Decker 52. Dora's father did actually have syphilis before he was married, but does not seem to have infected his wife with it; see Decker 51.
67. "Psychogenesis" (1920a), *SE* 18: 146 (the editor's introduction).
68. Freud discusses the Oedipus complex in girls in "Psychogenesis" (1920a), *SE* 18: 155, 157, 167–68, 192; "Beyond" (1920g), *SE* 18: 106; "Dreams and" (1922a), *SE* 18: 214–15; "Ego" (1923b), *SE* 19: 31–32; "Dissolution" (1924d), *SE* 19: 173, 177–79; "Some" (1925j), *SE* 19: 244–47, 251–52, 256–57; "New" (1933a), *SE* 22: 118–19, 120, 128–30, 133–34.
69. See my analysis of Kate Millett's discussion of Mailer in Chapter 6, "Questioning the Heterosexual Mystique."
70. "Universal (1912d), *SE* 11: 189.
71. "Fragment" (1905e), *SE* 7: 56.
72. See the many references to the Oedipus complex in the "General Subject Index" of Freud's works.
73. On the "dissolution" of the Oedipus complex see "Ego" (1923b), *SE* 19: 31–39; "Dissolution" (1924d), *SE* 173–74, 176–77, 179; "Some" (1925j), *SE* 19: 244–45, 256–57; "New" (1933a), *SE* 22: 92, 129.
74. See Decker on "countertransference" in Freud's treatment of Dora: 116–23, 136–36, 147.
75. "Fragment" (1905e), *SE* 7: 9.
76. "Fragment" (1905e), *SE* 7: 48.
77. "Fragment" (1905e), *SE* 7: 9.
78. See Decker.
79. "Three" (1905d), *SE* 7: 148.

Chapter 5
The Heterosexual Comes Out
From Doctor Discourse to the Mass Media

1. See D'Emilio and Freedman, *Intimate Matters: A History of Sexuality in America* (NY: Harper & Row, 1988), 194–201, 231, 241, 295–96; Ellen Kay Trimberger, "Feminism, Men, and Modern Love: Greenwich Village, 1900–1925," in Ann Snitow, Christine Stansell, Sharon Thompson, eds., *Powers of Desire: The Politics of Sexuality* (NY: Monthly Review Press, 1983), 131–52; Kathy Peiss, " 'Charity Girls' and City Pleasures: Historical Notes on Working Class Sexuality, 1880–1920," in *Powers of Desire,* 74–87; and Peiss's *Cheap Amusements: Working Women and Leisure in Turn-of-the-Century New York* (Philadelphia: Temple University Press, 1986). See also Christine Stansell, "Conclusion," *City of Woman: Sex and Class in New York, 1789–1860* (NY: Alfred A. Knopf, 1986), 217–21; Mary P. Ryan, "The Sexy Saleslady: Psychology, Heterosexuality, and Consumption in the Twentieth Century," in her *Womanhood in America,* 2nd ed. (NY: Franklin Watts: 1979), 151–82; and Joanne J. Meyerowitz, *Women Adrift: Independent Wage Earners in Chicago, 1880–1930* (Chicago: University of Chicago Press, 1988).

2. The heterosexual's coming out, sketched here in brief, broad strokes, is a history ripe for future fleshing out, so to speak. A few historical works are already beginning that work. See, for example, Kevin White, *The First Sexual Revolution: The Emergence of Male Heterosexuality in Modern America* (1993); and Ellen Kay Trimberger, "Feminism, Men, and Modern Love: Greenwich Village." The bibliography in White's book is useful.

3. Dr. Charles H. Hughes, "Erotopathia—Morbid Eroticism," read at the Pan-American Medical Congress, September, 1893; *Alienist and Neurologist,* 14: 4 (October 1893), 531–78.

4. Marc-André Raffalovich, "Uranism, Congenital Sexual Inversion. Observations and Recommendations," *Journal of Comparative Neurology,* vol. 5 (March 1895), 33-65. On Raffalovich see Brian Reade, *Male Homosexuality in English Literature from 1850 to 1900: An Anthology* (NY: Coward-McCann, 1971), 32–35, 38, 40, 50, 53, and Richard Ellman, *Oscar Wilde* (NY: Alfred A. Knopf, 1988), 61, 71n, 94, 112, 218, 253, 263, 282, 388, 462n, 472, 532, 572.

5. Raffalovich 42.

6. Raffalovich 50.

7. Krafft-Ebing 56.

8. Krafft-Ebing 49.

9. Krafft-Ebing 52.

10. Krafft-Ebing 53.

11. W[illiam] A[lexander] Dorland, *The American Illustrated Medical Dictionary*, second ed. (Philadelphia: W. B. Saunders, 1901), 300.

12. James A. H. Murray, Henry Bradley, W. A. Craigie, C. T. Onions, eds., *A Supplement to the Oxford English Dictionary* (Oxford, England: Clarendon Press, 1933), p. 460.

13. Sigmund Freud, *Three Contributions to the Sexual Theory*, trans. A. A. Brill, intro. James J. Putnam (NY: The Journal of Nervous and Mental Disease Publishing Company, 1910); retranslated in *The Standard Edition of the Complete Psychological Writings of Sigmund Freud*, edited by James Strachey, volume 7. Freud's American lectures of 1909 are published as "Five Lectures on Psycho-Analysis" in *SE* 11: 3–55. The fourth lecture focuses on sex.

14. Havelock Ellis, *Studies in the Psychology of Sex*, Volume I, *The Evolution of Modesty, The Phenomena of Sexual Periodicy, Auto-Eroticism* (Phila.: F. A. Davis, 1900). This volume was later incorporated into Ellis's four-volume *Studies in the Psychology of Sex* (NY: Random House. 1936).

15. The first edition of Ellis's *Sex in Relation to Society* was published in Philadelphia by F. A. Davis in 1910, as Volume VI of *Studies in the Psychology of Sex*. That edition is reprinted in *Studies in the Psychology of Sex*, Volume IV, *Sex in Relation to Society* (NY: Random House, 1936), and the quote is from p. 133.

16. The 1915 edition of Ellis's *Sexual Inversion* is reprinted in the Random House edition of 1936; for Ellis's use of "heterosexual" in 1915 see his *Studies in the Psychology of Sex*, Volume 4, Part Two, *Sexual Inversion* (NY: Random House, 1936), 2, 3, 27, 43, 53, 59, 68 (two uses), 71, 72, 73.

17. Havelock Ellis, *Studies in the Psychology of Sex*, Volume I, Part Two, "Analysis of the Sexual Impulse" (NY: Random House, 1936), 25, 63, 65. Ellis's term "tumescence" is derived from Moll, another early German sexologist. Ellis emphatically rejects the old equation of the "sexual instinct" with the "reproductive instinct." See *Studies*, above, 19-20. Also see Ellis's *Studies in the Psychology of Sex*, Volume III, Part One, "The Mechanism of Detumescence," 115–200 (NY: Random House, 1936).

18. Dr. James Weir, Jr., "The Effects of Female Suffrage on Posterity," *American Naturalist* 24:345 (Sept. 1995), 823–25.

19. This preacher's coining of derogatory, scientific-sounding names for women who stepped out of line was an attempt to appropriate for the clergy the power of the doctor profession's med-speak. See [Rev. Charles Parkhurst], "Woman. Calls Them Andromaniacs. Dr. Parkhurst

So Characterizes Certain Women Who Passionately Ape Everything That Is Mannish. Woman Divinely Preferred. Her Supremacy Lies in Her Womanliness, and She Should Make the Most of It—Her Sphere of Best Usefulness the Home," *New York Times,* May 23, 1897, 16:1.

20. *New York Times Book Review,* March 30, 1913, p. 175; reviewing J. Lionel Taylor's *The Nature of Woman* (NY: Dutton).

21. *New York Times Book Review,* Oct. 19, 1913, p. 56, reviewing Walter Heape's *Sex Antagonism* (NY: Putnam's).

22. See Carroll Smith-Rosenberg, "The New Woman as Androgyne: Social Disorder and Gender Crisis, 1870-1936," in her *Disorderly Conduct: Visions of Gender in Victorian America* (NY: Alfred A. Knopf, 1985), 245–96, 342–49. For the woman of pleasure see Jonathan Ned Katz, *Gay/Lesbian Almanac* (NY: Harper & Row, 1983), 169.

23. See, for example, D'Emilio and Freedman on "The Sexualized Society," in Part IV of *Intimate Matters;* Peter Gardella on "Redemption Through Sex," in *Innocent Ecstasy: How Christianity Gave America an Ethic of Sexual Pleasure* (NY: Oxford University Press 1985); Stephen Seidman on "Sexualizing Love, Eroticizing Sex" and "Bringing Sex Back In: The Birth of a Culture of Eroticism," Part Two of his *Romantic Longings: Love in America, 1830–1980* (NY: Routledge, 1991); and Mary P. Ryan, "The Erosion of Woman's Sphere: Heterosexuality and the Streamlined Home, 1910–1940," Chapter 5 in her *Womanhood in America from Colonial Times to the Present,* 3rd ed. (NY: Franklin Watts, 1983).

24. See Lisa Duggan, "The Social Enforcement of Heterosexuality and Lesbian Resistance in the 1920s," in Amy Swerdlow and Hannah Lessinger, eds., *Class, Race, and Sex: The Dynamics of Control* (Boston: G. K. Hall, 1983), 75–92; Rayna Rapp and Ellen Ross, "The Twenties Backlash: Compulsory Heterosexuality, the Consumer Family, and the Waning of Feminism," in Swerdlow above; Christina Simmons, "Companionate Marriage and the Lesbian Threat," *Frontiers* 4:3 (Fall 1979), 54–59; and Lillian Faderman, *Surpassing the Love of Men* (NY: William Morrow, 1981).

25. Robert H. Wiebe's *The Search for Order, 1877–1920* (NY: Hill and Wang, 1967), documents the normalization of track widths, time zones, and business practices: 22–23. See also Wiebe's comments on "scientific management" (151, 154–55); the 1896 "Battle of the Standards" (silver versus gold as the monetary standard, 100); the rise of a "quantitative ethic" (40); and Simon Nelson Patten's explanation around 1900 that a "scarcity or Pain Economy" had been supplanted by a "surplus or Pleasure Economy" (141). Would it were so. For the standardization of manufacturing, check out "scientific management" and "Taylorism" in

Harry Braverman's *Labor and Monopoly Capital: The Degradation of Work in the Twentieth Century* (NY: Monthly Review Press, 1974).

For the attempt to test, quantify, measure, and standardize intelligence, see Lewis Terman's *Stanford-Binet Intelligence Scale* (Boston: Houghton Mifflin, 1916). For Terman's attempt to do for an insufficiently regularized gender what he'd already done for a standardized intelligence, see Terman's and C. C. Miles' *Sex and Personality, Studies in Femininity and Masculinity* (NY: McGraw-Hill, 1936). For a feminist critique of Terman and other attempts to measure masculinity and femininity, see Miriam Lewin's two articles in the anthology she edited: *In the Shadow of the Past: Psychology Portrays the Sexes: A Social and Intellectual History* (NY: Columbia University Press, 1984).

26. J. R. Ackerley, *My Father and Myself* (NY: Coward-McCann, 1968; paperback San Diego: Harcourt Brace Jovanovich), 117. Ackerley says (101) that he was in Switzerland until the end of the First World War, when he met Lund. On Ackerley's virginity, see 113.

27. See David Loth, *The Erotic in Literature: A Historical Survey of Pornography as Delightful as It Is Indiscreet* (London: Secker & Warburg, 1962), ch. IX, "The Bars Begin to Drop," 145–70.

28. Brett P. Palmer, of Merriam-Webster Inc., Springfield, MA, to Katz, September 17 and October 28, 1993. Mr. Palmer assures me that "homosexuality" and "homosexual" appear on p. 1030 of the 1909 edition of *Webster's New International Dictionary,* that "heterosexuality" first appears on p. xcii of the 1923 supplement of *Webster's New International Dictionary,* and that the contemporary definition of *heterosexual* first appears in the 1934 Second Edition *Webster's.* I am grateful to Mr. Palmer for this information and for photocopies of these pages.

29. A hyphen still linked the newly welded concepts of sex-difference and sex-pleasure, the hetero and the sexual. See Mary Keyt Isham, review of Sigmund Freud's *Beyond the Pleasure Principle* and his *Group Psychology and the Analysis of the Ego, New York Times Book Review,* Sept. 7, 1924, 12, 16. It's relevant to note that in Freud's *Group Psychology* he speaks of "the truly magical power of words; they can evoke the most formidable tempests in the group mind" (80). Freud also speaks here of "sexual-love" (90–91), and "the libidinal structure" of the church and the army (93–99): see *SE* 18.

30. Her exact words are: "again and again in the history of achievement the fact of a fine flow of mature love toward a person of the opposite sex who rendered little response . . . finally struggled out again as a perfectly productive love."

31. Mary Ware Dennett, *The Sex Side of Life, An Explanation for Young People* (Astoria, NY: Published by the Author, 1928).

32. Louis Kronenberger, review of André Gide's *The Immoralist,* translated by Dorothy Bussy (NY: Knopf), *New York Times Book Review,* April 20, 1930, 9.

The first non-medical, English-language, mass media use of "heterosexual" listed by the *Oxford English Dictionary* occurred on October 1, 1927, on page 3 of the *Scots Observer,* which explained to its readers that "A certain proportion of people . . . are as instinctively homosexual as the normal individual is heterosexual." The idea that the "normal" equals "heterosexual" was being distributed around the English-speaking world. See R. W. Burchfield, ed., *A Supplement to the Oxford English Dictionary,* Volume II, H-N, (Oxford, England: Clarendon Press, 1976), 80.

33. Henry James Forman, review of Floyd Dell's *Love in the Machine Age* (NY: Farrar & Rinehart), *New York Times Book Review,* September 14, 1930, 9.

34. Burchfield, ed., *A Supplement to the Oxford English Dictionary* II, 80, citing E. Arnot Robertson, *Ordinary Families* (copyright 1933; reprinted London: Virago Press, 1986), 272.

35. Robertson 218.

36. Robertson 270.

37. Robertson 272.

38. Robertson 272.

39. The idea of such a thing as a heterosexual identity (and a publicly self-proclaimed one) documents the historically specific twentieth-century incitement and proliferation of heterosexuality. That this lyrical declaration of heterosexual identity was written by Lorenz Hart, a guilt-ridden, closeted homosexual is another of heterosexual history's ironies. The Rodgers & Hart estate denied me permission to quote the lyrics of the song.

40. This is the earliest use of "straight," meaning heterosexual, listed in the *OED;* see R. W. Burchfield, ed., *A Supplement to the Oxford English Dictionary* (Oxford: Clarendon Press, 1986), Volume IV, "Se-Z." The original source cited by the *OED* is G. W. Henry, *Sex Variants: A Study of Homosexual Patterns* (NY: Paul B. Hoeber, 1941), 2 volumes, II: 1176.

41. Here, what was once simply an erotic *act* of men and women has been converted into heterosexuality, a *thing* in which one may "indulge" or "re-indulge."

42. See Allan Bérubé, *Coming Out Under Fire: The History of Gay Men and Women In World War Two* (NY: Macmillan, 1990), 107, 193.

43. Ferdinand Lundberg and Dr. Marynia F. Farnham, *Modern Woman: the Lost Sex* (NY: Harper, 1947), 381–82.

44. For the term "sterile," see Katz, *G/LA*, 630–32, 646–48.

45. Dr. Howard A. Rusk, *New York Times Book Review*, January 4, 1948, 3.

46. He thereby contradicted the older idea of a monolithic, qualitatively defined, natural procreative act, experience, and person.

47. Kinsey and others, *Sexual Behavior in the Human Male* (Philadelphia: W. B. Saunders, 1948), 199–203, and see "Normal" in that book's index.

48. Kinsey, *Male*, 637, 639.

49. On the "heterosexual-homosexual rating scale," see "The Heterosexual-Homosexual Balance," in Kinsey, *Male*, 636–66.

50. See Steve Epstein, "Gay Politics, Ethnic Identity: The Limits of Social Constructionism," *Socialist Review* 17 (1987), 9–54. I am more critical than Epstein of the concept of "identity" in both its psychological and political uses, and as an analytical term used in history. We need numbers of other analytical terms.

51. Gore Vidal, "Someone to Laugh at the Squares With" [Tennessee Williams], *New York Review of Books,* June 13, 1985; reprinted in *At Home: Essays, 1982–1988* (NY: Random House, 1988), 48.

52. James Baldwin, "Preservation of Innocence," *Zero* 1:2 (Summer 1949); reprinted *Outlook* 2:2 (Fall 1989), 40–45 (quoted here from *Outlook*). For comment on Baldwin and this essay, see Melvin Dixon, "This Light, This Fire, This Time," in the same issue of *Outlook,* 38–39; and Katz, *G/LA* 161–62, 171, 591, 598, 647–51.

53. Baldwin 45.

54. Baldwin 41.

55. Baldwin 41.

56. Baldwin 42.

57. Baldwin 45.

58. Baldwin 43.

59. Baldwin 43.

60. Baldwin 44.

61. Heterosexuality's symbolic victory, its capture of a "normal [probably white] man," is brought to us via a Spanish woman, surely grist for the cultural critic's mill.

62. Baldwin 44.

63. Baldwin 44.

64. Baldwin 44–45.

65. Baldwin 45.

66. James Baldwin and Nikki Giovanni, *A Dialogue* (Philadelphia: J. B. Lippincott, 1973), 88–89. This *Dialogue* is transcribed from a conversa-

tion between Baldwin and Giovanni taped in London, November 4, 1971.

67. James Baldwin, " 'Go the Way Your Blood Beats': An Interview ..." by Richard Goldstein, *Village Voice,* June 26, 1984: 13–14, 16.

68. Katz, *G/LA* 161, 171, 591–95, 597–604.

69. The conflict between the category-busting tendency of gay liberation and its category-affirming impulse remains an ongoing tension within this major contemporary movement for social change.

70. Clyde Kluckhohn, "The Complex Kinsey Study and What It Attempts," Section VII, *New York Times Book Review,* September 13, 1953, 3.

71. Brooks Atkinson, *New York Times,* October 1, 1953, 35:1.

72. Robert C. Doty, "Growth of Overt Homosexuality in City Provokes Wide Concern," *New York Times,* December 17, 1963, pp. 1, 33. Doty's report is reprinted in part in Martin Duberman, *About Time: Exploring the Gay Past,* revised and expanded ed. (NY: Meridian/Penguin, 1991).

73. The need to explain that "straight" means "heterosexual" in gaytalk sets this report firmly in the past. And the mention in *The Times* of " 'straight' . . . speakers" (along with amused "gay" signifiers) marks the emergence in that paper of homosexuals as a minority with a special language, a new voice, and organizations of their own.

74. Rosalyn Regelson, "Up the Camp Staircase," *New York Times,* March 3, 1968, Section II, 1:5.

75. Clive Barnes, *New York Times,* March 22, 1968, 52:1.

76. Judy Klemesrud, "You Don't Have to Be One to Play One," *New York Times,* September 29, 1968, Section II, 1:2. The nasty subtext of Klemesrud's humor suggested that the actor did protest too much. His uneasy heterosex, she implied, revealed a hint of the homo. But whatever private psychodramas were performed on the stage of this particular male's mind, the exquisite anguish of the actor, desperate to dissociate himself from a homosexual role, was just an extreme example of many men's new need to publicly proclaim their heterosexuality—to define themselves to the world as *not* one of those "perverts" now more openly portrayed in the media. The coming out of the homo provoked the coming out of the hetero.

77. Peter and Barbara Wyden, *Growing Up Straight: What Every Thoughtful Parent Should Know About Homosexuality* (NY: Stein and Day, 1968).

78. Wyden 236.

79. Wyden 237.

80. Wyden 237.

81. Wyden 239.

82. Wyden 245.

83. Wyden 246.

84. Wyden 246.

85. In the 1990s it's dangerous to read chapter after chapter of the Wydens' utter, abject "expert" worship, their unquestioning belief in "adjustment," their unexamined belief in the "normal," and their pernicious deification of essential male and female roles to which children *must* conform or risk homosexual hell. The book's perfect banality causes brain death: "The child who becomes a homosexual is usually overprotected and *preferred* by his mother. In other cases he may be underprotected" (Wyden 48).

Chapter 6
Questioning the Heterosexual Mystique
Some Liberal Feminist and Radical Feminist Verdicts

1. Alice Echols, *Daring To Be Bad: Radical Feminism in America, 1967–1975* (Minneapolis: University of Minnesota Press, 1989), 4–5; Betty Friedan, *The Feminine Mystique* (NY: W. W. Norton, 1963; future references are to this edition).

2. See Betty Friedan, *It Changed My Life: Writings on the Women's Movement* (NY: Random House, 1976), especially "Introduction: Critique of Sexual Politics (Nov. 1970)," 155–64.

3. Echols 15. Echols also discusses another influential feminist analysis and activism: cultural feminism. The analysis produced by cultural feminists, emerging about 1975, at the end of the years covered here, posited an essential, valuable difference of women from men. Trying to turn the idea of the eternal feminine and essential female to the cause of women's emancipation, cultural feminists focused on the ill effects of " 'male' values." They stressed the importance of creating an alternative "female counterculture" in which " 'female' values" would be nurtured. Echols 6–8, 9, 22, 243, 257, 281–84.

4. "The Sex-Seekers" is Chapter 11, and "The Sexual Sell" is Chapter 9 of *The Feminine Mystique.*

5. Ti-Grace Atkinson, *Amazon Odyssey* (NY: Links Books, 1974); Kate Millett, *Sexual Politics* (NY: Doubleday, 1970; reprinted NY: Avon, 1971); Gayle Rubin, "The Traffic in Women: Notes on the 'Political Economy' of Sex," in Rayna [Rapp] Reiter, ed., *Toward an Anthropology of Women* (NY: Monthly Review Press, 1975), 157–210. On heterosexuality also see Anne Koedt, "The Myth of the Vaginal Orgasm," in Anne Koedt, Ellen Levine, and Anita Rapone, eds., *Radical Feminism* (NY: Quadrangle

Books, 1973), 198–207 and Shulamith Firestone, *The Dialectic of Sex: The Case for Feminist Revolution* (NY: William Morrow, 1970).

6. In 1968, Atkinson is already hinting that the distinction between biological sex and social gender is problematic. The assumption of two biological sexes, she argues, will have to go for "women" to become "human." For another early and brilliant deconstruction of biological "sex" differences, see Suzanne J. Kessler and Wendy McKenna, *Gender: An Ethnomethodological Approach* (John Wiley, 1978; reprinted Chicago: University of Chicago Press, 1985).

7. As feminist anthropologist Carole S. Vance later explained, modern women's response to sexuality has negotiated a difficult field of desire and danger, pleasure and fear. See her "Pleasure and Danger: Toward a Politics of Sexuality," in *Pleasure and Danger: Exploring Female Sexuality* (Boston: Routledge & Kegan Paul), 1–28.

8. In this and the following chapter I do not intend to offer a comprehensive history of the early years of the modern feminist comment on heterosexuality. I say nothing of the neo-Freudian, psychoanalytic feminism inspired by Juliet Mitchell's *Psychoanalysis and Feminism* (NY: Pantheon, 1974) and Nancy Chodorow's *The Reproduction of Mothering: Psychoanalysis and the Sociology of Gender* (Berkeley: University of California Press, 1978). I say nothing about the implications for heterosexuality of a specifically socialist feminist analysis—though Rubin's "The Traffic in Women" is strongly informed by Marx, among others. I do not discuss the antipornography feminism of Andrea Dworkin, Catherine MacKinnon, and others, or the anticensorship, sex radical feminism represented in the anthologies by Carole S. Vance and Ann Snitow, et al. Nor do I touch in these chapters on the African-American feminist analysis of heterosexuality, or the more recent takes on heterosexuality influenced by literary criticism and critical theory offered in the queer feminist works of Eve Kosofsky Sedgwick, Judith Butler, and Diana Fuss. Neither do I discuss the multidisciplinary feminist analyses offered recently by the Canadian periodical *Resources for Feminist Research*, in its "Confronting Heterosexuality" double issue (September/December 1990) or the English scholarly journal *Feminism and Psychology* in its special "Heterosexuality" issue (October 1992). As the last texts indicate, book-length works about feminism and heterosexuality are already appearing, and I hope will continue to multiply.

The feminist texts in this chapter (and those analyzed next) discuss complex ideas, and are more abstract and elaborated than some other discourses on heterosexuality examined in this book. These feminist analyses may require concentrated attention, but they are worth the effort, for these critical reviews of holy heterosexuality began to divest it of its sacred status, its mysterious immunity to questions.

9. "The Problem That Has No Name" is a chapter title in Friedan's *The Feminine Mystique*. The paperback edition of Friedan's book (NY: Dell, 1964) calls it a "bestseller" and says "over 1 million" copies in print.

10. Judith Hole and Ellen Levine, *Rebirth of Feminism* (NY: Quadrangle, 1971), 85.

11. Friedan, *Feminine Mystique* 241.

12. Friedan, *Feminine Mystique* 241.

13. For example, see Christopher Lasch, *The Culture of Narcissism* (NY: W. W. Norton, 1979).

14. Friedan, *Feminine Mystique*, 242.

15. Friedan, *Feminine Mystique* 251.

16. Friedan, *Feminine Mystique* 294–305.

17. Friedan, *Feminine Mystique* 257–58.

18. Friedan, *Feminine Mystique* 256.

19. Friedan, *Feminine Mystique* 75–76.

20. Friedan, *Feminine Mystique* 79.

21. See Ellen Carol DuBois and Linda Gordon, "Seeking Ecstasy on the Battlefield: Danger and Pleasure in Nineteenth-century Feminist Sexual Thought," in Vance, ed., *Pleasure and Danger* 31–49. On intimacies between nineteenth century feminists, see Lillian Faderman, *Surpassing the Love of Men: Romantic Friendship and Love Between Women from the Renaissance to the Present* (NY: William Morrow, 1981).

22. Friedan, *Feminine Mystique* 80.

23. Friedan, *Feminine Mystique* 74.

24. See especially Radicalesbians, "The Woman-Identified Woman" in Koedt, Levine, and Rapone, eds., *Radical Feminism*, discussed in the following chapter.

25. Friedan, *Feminine Mystique* 97.

26. Friedan, *Feminine Mystique* 115.

27. Friedan, *Feminine Mystique* 115.

28. See Friedan's chapter 5, "The Sexual Solipsism of Sigmund Freud," *Feminine Mystique* 96–116.

29. Friedan, *Feminine Mystique* 110.

30. Friedan, *Feminine Mystique* 110.

31. See Friedan's Chapter 6: "The Functional Freeze, The Feminine Protest, and Margaret Mead," *Feminine Mystique* 117–38.

32. Friedan, *Feminine Mystique* 126–27.

33. Friedan, *Feminine Mystique* 126–27.

34. Friedan, *Feminine Mystique* 133.

35. "Vaginal Orgasm" was given as a talk at the National Conference, Medical Committee for Human Rights, Philadelphia, April 5, 1968, and reprinted in Atkinson 5–7. "The Institution of Sexual Intercourse" was written November 1968, and published by *The New York Free Press*, December 13, 1968; reprinted in Shulamith Firestone and Anne Koedt, eds., *Notes from the Second Year* (NY: New York Radical Women, 1970), 42–47; and reprinted in Atkinson 13–23.

Atkinson's pointed comments on the social ordering of women's and men's erotic relations also appear in her "Radical Feminism and Love (April 12, 1969), Atkinson 41–45. Also see her articles on the heated conflict between lesbians and heterosexual feminists: "Lesbianism and Feminism" (Feb. 21, 1970), Atkinson 83–88; "Lesbianism and Feminism: Justice for Women as 'Unnatural' " (Dec. 31, 1970), Atkinson 131–34.

36. Atkinson xxii. Atkinson helped to found the New York chapter of the National Organization for Women and served as that chapter's first president; she quit that post and the organization after a failed attempt to radically democratize its internal power structure: Atkinson 9–11.

37. Atkinson 66–67. But as women become "more independent" their "interest in" and "need for" men decreases, she thinks (13–14). In a rare, explicit reference to heterosexuality, Atkinson says, "in a society which is militantly heterosexual, homosexuality must be, at some point, a conscious *choice*" (85). An element of decision-making, she suggests, is involved whenever a person with homosexual feelings pursues an active homosexual life in a society officially dedicated to heterosexuality. But Atkinson doesn't elaborate her insight into the social enforcement of heterosexuality.

38. Atkinson 13.

39. Atkinson 85.

40. Atkinson 19.

41. Atkinson 135.

42. Atkinson 20.

43. Atkinson 20.

44. Atkinson 21.

45. Atkinson 13.

46. Atkinson 53.

47. Atkinson 71.

48. Atkinson 49, 114.

49. Atkinson's ideas resonate with early gay liberation analyses contending that homosexuals, to liberate themselves, must do away with the homosexual/heterosexual distinction (though she doesn't make this

connection). (See, for example, the quotes from the Radicalesbians and from Dennis Altman in Chapter 1.) All those analyses resonate with Marx's idea of capitalist society's proletarians as the class that will do away with the capitalist class, and itself.

50. Atkinson 49. Atkinson adapts the old, middle-class ideology of individualism to the cause of women's radical liberation from the category of sex.

51. Atkinson 44–45.

52. Atkinson 105.

53. Atkinson 43.

54. Atkinson 105.

55. Atkinson 44–45.

56. Millett on the "heterosexual caste system," 275; on "heterosexual orthodoxy," 333, 342; on "heterosexual posturing," 331; and on "rabid heterosexual activism," 333.

57. See Wilhelm Reich, *Sex-Pol: Essays 1919–1934,* ed. by Lee Baxandall, trans. Anna Bostock, Tom DuBose, Lee Baxandall (NY: Vintage Books/ Random House, 1972); and Wilhelm Reich, *The Sexual Revolution: Toward a Self-Governing Character Structure,* rev. ed., trans. by Theodore P. Wolfe (NY: Farrar, Straus and Giroux, 1969).

58. Millett 10.

59. Millett 10.

60. Millett 10.

61. Millett 11–12.

62. Millett 13.

63. Millett 331.

64. Millett 333.

65. Millett 335. That a revolutionary abolition of the fear of homosexuality would challenge the heterosexual/homosexual division itself, Millett does not consider.

66. Millett 333.

67. Millett 50–51. She apparently refers to the French historian Charles Seignebos (1854–1942), but does not specify his "famous dictum."

68. Millett 53.

69. Millett 17.

70. Millett 17.

71. Millett 17.

72. The distinction between biological "sex" and socially constructed "gender" is basic to both the radical feminist and liberal feminist argument that societal organization, not female anatomy, presents women with culturally ordained destinies—in regard to which they can con-

form or rebel. Millett's radical feminist analysis also suggests, without pushing the point, that the social production of masculine and feminine sexes is linked to society's hierarchizing of different-sex and same-sex eroticism.

73. Millett 19.
74. Millett 20.
75. Millett 22.
76. Millett 363.
77. Sidney Abbott and Barbara Love, *Sappho Was a Right-On Woman: A Liberated View of Lesbianism* (NY: Stein and Day, 1972), 121; Hole and Levine 241.
78. Hole and Levine 241.
79. Rubin 8.
80. Rubin 178.
81. Rubin 179.
82. Rubin 178.
83. Rubin 178.
84. Rubin 180–81.
85. Rubin 180–81. She adds: "The sexual division of labor is implicated in both aspects of gender—male and female it creates them, and it creates them heterosexual." She explains that the "suppression of the homosexual component of human sexuality, and by corollary, the oppression of homosexuals, is therefore a product of the same system whose rules and relations oppress women."
86. Rubin 181.
87. Rubin 180–81.
88. Rubin 181. Her analysis stresses the difference between "our" standard of "heterosexual" and "homosexual," based on the anatomical sex of partners, and the Mojave distinction between "heterosexual" and "homosexual" based on social role, behavior, and dress. That this Mojave organization of sex might not include any internal "heterosexual/homosexual" distinction is not considered by Rubin.
89. That is still the dominant understanding of heterosexuality and homosexuality. The alternative conception I offer presents heterosexuality as one historically specific and limited arrangement of sex difference and eroticism. I suggest that heterosexual and homosexual are *not* universal, but are historically specific ways of combining gender and eroticism.
90. Rubin's analysis of the exchange of women is adapted from Lévi-Strauss.
91. Rubin 176.

92. Rubin 177.
93. Rubin 172, 174.
94. Rubin 186.
95. Rubin 186–88.
96. Rubin 193.
97. Gayle Rubin, "Thinking Sex: Notes for a Radical Theory of the Politics of Sexuality," in Vance, ed., *Pleasure and Danger*, 307.
98. Rubin developed the concept of a sex/gender system "to counter a certain tendency to explain sex oppression as a reflex of economic forces" ("Traffic" 203).
99. Rubin, "Traffic" 207.
100. Rubin, "Traffic" 177.
101. Rubin, "Traffic" 210.
102. Rubin, "Traffic" 157.
103. Rubin, "Traffic" 204.

Chapter 7
The Lesbian Menace Strikes Back
Some Lavender Feminist Critiques

1. Alice Echols, *Daring to Be Bad: Radical Feminism in America 1967–1975* (Minneapolis: University of Minnesota Press, 1989), 16 (n. 59), 305, 212 (n. 44), 345. As the source of the Friedan quote Echols cites Susan Brownmiller, "Sisterhood Is Powerful," *New York Times Magazine,* March 15, 1970, 140. Friedan discusses her attitude toward lesbianism in "Critique of Sexual Politics," *Social Policy Magazine,* Nov. 1970, reprinted in *It Changed My Life* (NY: Random House, 1976), 161–64; and amends her views somewhat in the introduction to the above essay, 154–60.
2. This chapter, like the last, by no means offers a complete history, in this case, of lesbian-feminist analyses of heterosexuality. It also makes little attempt to comment on the lesbian input into antipornography feminists' take on heterosexuality, or the lesbian input into the critical response of feminist sex radicals and anti-censorship feminists, and the ensuing feminist "sex wars" of the '80s and '90s. Neither is my focus on the actual, internal feminist movement politics around heterosexuality and lesbianism. For that, see Echols on "the gay/straight split" (*Daring to Be Bad*, 210–41).
3. Donn Teal, *The Gay Militants* (NY: Stein and Day, 1970), 179.
4. Radicalesbians, "The Woman-Identified Woman," in Anne Koedt, Ellen Levine, and Anita Rapone, eds., *Radical Feminism* (NY: Quadrangle Books, 1973), 240–45; Echols, 215–16.

5. Radicalesbians 241.

6. Radicalesbians 245.

7. Radicalesbians 242.

8. Radicalesbians 241.

9. Radicalesbians 242.

10. Radicalesbians 242.

11. Radicalesbians 245.

12. Radicalesbians 240, 244.

13. Radicalesbians 241–42.

14. Radicalesbians 242–43.

15. Radicalesbians 243.

16. Radicalesbians 243.

17. Radicalesbians 243–44.

18. Radicalesbians 240.

19. Nancy Myron and Charlotte Bunch, eds., *Lesbianism and the Women's Movement* (Baltimore: Diana Press, 1975).

20. "The Myth of the Vaginal Orgasm" by Anne Koedt was an early influential feminist essay that questioned the Freudian-inspired ideal of vaginal intercourse, as opposed to clitoral stimulation, as the source of women's erotic pleasure; "The Myth" is reprinted in Anne Koedt, Ellen Levine, Anita Rapone, eds., *Radical Feminism* (NY: Quadrangle Books/ New York Times, 1973): 198–207.

21. Coletta Reid, "Coming Out in the Women's Movement," in Myron and Bunch, 91–93.

22. Myron and Bunch, 93.

23. Myron and Bunch, 101.

24. Myron and Bunch, 95–96.

25. Myron and Bunch, 101.

26. Myron and Bunch, 101.

27. Myron and Bunch, 101.

28. Myron and Bunch, 101.

29. Myron and Bunch, 103.

30. Myron and Bunch, 103. Another autobiographical essay in this anthology, "Such a Nice Girl" by Sharon Deevey, describes how a middle-class American housewife became an angry, militant lesbian-feminist-separatist (see Myron and Bunch, 21–28).

31. Margaret Small, "Lesbians and the Class Position of Women," in Myron and Bunch, 49–62. Her talk was delivered at the Institute for Policy Studies, a left-leaning thinktank in Washington, D.C.

32. Myron and Bunch, 58.

33. Myron and Bunch, 58.

34. Myron and Bunch, 59–60.
35. Myron and Bunch, 59–60.
36. Myron and Bunch, 60–61.
37. Myron and Bunch, 59.
38. Myron and Bunch, 61.
39. Purple September Staff, "The Normative Status of Heterosexuality," in Myron and Bunch, 79–84.
40. Myron and Bunch, 80 (the single quote marks are in the original).
41. Myron and Bunch, 81.
42. Myron and Bunch, 81.
43. Myron and Bunch, 82.
44. Myron and Bunch, 82.
45. Myron and Bunch, 83.
46. Myron and Bunch, 83.
47. Nancy Myron and Charlotte Bunch, "Introduction," in Myron and Bunch, 12.
48. Myron and Bunch, 12.
49. Myron and Bunch, 35–36.
50. Monique Wittig, *The Straight Mind and Other Essays* (Boston: Beacon Press, 1992), hereafter cited as Wittig; and Wittig's "Paradigm" in George Stambolian and Elaine Marks, eds., *Homosexualities and French Literature: Cultural Contexts/Critical Texts* (Ithaca: Cornell University Press, 1979), 114–21, hereafter cited as Stambolian and Marks.
51. Wittig 6.
52. Wittig 2.
53. Stambolian and Marks, 115.
54. Wittig 8.
55. Wittig 30.
56. Stambolian and Marks, 120.
57. Wittig 61.
58. Wittig 5. She here also speaks of the "compulsory character of the category [of sex] itself," suggesting that to speak of a "compulsory" sex distinction is redundant. The idea is that the category of sex already assumes a division of sexes, making that distinction obligatory as one employs the concept. I make a similar critique of the now-common use of "compulsory heterosexuality" (see my comments on Adrienne Rich that follow in this chapter).
59. Wittig, xvi.
60. Wittig 6.
61. Wittig 13.
62. Wittig 32.

63. Wittig 13.

64. Stambolian and Marks 117.

65. Into exactly what other "dimension" lesbianism opens, into what universe, is not clear. This is sex utopianism losing touch.

66. Stambolian and Marks 115–16.

67. Wittig 5–6; see also Stambolian and Marks 116, 118.

68. Stambolian and Marks 118.

69. Wittig 43.

70. Wittig 41, 43, 44. Wittig equates women's "pleasure in sex" with men with "happiness in slavery" (101). The modern ideal of women as "sexual beings" (actually, heterosexual beings) is, simply, a bad thing for women, she claims (7). The twentieth-century heterosexualizing of women is, unambiguously and only, disempowering (6). She declares: "sexuality is not for women an individual and subjective expression, but a social institution of violence" (19). Such overstatement expresses an undialectical feminism; in this, sex pleasure is one thing with one meaning, a tool only of women's victimization (7, 8). Wittig's analysis denies the feminist sex radical's claim that women's heteroerotic and homoerotic desires provide powerful emotional sources of self-affirmation and feminist agency.

Wittig also consistently fails to distinguish "sex," meaning sex difference, from "sexuality," meaning sex pleasure. When she suggests that lesbians and feminists are fighting for a "sexless society," that "sexless" conflates a sex-blind society and an antisex society (13). Ignoring the strong antipleasure, body-denying, puritanical tradition within American culture, she ignores also the way this culture has denied women, in particular, a valid, autonomous eroticism. See Carole S. Vance, "Pleasure and Danger: Toward a Politics of Sexuality," in Vance, ed., *Pleasure and Danger: Exploring Female Sexuality* (Boston: Routledge & Kegan Paul, 1984), 1–28.

71. Stambolian and Marks, 117. Wittig's reference to Baudelaire as "the lesbian poet" is a serious joke. If lesbianism equals pleasure-seeking apart from sex differences, there's no reason why Baudelaire can't be a lesbian.

72. Stambolian and Marks 119.

73. Wittig 27; also see 10, 20.

74. Wittig 65.

75. Wittig 25.

76. Wittig 31.

77. Wittig, "Social Contract" (1989), 40. See also her comments on the

social contract in "The Straight Mind" (read 1978; published 1980), and in "One Is Not Born a Woman" (1981).

78. Wittig 41.

79. Wittig 40–41, 44.

80. Wittig 43.

81. Wittig 27. Throughout numbers of her essays Wittig protests the naturalizing of heterosexuality (see, for example, 2, 3, 9, 10, 11, 13, 27, 59, 77, 104).

82. Wittig 28.

83. Wittig 24.

84. Wittig 42; see also 27.

85. Wittig 10, 40. She also refers to the "social contract and heterosexuality as two superimposable notions" (40). But if the social contract and heterosexuality are identical, it's difficult to imagine a nonheterosexual society, for it's hard to picture a society without any established rules.

86. Wittig 27.

87. Wittig's concept of heterosexuality remains resolutely dateless, though she recognizes the historicity of the term. She twice remarks, first in a backnote, then in a text, that "heterosexuality" is "a word which first appears in the French language in 1911" (Wittig 103 and Stambolian and Marks 115). Though she's fascinated by this datum and can't leave it alone, she doesn't know what to do with it. The term's recent emergence does *not* lead her to wonder about the temporal specificity of the heterosexual system (103).

88. Stambolian and Marks, 116. A historically specified analysis would show that it was not precisely a "heterosexual romance" with which Ovid tried to saddle Sappho. For an analysis of Sappho that tries to understand her in the context of her time, without importing our concepts of heterosexual and homosexual, see John J. Winkler, "Double Consciousness in Sappho's Lyrics," in *The Construction of Desire: The Anthropology of Sex and Gender in Ancient Greece* (NY: Routledge, 1990), 162–87.

89. Her argument simultaneously establishes the possibility of an alternative to heterosexuality and the existence in ancient Greece of a timeless, eternal heterosexuality. Wittig refers to the "thought which throughout the centuries built heterosexuality as a given" (xvi). Here, she simultaneously posits heterosexuality as historically "built," and presents it as "centuries" old. Her understanding of heterosexuality arises from a feminism that is dialectical materialist but not rigorously historical materialist. Wittig's allusions to history are offhand.

90. Wittig 25–26.

91. Wittig 25–26.

92. For a succinct history of the feminist antiporn movement and the feminist sex radical response, see Carole S. Vance, "Introduction" to the second edition of *Pleasure and Danger: Exploring Female Sexuality* (London: Pandora Press, 1992).

93. Wittig republished her antiporn paragraphs in 1992 with no reference to the collusion of antipornography feminists with the right. Neither does she refer to the, by then, influential critique of antiporn feminists by feminist sex radicals and anti-censorship feminists. The subversive inconoclasm of Wittig's abstract theorizing contrasts sharply, then, with the conservative character of her practical antiporn politics. We can reject Wittig's use of pornography as example of the injurious, material effect of discourse, without rejecting her idea that the discourse on heterosexuality causes real-life damage.

94. Wittig 28–29.

95. Wittig 29.

96. Wittig 45.

97. Wittig 34, 35, 40.

98. Wittig 44, 49.

99. Adrienne Rich, "Compulsory Heterosexuality and Lesbian Existence," *Signs* 5:4 (Summer 1980), 631–60; reprinted in Ann Snitow, Christine Stansell, and Sharon Thompson, eds., *Powers of Desire: The Politics of Sexuality,* (NY: Monthly Review Press, 1983), 177–205; reprinted with a new Foreword and Afterword in Rich's *Blood, Bread, and Poetry: Selected Prose 1979–1985* (NY: W. W. Norton, 1986), 23–75. Hereafter quoted from Snitow, Stansell, and Thompson.

100. Rich made this point explicit: "the failure to examine heterosexuality as an institution is like failing to admit that the economic system called capitalism or the caste system of racism is maintained by a variety of forces, including both physical violence and false consciousness," 192.

101. Rich 178, 187, 192, 199, 201.

102. Rich 182, 202.

103. Rich 197. See also 183, 185.

104. Rich 183.

105. Rich 183. She approvingly quotes Catherine MacKinnon's analysis of the "sexulization" of women as a normal, negative aspect of women's wage work under contemporary capitalism (186–187).

106. Rich characterizes as "false consciousness" some women's experience of heterosexuality as a "choice" or "preference" (192). Women's

experience of freedom and pleasure in sex relations with men denies, she thinks, the social forces that have imposed that heterosexual attraction.

107. Rich 179, 192.

108. Rich 192.

109. Inspired by Rich's analysis, numbers of writers on women's history now regularly refer to "compulsory heterosexuality" (or "institutionalized" or "normative" heterosexuality), implicitly suggesting the possibility of a noncompulsory (noninstitutionalized, non-normative) heterosexuality. See, for example, the references to "institutionalized heterosexuality" and "normative heterosexuality" in Echols 285–286.

110. Rich 179.

111. Rich 195.

112. Rich 178, 193.

113. Rich 184.

114. Rich 201. She criticizes an anthropologist's book on "sexual arrangements" for being "utterly ahistorical" (180).

115. Rich 192.

116. Audre Lorde, "The Master's Tools Will Never Dismantle the Master's House," in *Sister Outsider: Essays and Speeches* (Freedom, CA: Crossing Press, 1984), 110–13.

117. Lorde 112.

Chapter 8
Toward a New Pleasure System
Looking Forward

1. *New York Times Book Review,* August 8, 1982, 10–11.

2. *New York Times Book Review,* October 3, 1982, 7.

3. Stephen Farber, "How Conflict Gave Shape to 'Tootsie,' " *New York Times,* December 19, 1982, 1:1.

4. Stanley Keleman, *In Defense of Heterosexuality* (Berkeley, CA: Center Press, 1982), dedicated to "Gail," and to "those who understand that anatomy means the dynamic structure of experience." In the early 1980s heterosexuality's troubles were more and more often a matter of explicit public comment. In 1983 a proposal to investigate and treat our society's "heterosexual conflict" appeared in a U.S. Justice Department memo by Alfred S. Regnery, then administrator of the Office of Juvenile Justice and Delinquency Prevention (also, of ultraconservative fame). His memo warned that the American family is threatened: "heterosexual conflicts . . . are growing and spreading in both virulence and

social normalcy" (quoted by Larry Bush, "Big Brother Is Watching You," *Village Voice,* August 7, 1984, 23).

5. William H. Masters, Virginia Johnson, Robert Kolodny, *Crisis: Heterosexual Behavior in the Age of AIDS* (NY: Grove Press, 1988).

6. Michael Fumento, *The Myth of Heterosexual AIDS* (NY: A New Republic Book/Basic Books, 1990).

7. Pete Hamill, "American Journal: Confessions of a Heterosexual," *Esquire* (Aug. 1990), 55–57.

8. Hamill 56.

9. Hamill 56.

10. Hamill 56.

11. Front page, *New York Newsday,* March 16, 1989.

12. Bruce Weber, "About Men: My Best Friend's Girlfriend," *New York Times Magazine,* April 16, 1989, 18–20.

13. See Karen Houpaert's review of "Heterosexuals in Crisis," *Village Voice,* Aug. 7, 1990, 100.

14. Michel Foucault, *The History of Sexuality: Volume I: An Introduction,* trans. from the French by Robert Hurley (NY: Pantheon, 1978); *The Use of Pleasure: Volume 2 of the History of Sexuality* (NY: Pantheon, 1985; Vintage Books Edition, March 1990); *The Care of the Self: Volume 3 of The History of Sexuality* (NY: Pantheon 1986; Vintage Books Edition, Nov. 1988).

I also consulted Foucault's major essays and interviews on sexuality and pleasure. See: "Power and Sex: An Interview with Michel Foucault," *Telos,* No. 32 (Summer 1977), 152–61.

"The History of Sexuality" (Jan. 1977) and "The Confessions of the Flesh" (July 10, 1977), both in Colin Gordon, ed., *Power/Knowledge: Selected Interviews and Other Writings 1972–1977: Michel Foucault* (NY: Pantheon, 1980).

"Power and Sex" (March 12, 1977), "Sexual Morality and the Law" (April 4, 1978), "The Battle for Chastity" (1982), "Sexual Choice, Sexual Act: Foucault and Homosexuality" (Fall 1982), "The Return of Morality," (June 28, 1984), "The Concern for Truth" (May 1984), all in Lawrence D. Kritzman, ed., *Michel Foucault: Politics, Philosophy, Culture, Interviews and Other Writings 1977–1984* (NY: Routledge, 1988).

"Sexuality and Solitude," *London Review of Books,* May 21–June 3, 1981, 3, 5–6; reprinted in David Rieff, ed., *Humanities in Review* I (NY: Cambridge University Press, 1982), 3–21.

Bob Gallagher and Alexander Wilson, "Michel Foucault: An Interview: Sex, Power and the Politics of Identity," *The Advocate,* No. 400, Aug. 7, 1984, 26–30, 58; reprinted in Mark Thompson, ed., *Gay Spirit: Myth and Meaning,* (NY: St. Martin's Press, 1987), 25–35.

"The Social Triumph of the Sexual Will," *Christopher Street* 64, May 1982, pp. 36–41 (a conversation with Gilles Barbedette, tr. Brendan Lemon).

The three major biographies of Foucault are James Miller, *The Passion of Michel Foucault* (NY: Simon & Schuster, 1993); Didier Eribon, *Michel Foucault* (Cambridge, MA: Harvard University Press, 1991); and David Macey, *The Lives of Michel Foucault: A Biography* (NY: Pantheon, 1993).

Also valuable are: Jeffrey Weeks, "Foucault for Historians," *History Workshop*, No. 14 (Autumn 1982), 106–19; and Irene Diamond and Lee Quinby, eds., *Feminism and Foucault: Reflections on Resistance* (Boston: Northeastern University Press, 1988).

I am grateful to David M. Halperin for advance copies of his two essays "The Queer Politics of Michel Foucault" and "The Describable Life of Michel Foucault."

15. See especially Foucault, "The Repressive Hypothesis," Part Two of *History of Sexuality* I, 15–50.

16. Foucault's historical analysis of different discourses anchors them in particular institutions—the insane asylum, the hospital, the prison, the legal system, the school, the family, the medical and psychiatric professions, the capitalist class, the working class. Only his histories of sexuality and pleasure fail to as clearly connect sex-talk to particular social institutions. See, for example, Foucault's *Madness and Civilization* (NY: Pantheon, 1965); *The Birth of the Clinic* (NY: Pantheon, 1973); *Discipline and Punish* (NY: Pantheon, 1977), *I, Pierre Rivière, Having Slaughtered My Mother, My Sister, and My Brother . . .* (NY: Pantheon, 1975); and "Introduction" to *Herculine Barbin* (Brighton: Harvester, 1980).

17. He doubts the claim of today's scientific sexperts to be neutral tellers of sexuality's objective, apolitical truth. See especially Foucault, "Scientia Sexualis," Part Three in *History of Sexuality* I, 51–74.

18. See especially Foucault, *History of Sexuality* I, 36–49, 101.

19. On "normalization," "normalizing," "normality," "normativity," the "norm" and "normal," see especially Foucault *History of Sexuality* I, 3, 5, 36, 38, 54, 65, 67, 68, 71, 89, 105, 117, 119, 144, 148, 149; *The Use of Pleasure* II, 4, 12, 36.

See also "Power and Norm" (notes taken at a lecture given by Foucault on March 28, 1973), in Meaghan Morris and Paul Patton, eds., *Michel Foucault: Power, Truth, Strategy* (Sydney, Australia: Ferral Publications, 1979), 59–66, and Foucault. "Introduction" to Georges Canguilhem, *The Normal and the Pathological* (NY: Zone Books, 1989), 7–24.

20. Foucault, *History of Sexuality* I, 5, 36.

21. Foucault, *History of Sexuality* I, 105.

22. On the making of "sexuality," see especially Foucault, *The Use of Pleasure* II, 3, 31, 35, 46; and *History of Sexuality* I, 68, 108, 124, 152.

23. Foucault, *History of Sexuality* I, 69, 72, 108, 154; *The Use of Pleasure* II, 244.

24. Contending against the political economy of joy, the governmental organization of immiseration remained an important concern, and an object of Foucault's active political protests. He analyzes the ways in which the body, its pains and pleasures, are fitted historically into a variety of powerful, moralizing institutions.

25. Foucault, *History of Sexuality* I, 43.

26. Foucault, *History of Sexuality* I, 101.

27. See especially Foucault, *History of Sexuality* I, 101; and Gallagher and Wilson, "Michel Foucault: An Interview."

28. Foucault, *History of Sexuality* I, 38.

29. Foucault, *History of Sexuality* I, 144, 148.

30. I am here using Foucault's critique of the gay liberationist's reverse affirmation to understand his own focus on homosexuality and his disregard of heterosexuality.

31. Questioning the "minoritizing" and "universalizing" tendencies of gay, lesbian, and queer analyses of the homosexual/heterosexual order is one of Eve Kosofsky Sedgwick's main projects in *Epistemology of the Closet* (Berkeley: University of California Press, 1990).

32. See Boswell, "Categories, Experience and Sexuality" in Edward Stein, ed., *Forms of Desire: Sexual Orientation and the Social Constructionist Controversy* (NY: Garland 1990), 161.

33. The sociologist Richard Sennett was also a speaker. The date of this talk is listed in Macy 560, number 313.

34. See "Bloodbath in Village," *New York Post*, November 20, 1980, front page, 2, 3; "Throng of Gays March for Gun Victims" and "Pastor's Family Torn Apart by Murderous Nightmare," *New York Post*, Nov. 21, 1980, 4; "Former Transit Officer Held As Slayer of Two in Village," *New York Times*, Nov. 21, 1980, B2.

35. Foucault, *History of Sexuality* I, 105, 108.

36. I borrow "invented tradition" from the historian Eric Hobsbawm. See Hobsbawm and Terence Ranger, eds., *The Invention of Tradition* (London: Cambridge University Press, 1983), especially Hobsbawm's essay "Mass-Producing Traditions: Europe, 1870–1914," pp. 263–307.

37. D'Emilio and Freedman, 332.

38. D'Emilio and Freedman 349.

39. D'Emilio and Freedman 358.
40. D'Emilio and Freedman 338.
41. D'Emilio and Freedman 338, 339.
42. D'Emilio and Freedman 331.
43. D'Emilio and Freedman 331.
44. D'Emilio and Freedman 331.
45. D'Emilio and Freedman 336.
46. D'Emilio and Freedman 337.
47. D'Emilio and Freedman 358.
48. D'Emilio and Freedman 362.
49. D'Emilio and Freedman 359.
50. Dennis Altman, *The Homosexualization of America, The Americanization of the Homosexual* (NY: St. Martin's Press, 1981).
51. D'Emilio and Freedman 300.
52. I pay homage to Monique Wittig's analysis of the master/slave, heterosexual/homosexual connection in Chapter 7, "The Lesbian Menace Strikes Back."
53. Gore Vidal, "The Tree of Liberty: Notes on Our Patriarchal State," *The Nation*, August 27/September 3, 1990, 1, 202, 204.

BIBLIOGRAPHY

The author would like to hear of striking references to heterosexuality and of materials relevant to heterosexual history: c/o Diane Cleaver, Literary Agent, 55 Fifth Avenue, 15th Floor, New York, NY 10011.

Included here are some important works cited in the text and backnotes and other works that help us interrogate the heterosexual category and system. Explicit references to **"heterosexual"** and **"straight"** are in bold type.

ABELOVE, HENRY. "Freud, Male Homosexuality, and the Americans." *Dissent* (Winter 1986): 59–69.

————. "Some Speculations on the History of 'Sexual Intercourse' During the 'Long Eighteenth Century' in England." *Genders* 6 (November 1989): 125–30; rev. in Andrew Parker and others, eds., *Nationalisms and Sexualities*. NY: Routledge, 1992: 335–42.

ACKERLEY, J. R. *My Father and Myself.* NY: Coward-McCann, 1968.

ADAMS, MARY LOUISE, et al., eds., "Confronting **Heterosexuality**." (Issue of) *Resources for Feminist Research* (Toronto), 19:3/4 (Sept./Dec. 1990).

ALTMAN, DENNIS. *The Homosexualization of America, The Americanization of the Homosexual.* NY: St. Martin's Press, 1981.

―――. *Homosexual Oppression and Liberation.* NY: Outerbridge & Dienstfrey, 1971.

ANDERSON, MARTY (MARTHA SHELLEY). "Is **Heterosexuality** 'Natural'?" *The Ladder* (June/July 1969): 4–7; reprinted (and attributed to Shelley) in Barbara Grier and Coletta Reid, eds., *The Lavender Herring: Lesbian and Gay Essays from The Ladder.* Baltimore: Diana Press, 1976: 55–60.

APPIAH, ANTHONY. "The Uncompleted Argument: Du Bois and the Illusion of Race." In Gates, ed.: 21–37.

ARIÈS, PHILIPPE. *Centuries of Childhood: A Social History of Family Life.* Trans. Robert Baldick. NY: Random House, 1962. (See on the invention of "adolescence" and "childhood" and the critique summarized by Vann.)

ATKINSON, TI-GRACE. *Amazon Odyssey.* NY: Links Books, 1974.

BAILY, BETH L. *From Front Porch to Back Seat: Courtship in Twentieth-Century America.* Baltimore: Johns Hopkins University Press, 1988.

BALDWIN, JAMES. " 'Go the Way Your Blood Beats': An Interview . . . by Richard Goldstein." *Village Voice* (June 26, 1984): 13–14, 16.

―――. "Preservation of Innocence." *Zero* (Tangier, Morocco) 1:2 (Summer 1949); reprinted *Outlook* 2:2 (Fall 1989): 40–45.

―――, and NIKKI GIOVANNI. *A Dialogue.* Philadelphia: J. B. Lippincott, 1973.

BARKER-BENFIELD, G. J. *The Horrors of the Half-Known Life: Male Attitudes Toward Women and Sexuality in Nineteenth-Century America.* NY: Harper and Row, 1976.

―――. "The Spermatic Economy." *Feminist Studies* 1 (Summer 1972): 45–74.

BATTAN, JESSE F. " 'The Word Made Flesh': Language, Authority, and Sexual Desire in Late Nineteenth-Century America." *Journal of the History of Sexuality* 3:2 (1992); reprinted in Fout and Tantillo: 101–40.

BAYER, RONALD. *Homosexuality and American Psychiatry: The Politics of Diagnosis.* NY: Basic Books, 1981.

BEAUVOIR, SIMONE DE. *The Second Sex* (1949). NY: Knopf, 1953. (See **"heterosexual"** in index.)

BERGER, PETER L., and THOMAS LUCKMAN. *The Social Construction of Reality.* NY: Doubleday, 1966.

BERNHEIMER, CHARLES, and CLAIRE KAHANE, eds. *In Dora's Case: Freud, Hysteria, Feminism.* NY: Columbia University Press, 1985.

BÉRUBÉ, ALLAN. *Coming Out Under Fire: The History of Gay Men and Women*

In World War Two. NY: Macmillan, 1990. (See **"heterosexuals"** in index.)

BETHEL, LORRAINE, and BARBARA SMITH, eds. *Conditions: Five, The Black Women's Issue* 2:2 (Autumn 1979).

BIRKEN, LAWRENCE. *Consuming Desire: Sexual Science and the Emergence of a Culture of Abundance, 1871–1914.* Ithaca: Cornell University Press, 1988. (See **"Heterosexuality"** in index.)

BLOCK, R. HOWARD. *Medieval Misogyny and the Invention of Western Romantic Love.* Chicago: University of Chicago Press, 1991.

BLUMIN, STUART M. *The Emergence of the Middle Class: Social Experience in the American City, 1760–1900.* NY: Cambridge University Press, 1989.

———. "The Hypothesis of Middle-Class Formation in Nineteenth-Century America: A Critique and Some Proposals." *American Historical Review* 90 (April 1985): 299–338.

BOSWELL, JOHN. "Categories, Experience and Sexuality." In Stein, ed. 133–73. An abridged version of this essay appears in *differences* 2:1 (Spring 1990): 67–87.

———. *Christianity, Social Tolerance, and Homosexuality: Gay People in Western Europe from the Beginning of the Christian Era to the Fourteenth Century.* Chicago: University of Chicago Press, 1980.

———. "Gay History" (review of David Greenberg's *The Construction of Homosexuality*). *The Atlantic* (Feb. 1989): 74–78.

———. "Jews, Bicycle Riders, and Gay People: The Determination of Social Consensus and Its Impact on Minorities." *Yale Journal of Law and the Humanities* 1 (1989).

———. "Sexual Categories, Sexual Universals: A Conversation with John Boswell." In *Christopher Street* 13:6 (1990): 23–40; reprinted in Mass, Vol. 2: 202–33.

———. "Toward the Long View: Revolutions, Universals and Sexual Categories." *Salmagundi* Nos. 58–59 (Fall-Winter 1982–83): 89–113; in Duberman, et al.: 17–36.

BOYER, PAUL. *Purity in Print: The Vice-Society Movement and Book Censorship in America.* NY: Scribner's, 1968.

———. *Urban Masses and Moral Order in America, 1820–1920.* Cambridge, MA: Harvard University Press, 1978.

BOYLE, THOMAS. "Morbid Depression Alternating with Excitement: Sex in Victorian Newspapers." In Don Cock, ed., *Sexuality and Victorian Literature.* Knoxville: University of Tennessee Press, 1984.

BRAY, ALAN. *Homosexuality in Renaissance England.* London: Gay Men's Press, 1982.

BRIDENTHAL, RENATA. "The Dialectics of Production and Reproduction in History." *Radical America* 10:2 (1976): 3–11.

BRONSKI, MICHAEL. "The Theory of the Pleasure Class." In his *Culture Class: The Making of a Gay Sensibility.* Boston: South End Press, 1984.

BROWN, RITA MAE. *A Plain Brown Wrapper.* Baltimore: Diana Press, 1976.

BUCHBINDER, HOWARD, et al., eds. *Who's on Top? The Politics of **Heterosexuality**.* Toronto: Garamond, 1987.

BULKIN, ELLY, MINNI BRUCE PRATT, and BARBARA SMITH. *Yours in Struggle: Three Feminist Perspectives on Anti-Semitism and Racism.* Brooklyn, N.Y.: Long Haul Press, 1984.

BULLOUGH, VERN L. "The Physician and Research Into Human Sexual Behavior in Nineteenth Century Germany." *Bulletin of the History of Medicine* 63 (1989): 247–67.

———. *Sex, Society, and History.* NY: Science History Publications, 1976.

———. *Sexual Variance in Society and History.* NY: John Wiley and Sons, 1976.

———, and BONNIE BULLOUGH. "Lesbianism in the 1920s and 1930s: A Newfound Study." *Signs* 2:4 (Summer 1977): 895–904.

BUNCH, CHARLOTTE. *Building Feminist Theory: Essays from Quest.* NY: Longman, 1981.

———. *Passionate Politics: Essays, 1968–1986.* NY: St. Martin's Press, 1987. (See especially "Not for Lesbians Only" [Fall 1975]: 174–81; "Learning from Lesbian Separatism" [Nov. 1976]: 182–91; "Lesbian-Feminist Theory" [1978]: 196–202.)

BURNHAM, JOHN C. *Paths Into American Culture: Psychology, Medicine, and Morals.* Philadelphia: Temple University Press, 1988.

———. *Psychoanalysis and American Medicine, 1894–1918: Medicine, Science and Culture. Psychological Issues* 5:4, Monograph 20. NY: International Unversities Press, 1967.

———. "The Progressive Era Revolution in American Attitudes Towards Sex." *Journal of American History* 59 (March 1973): 885–903.

BUTLER, JUDITH. *Gender Trouble: Feminism and the Subversion of Identity.* NY: Routledge, 1990. (See especially ch. 2: "Prohibition, Psychoanalysis, and the Production of the **Heterosexual** Matrix").

CADE, TONI, ed. *The Black Woman: An Anthology.* NY: Signet, 1970.

CAMERON, DEBORA. " 'Compulsory **Heterosexuality**' 10 Years On." *Women: A Cultural Review* 3 (1992).

CANGUILHEM, GEORGES. *The Normal and the Pathological.* Introduction by Michel Foucault. NY: Zone Books, 1989.

CARNES, MARK C., and CLYDE GRIFFEN, eds. *Meanings for Manhood: Construc-*

tions of Masculinity in Victorian America. Chicago: University of Chicago Press, 1990.

CHAUNCEY, GEORGE, JR. "Christian Brotherhood or Sexual Perversion? Homosexual Identities and the Construction of Sexual Boundaries in the World War One Era." *Journal of Social History* 19 (1985): 189–211; in Duberman, et al.: 294–317.

———. "From Sexual Inversion to Homosexuality: Medicine and the Changing Conceptualization of Female Sexual Deviance." *Salmagundi* Nos. 58–59 (Fall 1982–Winter 1983): 114–46.

———. *Gay New York: Gender, Urban Culture, and the Making of the Gay Male World (1890–1940).* NY: Basic Books, June 1994. (See ch. 4, "The Forging of Queer Identities and the Emergence of **Heterosexuality** in Middle-Class Culture," and, in index, **"Heterosexuality,** concept of, absence of . . . ; emergence of, in middle-class culture . . . ; homo-**heterosexual** binarism.")

CHODOROW, NANCY J. *Femininities, Masculinities, Sexualities: Freud and Beyond.* Lexington, KY: The University Press of Kentucky, 1994. (Includes **"Heterosexuality** as a Compromise Formation: Reflections on the Psychoanalytic Theory of Sexual Development.")

———. *Feminism and Psychoanalytic Theory.* New Haven: Yale University Press, 1989. (Includes "Oedipal Asymmetries and **Heterosexual** Knots.")

———. *The Reproduction of Mothering: Psychoanalysis and the Sociology of Gender.* Berkeley: University of California Press, 1978.

COHEN, ED. *Talk on the Wilde Side: Toward a Genealogy of a Discourse on Male Sexualities.* NY: Routledge, 1993. (See **"heterosexual"** in index.)

COMINOS, PETER T. "Innocent Femina Sensualis in Unconscious Conflict." In Vicinus, *Suffer:* 155–72, 229–31.

———. "Late-Victorian Respectability and the Social System." *International Review of Social History* 8 (1963): 18–48, 216–50.

COSTELLO, JOHN. *Virtue Under Fire: How World War II Changed Our Social and Sexual Attitudes.* NY: Fromm International Publishing, 1985.

COTT, NANCY F. *The Bonds of Womanhood: "Women's Sphere" in New England, 1780–1835.* New Haven: Yale University Press, 1977.

———. *The Grounding of Modern Feminism.* New Haven: Yale University Press, 1987.

———. "Passionlessness: An Interpretation of Victorian Sexual Ideology, 1790–1850." *Signs* 4:2 (Winter 1978): 219–36; reprinted in Cott and Pleck: 162–81.

———, and ELIZABETH H. PLECK, eds. *A Heritage of Their Own: Toward a New Social History of American Women.* NY: Simon and Schuster, 1979.

DAVIDOFF, LEONORE. "Class and Gender in Victorian England: The Diaries of Arthur J. Munby and Hannah Cullwick." *Feminist Studies* 5 (Spring 1979): 87–141.

DAVIDSON, ARNOLD I. "Closing Up the Corpses: Diseases of Sexuality and the Emergence of the Psychiatric Style of Reasoning." In George Boolos, ed. *Meaning and Method: Essays in Honor of Hilary Putnam.* NY: Cambridge University Press, 1990: 295–325.

———. "How to Do the History of Psychoanalysis: A Reading of Freud's *Three Essays on the Theory of Sexuality.*" *Critical Inquiry* (Winter 1987): 252–77.

———. "Sex and the Emergence of Sexuality." *Critical Inquiry* 14 (Autumn 1987): 16–48; reprinted in Stein, ed.

DAVY, KATE. "Reading Past the **Heterosexual** Imperative." *The Drama Review* 33:1 (Spring 1989): 153–70.

DECKER, HANNAH S. *Freud, Dora, and Vienna 1900.* NY: The Free Press, Macmillan, 1991.

DEEVEY, SHARON, "Such a Nice Girl." In Myron and Bunch, eds. (1975): 21–28.

DEGLER, CARL N. *At Odds: Women and the Family in America from the Revolution to the Present.* NY: Oxford University Press, 1980.

———. "What Ought to Be and What Was: Women's Sexuality in the Nineteenth Century." *American Historical Review* 79:5 (Dec. 1974): 1467–90.

DE LAURETIS, TERESA. "The Female Body and **Heterosexual** Presumption." *Semiotica* 67:3/4 (1987): 259–79.

D'EMILIO, JOHN. *Making Trouble: Essays on Gay History, Politics, and the University.* NY: Routledge, 1992.

———. *Sexual Politics, Sexual Communities: The Making of a Homosexual Minority in the United States, 1940–1970.* Chicago: University of Chicago Press, 1983.

———, and ESTELLE FREEDMAN. "Dialogue of the Sexual Revolutions: A Conversation with John D'Emilio and Estelle Freedman." In Mass, 2: 170–201.

———. *Intimate Matters: A History of Sexuality in America.* NY: Harper and Row, 1988.

DENSMORE, DANA. "Independence from the Sexual Revolution. In Koedt, Rapone, and Levine, eds.

DIAMOND, IRENE, and LEE QUINBY, eds. *Feminism and Foucault: Reflections on Resistance.* Boston: Northeastern University Press, 1988.

DITZION, SIDNEY HERBERT. *Marriage, Morals and Sex in America: A History of Ideas.* NY: Bookman, 1953. Rev. ed. 1969.

DIXON, MELVIN. "This Light, This Fire, This Time" (on James Baldwin). *Outlook* 2:2 (Fall 1989): 38–39.

DOLLIMORE, JONATHAN. *Sexual Dissidence: Augustine to Wilde, Freud to Foucault.* Oxford: Clarendon Press, 1991. (See **"heterosexuality"** in index and scattered references throughout.)

DORLAND, WILLIAM ALEXANDER, *The American Illustrated Medical Dictionary.* Second ed. Philadelphia: W. B. Saunders, 1901. (See **"heterosexual,"** 300.)

DOUGLAS, CAROL ANN. *Love and Politics: Radical Feminist and Lesbian Theories.* San Francisco: ism press, 1990. (See especially: "The Critique of **Heterosexuality**": 156–84, which includes a useful summary of what some "Feminists of Color" have said about **heterosexuality:** 175–80. See also **"heterosexism"** and "**heterosexual** feminists" in index.)

———. "Confessions of an Ex-**heterosexual**." *off our backs* 4:9 (Oct. 1979): 13.

DUBERMAN, MARTIN B. " 'Writhing Bedfellows' in Ante-bellum South Carolina: Historical Interpretations and the Politics of Evidence." In Duberman, et al.: 169–85.

———, MARTHA VICINUS, and GEORGE CHAUNCEY, JR., eds., *Hidden from History.* NY: New American Library, 1989.

DUBINSKY, KAREN. *Improper Advances: Rape and Heterosexual Conflict in Ontario, 1880–1929.* Chicago: University of Chicago Press, 1993. (See **"heterosexuality"** in index.)

DUBOIS, ELLEN CAROL, and LINDA GORDON. "Seeking Ecstasy on the Battlefield; Danger and Pleasure in Nineteenth Century Feminist Thought." *Feminist Studies* 9 (1983): 7–25; in Vance, ed.: 31–49.

DUCILLE, ANN. *The Coupling Convention: Sex, Text, and Tradition in Black Women's Fiction.* NY: Oxford University Press, 1993.

DUGGAN, LISA. "Biography = Death: Michel Foucault, Passion's Plaything" (review of James Miller, *The Passion of Michel Foucault*). *Village Voice* (May 4, 1993): 90–91.

———. "History's Gay Ghetto: The Contradictions of Growth in Lesbian and Gay History," in Susan Porter Benson, et al., eds., *Presenting the Past: Essays on History and the Public.* Philadelphia: Temple University Press, 1986: 281–90.

———. "Making It Perfectly Queer." *Socialist Review* 22 (1992).

———. "Review Essay. From Instincts to Politics: Writing the History of Sexuality in the U.S." *Journal of Sex Research* 27:1 (Feb. 1990): 95–109.

———. "The Social Enforcement of **Heterosexuality** and Lesbian Resistance in the 1920s," in Swerdlow: 76–92.

———. "The Trials of Alice Mitchell: Sensationalism, Sexology and the

Lesbian Subject in Turn-of-the-Century America." Ph.D. Thesis, University of Pennsylvania, 1992.

———. "The Trials of Alice Mitchell: Sensationalism, Sexology, and the Lesbian Subject in Turn-of-the-Century America." *Signs* 18:4 (Summer 1993), 791–814.

DWORKIN, ANDREA. *Intercourse.* NY: The Free Press, 1987.

———. *Our Blood: Prophecies and Discourses on Sexual Politics.* NY: Harper and Row, 1976.

———. *Right-wing Women.* NY: Wideview/Perigree Books, 1983.

———. *Woman Hating.* NY: Dutton, 1974.

DYER, RICHARD. " 'I Seem to Find the Happiness I Seek': **Heterosexuality** and Dance in the Musical." In Helen Thomas, ed. *Dance, Gender and Culture.* London: Macmillan, 1993.

———. *The Matter of Images: Essays on Representation.* NY: Routledge, 1993. (See "**heterosexuality**" in index; "**Straight** Acting": 133–36; and "White": 141–63.)

DYNES, WAYNE R., **"Heterosexuality."** In Dynes, ed. *Encyclopedia of Homosexuality.* NY: Garland, 1990: 332–35.

ECHOLS, ALICE. *Daring to Be Bad: Radical Feminism in America: 1967–1975.* Minneapolis: University of Minnesota Press, 1989. (See **"heterosexuality"** in index.)

———. "The New Feminism of Yin and Yang." In Snitow, et al.: 439–59.

———. "The Taming of the Id: Feminist Sexual Politics, 1968–83." In Vance, ed.: 50–72.

EHRENREICH, BARBARA. *The Hearts of Men: American Dreams and the Flight from Commitment.* NY: Anchor Press/Doubleday, 1983.

———, and DEIRDRE ENGLISH. *For Her Own Good.* NY: Doubleday, 1978.

———, HESS, ELIZABETH, and GLORIA JACOBS. *Re-Making Love: The Feminization of Sex.* Garden City, NY: Anchor Press/Doubleday, 1987. (See especially "The Battle for Orgasm Equity: The *Heterosexual Crisis of the Seventies*": 74–102.

EISENSTEIN, HESTER. *Contemporary Feminist Thought.* Boston: G. K. Hall, 1983.

———, and ALICE JARDINE. *The Future of Difference.* NY: Columbia University Press, 1980.

EISENSTEIN, ZILLAH. *The Radical Future of Liberal Feminism.* NY: Longman, 1981.

———, ed. *Capitalist Patriarchy and the Case for Socialist Feminism.* NY: Monthly Review Press, 1979.

ELLIS, HAVELOCK. *Studies in the Psychology of Sex.* NY: Random House, 1936.

ENGLISH, DEIRDRE, AMBER HOLLIBAUGH, GAYLE RUBIN. "Talking Sex: A Conversation on Sexuality and Feminism." *Socialist Review* 58 (July/Aug. 1981): 43–62.

EPSTEIN, BARBARA. "Family, Sexual Morality, and Popular Movements in Turn-of-the-Century America." In Snitow, et al.: 117–30.

EPSTEIN, JOSEPH. "Homo/**Hetero:** The Struggle for Sexual Identity." *Harper's Magazine* 241:144 (Sept. 1970): 37–51.

EPSTEIN, JULIE, and KRININA STRAUB, eds. *Body Guards: The Cultural Politics of Gender Ambiguity.* NY: Routledge, 1991.

EPSTEIN, STEVEN. "Gay Politics, Ethnic Identity: The Limits of Social Constructionism." *Socialist Review* Nos. 93/94 (May/Aug. 1987): 9–54; in Stein.

ERENBERG, LOUIS A. *Steppin' Out: New York Nightlife and the Transformation of American Culture, 1890–1930.* Westport, CT: Greenwood Press, 1980.

ERIBON, DIDIER. *Michel Foucault.* Cambridge, MA: Harvard University Press, 1991.

EVANS, DAVID T. *Sexual Citizenship: The Material Construction of Sexualities.* NY: Routledge, 1993.

EVANS, SARAH. *Born to Liberty.* NY: The Free Press, 1989.

EWEN, STUART. *Captains of Consciousness: Advertising and the Social Roots of the Consumer Culture.* NY: McGraw-Hill, 1976.

FADERMAN, LILLIAN. "The Morbidification of Love Between Women by 19th-Century Sexologists." *Journal of Homosexuality* 4:1 (Fall 1978): 73–89.

———. *Odd Girls and Twilight Lovers: A History of Lesbian Life in Twentieth-Century America.* NY: Columbia University Press, 1991.

———. *Scotch Verdict.* NY: William Morrow, 1983.

———. *Surpassing the Love of Men: Romantic Friendship and Love Between Women from the Renaissance to the Present.* NY: William Morrow, 1981.

FASS, PAULA S. *The Damned and the Beautiful: American Youth in the 1920s.* NY: Oxford University Press, 1977. (See especially ch. 6, "Sexual Mores in the World of Youth": 260–90.)

FIELDS, BARBARA JEANNE. "Slavery, Race and Ideology in the United States of America." *New Left Review* No. 181 (May/June 1990): 95–118.

FELLMAN, ANITA CLAIR, and MICHAEL FELLMAN. *Making Sense of Self: Medical Advice Literature in Late Nineteenth-Century America.* Philadelphia: University of Pennsylvania Press, 1981.

FÉRAY, JEAN-CLAUDE, and MANFRED HERZER. "Homosexual Studies and Politics in the 19th Century: Karl Maria Kertbeny." Trans. Glen W. Peppel. *Journal of Homosexuality* 19:1 (1990): 23–47.

FÉRÉ, CHARLES SAMSON. *The Sexual Instinct: Its Evolution and Dissolution.*

Trans. H. Blanchamp. London: The University Press, 1900. (See "**hetero-sexuality**," 183.)

FERGUSON, ANN. *Sexual Democracy: Women, Oppression, and Revolution.* Boulder, CO: Westview Press, 1991. (See "**heterosexuality**, compulsory" and "**heterosexual** relationships" in index.)

————, JACQUELYN N. ZITA, KATHRYN PYNE ADDLESON. "On 'Compulsory **Heterosexuality** and Lesbian Existence': Defining the Issues." *Signs* 7:1 (Aut. 1981): 158–99. (Includes: Ann Ferguson, "Patriarchy, Sexual Identity, and the Sexual Revolution"; J. N. Zita, "Historical Amnesia and the Lesbian Continuum"; K. P. Addelson, "Words and Lives.")

FIEDLER, LESLIE. *Love and Death in the American Novel.* NY: Criterion Books, 1960.

FIRESTONE, SHULAMITH. *The Dialectic of Sex: The Case for Feminist Revolution.* NY: William Morrow, 1970; rev. ed. NY: Bantam, 1970.

———— and ANNE KOEDT, eds. *Notes from the Second Year.* NY: New York Radical Women, 1970.

FOUCAULT, MICHEL. "The Battle for Chastity" (1982). In Kritzman, 227–41.

————. *The Care of the Self: Volume 3 of The History of Sexuality* (1984). Trans. Robert Hurley. NY: Pantheon, 1986

————. "The Concern for Truth" (May 1984). In Kritzman: 255–67.

————. "The Confessions of the Flesh" (July 10, 1977). In Gordon, ed.: 194–228.

————. "A Conversation with Michel Foucault: The Social Triumph of the Sexual Will." Gilles Barbedette, interviewer. Trans. Brendan Lemon. *Christopher Street* 64 (May 1982): 36–41.

————. "Friendship as a Way of Life" (April 1981). In Sylvère Lotringer, ed. *Foucault Live.* NY: Semiotext(e), 1989: 203–11.

————. "The History of Sexuality" (January 1–15, 1977). In Gordon, ed. 183–93.

————. *The History of Sexuality, Volume I, An Introduction.* Trans. Robert Hurley. NY: Pantheon, 1978.

————. "Introduction" to Canguilhem.

————. "Introduction" to *Herculine Barbin: Being the Recently Discovered Memoirs of a Nineteenth-Century French Hermaphrodite.* Trans. Richard McDougall. NY: Pantheon, 1980.

————. *Michel Foucault: Politics, Philosophy, Culture: Interviews and Other Writings 1977–1984.* Ed. by Lawrence D. Kritzman. Trans by Alan Sheridan and Others. NY: Routledge, 1988.

————. "Michel Foucault, An Interview: Sex, Power and the Politics of Identity." Interview by Bob Gallagher and Alexander Wilson (June

1982). *The Advocate* No. 400 (August 7, 1984): 26–30, 58; reprinted in Mark Thompson, ed. *Gay Spirit: Myth and Meaning.* NY: St. Martin's Press, 1987: 25–35.

———. "Power and Norm." In Meaghan Morris and Paul Patton, eds. *Michel Foucault: Power, Truth, and Strategy.* Sydney: Ferral Publications, 1979: 59–66.

———. *Power/Knowledge: Selected Interviews and Other Writings 1972–1977.* Ed. by Colin Gordon. Trans. Colin Gordon, Leo Marshal, John Mepham, Kate Soper. NY: Pantheon, 1980.

———. "Preface to *The History of Sexuality Volume II.*" Trans. and abridged by William Smock in Paul Rabinow, ed. *The Foucault Reader.* NY: Pantheon, 1984: 33–39.

———. "Power and Sex" (March 12, 1977). In Kritzman: 110–24.

———. "The Return of Morality" (June 28, 1984). In Kritzman: 232–54.

———. "Sexual Choice, Sexual Act: Foucault and Homosexuality" (Fall 1992). In Kritzman: 286–303.

———. "Sexuality and Solitude" (Nov. 20, 1980). *London Review of Books* 21 (May/June 1981): 3, 5–6; reprinted in David Rieff, ed., *Humanities in Review I.* NY: Cambridge University Press, 1982: 3–21.

———. "Sexual Morality and the Law" (April 4, 1978). In Kritzman: 271–85.

———. "The Simplest of Pleasures" (April 1979). Trans. Mike Riegle and Gilles Barbedette. *Fag Rag* 29 (1979): 3.

———. *The Use of Pleasure: Volume 2 of The History of Sexuality* (1984). NY: Pantheon, 1985.

———. "The West and the Truth of Sex" (Nov. 5–6, 1976). *Sub/stance* 20 (1978).

FOUT, JOHN C., and MAURA SHAW TANTILLO, eds. *American Sexual Politics: Sex, Gender, and Race Since the Civil War.* Chicago: University of Chicago Press, 1993.

FRANK, BLYE. "Hegemonic **Heterosexual** Masculinity." *Studies in Political Economy* 24 (Autumn 1987): 159–69.

FREDERICSON, GEORGE. *The Black Image in the White Mind: The Debate on Afro-American Character and Destiny: 1817–1914.* NY: Harper and Row, 1971.

FREEDMAN, ESTELLE B. "Sexuality in Nineteenth-Century America: Behaviour, Ideology, and Politics." *Reviews in American History* 10:4 (Dec. 1982): 196–215.

———. " 'Uncontrolled Desires': The Response to the Sexual Psychopath, 1920–1960." *Journal of American History* 79:1 (June 1987): 83–106.

————, et al., eds. "The Lesbian Issue." *Signs* (1985).

FREUD, SIGMUND. *The Standard Edition of the Complete Psychological Works of Sigmund Freud.* 24 volumes. Edited by James Strachey. London: Hogarth Press, 1953–. (The following alphabetical list of titles of Freud's works refers to the volume number of the *Standard Edition.*)

————. "Analysis of a Phobia in a Five-Year-Old Boy [Little Hans]." (1909b), *SE* 10: 3–149.

————. "Analysis Terminable and Interminable." (1937c), *SE* 23: 211–53.

————. "An Autobiographical Study." (1925d), *SE* 20: 3–76.

————. *Beyond the Pleasure Principle.* (1920g), *SE* 18: 3–64.

————. "Character and Anal Eroticism." (1908d), *SE* 9: 169–75.

————. " 'A Child Is Being Beaten.' " (1919e), *SE* 17: 177–204.

————. *Civilization and Its Discontents* (1930a), *SE* 21: 59–145.

————. " 'Civilized' Sexual Morality and Modern Nervous Illness" (1908d), *SE* 9: 179–204.

————. "Claims of Psycho-Analysis to Scientific Interest" (1913f), Part II (C), "The Biological Interest of Psycho-analysis." *SE* 13: 179–82.

————. "Contributions to a Discussion on Masturbation" (1912f), *SE* 12: 243–54.

————. "The Disposition to Obsessional Neurosis." (1913i), *SE* 12: 313–26.

————. "The Dissolution of the Oedipus Complex." (1924d), *SE* 19: 173–79.

————. "The Economic Problem of Masochism." (1924c), *SE* 19: 157–70.

————. *The Ego and the Id.* (1923b), *SE* 19: 3–66.

————. "Family Romances" (1909c), *SE* 9: 237–41.

————. "Female Sexuality" (1931b), *SE* 21: 223–43.

————. "Fetishism" (1927e), *SE* 21: 149–57.

————. *Five Lectures on Psycho-Analysis* (1910a), *SE* 11: 3–55. (Especially Lecture IV on sexuality.)

————. "Fragment of an Analysis of a Case of Hysteria" (Dora) (1905d), *SE* 7: 3–122.

————. *Group Psychology and the Analysis of the Ego* (1921c), *SE* 18: 67–143.

————. "From the History of an Infantile Disorder" (Wolf Man) (1918b), *SE,* 17: 3–122.

————. "Hysterical Phantasies and Their Relation to Bisexuality" (1908a), *SE* 9: 157–66.

————. "The Infantile Genital Organisation" (1923e), *SE* 19: 141–45.

————. "Instincts and Their Vicissitudes" (1915c), *SE* 14: 111–40.

————. *Introductory Lectures on Psycho-Analysis* (1916–17), *SE* 16: Lecture XX, "The Sexual Life of Human Beings," 303–19; Lecture XXI, "The Development of the Libido and the Sexual Organizations," 320–38; Lecture XXII, "Some Thoughts on Development and Regression—Aetiology," 339–57.

————. "Leonardo da Vinci and a Memory of His Childhood" (1910c), *SE* 11: 59–63, 93–106. (See especially Ch. 3 about sexuality.)

————. "Libidinal Types" (1913a), *SE* 21: 216–20.

————. "My Views on the Part Played by Sexuality in the Aetiology of the Neuroses" (1906a), *SE* 7: 271–79.

————. *New Introductory Lectures on Psycho-Analysis* (1933a), Editor's Note; XXXII, "Anxiety and the Instinctual Life"; XXXIII, "Femininity." *SE* 3–4: 81–111; 112–35.

————. "Notes Upon a Case of Obsessional Neurosis" (Rat Man) (1909d), *SE* 10: 153–318.

————. "On Narcissism: an Introduction" (1914c), *SE* 14: 69–102.

————. "On the Sexual Theories of Children" (1908c), *SE* 9: 207–226.

————. "On Transformation of Instinct as Exemplified in Anal Erotism" (1917c), *SE* 17: 126–33.

————. "On the Universal Tendency to Debasement in the Sphere of Love" (1912d), *SE* 11: 178–90.

————. *An Outline of Psycho-Analysis* (1940a), Editor's Note; III, "The Development of the Sexual Function"; VII, "An Example of Psycho-Analytic Work." *SE* 23: 141–43; 152–56; 183–94.

————. "Preface to Bourke's *Scatologic Rites of All Nations* (1913k), *SE:* 12, 334–37.

————. "Preface to the Fourth Edition of *Three Essays on the Theory of Sexuality*" (1920), *SE* 7: 133.

————. "Psycho-Analytic Notes on an Autobiographical Account of a Case of Paranoia (Dementia Paranoides)" (Schreber) (1911), *SE* 12: 3–82.

————. "The Psychogenesis of a Case of Female Homosexuality," (1920a), *SE* 18: 146–72.

————. "The Sexual Enlightenment of Children" (1907c), *SE* 9: 131–39.

————. "Sexuality in the Aetiology of the Neuroses" (1898a), *SE* 3: 261.

————. "Some Neurotic Mechanism in Jealousy, Paranoia and Homosexuality" (1922b), *SE* 18: 222–32.

————. "Some Psychical Consequences of the Anatomical Distinctions Between the Sexes" (1925j), *SE* 19: 243–58.

———. "A Special Type of Choice of Object Made by Men" (1910h), *SE* 11: 165–75.

———. "Splitting of the Ego in the Process of Defense" (1940), *SE* 23: 273–78.

———. "Studies in Hysteria" (1893), *SE* 2: ix–xxvii; 48–181 (Freud's cases 2, 3, 4, 5.)

———. "The Taboo of Virginity" (1918a), *SE* 11: 192–208.

———. "Three Essays on the Theory of Sexuality" (1905d), *SE* 7: 125. (This was also published as *Three Contributions to the Sexual Theory*. Trans. A. A. Brill. NY: The Journal of Nervous and Mental Disease Publishing House, 1910.)

———. "Two Encyclopedia Entries" ("Libido Theory") (1923a), *SE* 18: 234–59.

FRIEDAN, BETTY. *The Feminine Mystique*. NY: W. W. Norton, 1963.

———. *It Changed My Life: Writings on the Women's Movement*. NY: Random House, 1976.

FUMENTO, MICHAEL. *The Myth of Heterosexual AIDS*. NY: Basic Books, 1990.

FUSS, DIANA. *Essentially Speaking: Feminism, Nature & Difference*. NY: Routledge, 1989. (See **"heterosexism," "heterosexuality"** in index.)

———, ed. *Inside/Out: Lesbian and Gay Theories*. NY: Routledge, 1990. (See especially "Inside Out" by Fuss.)

GADLIN, HOWARD. "Private Lives and Public Order: A Critical View of the History of Intimate Relations in the U.S." *Massachusetts Review* 17 (Summer 1976): 304–30.

GAGNON, JOHN. *Human Sexualities*. Glenview, IL: Scott, Foresman, 1977. (See especially ch. 9, "Learning **Heterosexuality**": 165–90, and **heterosexuality**" in index.)

———, and CATHY GREENBLATT. *Life Designs: Individuals, Marriages, Families*. Glenview, IL: Scott, Foresman, 1978. (See especially "The Learning and Practice of **Heterosexuality**": 137–43.)

———, and WILLIAM SIMON. *Sexual Conduct*. Chicago: Adline, 1973.

GALLAGHER, CATHERINE, and THOMAS LAQUEUR, eds. *Sexuality and the Social Body in the Nineteenth Century*. *Representations* 14 (Spring 1986). Reprinted as *The Making of the Modern Body: Sexuality and Society in the Nineteenth Century*. Berkeley: University of California Press, 1987.

GARBER, MARJORIE. *Vested Interests: Cross-Dressing and Cultural Anxiety*. NY: Routledge, 1992.

GARDELLA, PETER. *Innocent Ecstasy: How Christianity Gave America an Ethic of Sexual Pleasure*. NY: Oxford University Press, 1985.

GATES, HENRY LOUIS. "Editor's Introduction: Writing 'Race' and the

Difference It Makes." In *"Race," Writing and Difference*. Chicago: University of Chicago Press, 1986: 1–20.

GAY, PETER. *The Bourgeois Experience, Victoria to Freud*. 3 volumes. NY: Oxford University Press, 1984, 1986, 1993.

———. "Victorian Sexuality: Old Texts and New Insights." *American Scholar* (Summer 1980): 372–78.

GENOVESE, EUGENE. *Roll, Jordan, Roll: The World the Slaves Made*. NY: Pantheon, 1974. (On sexuality 458–75.)

GIDDINGS, PAULA. *When and Where I Enter: The Impact of Black Women on Race and Sex in America*. NY: Bantam Books, 1985.

GILFOYLE, TIMOTHY. *City of Eros: New York City, Prostitution, and the Commercialization of Sex, 1790–1920*. NY: W. W. Norton, 1992.

GILMAN, SANDER L. *The Case of Sigmund Freud: Medicine and Identity at the Fin de Siècle*. Baltimore: Johns Hopkins University Press, 1993.

———. *Difference and Pathology: Stereotypes of Sexuality, Race, and Madness*. Ithaca: Cornell University Press, 1985.

GOLDBERG, JONATHAN, ed. *Queering the Renaissance*. Durham: Duke University Press, 1994.

———. "Sodomy in the New World: Anthropologies Old and New." In Warner, ed.: 3–18.

———. " 'They Are All Sodomites': The New World." In his *Sodometries: Renaissance Texts, Modern Sexualities*. Stanford: Stanford University Press, 1992: 179–249. (See **"heterosexuality"** in index.)

GORDON, LINDA. *Women's Body, Woman's Right: A Social History of Birth Control in America*. NY: Grossman, 1976.

GORDON, MICHAEL, ed. *The American Family in Social-Historical Perspective*. 3rd ed. NY: St. Martin's Press, 1983.

———. "From an Unfortunate Necessity to a Cult of Mutual Orgasm: Sex in American Marital Education Literature, 1830–1940." In James Henslin, ed., *Studies in the Sociology of Sex*. NY: Appleton-Century-Crofts, 1971: 53–77.

———. "The Ideal Husband as Depicted in the Nineteenth-Century Marriage Manual." In Pleck and Pleck: 145–57.

GORNICK, VIVIAN. *Essays in Feminism*. NY: Harper and Row, 1978.

———, and BARBARA K. MORGAN, eds. *Woman in Sexist Society*. NY: Basic Books, 1971.

GOSSETT, THOMAS F. *Race: The History of an Idea in America*. Dallas, TX: Southern Methodist University Press, 1963.

GREENBERG, DAVID. *The Construction of Homosexuality*. Chicago: University of Chicago Press, 1988. (See **"heterosexuality"** in index.)

GUTMAN, HERBERT G. *The Black Family in Slavery and Freedom, 1750–1925*.

NY: Pantheon, 1976. (See "sex education," "sexual practices," and "sexual punishment" in index.)

——, and RICHARD SUTCH. "Victorians All? The Sexual Conduct of Slaves and Their Masters." In Paul A. David, et al., eds. *Reckoning with Slavery: A Critical Study of the Quantitative History of American Negro Slavery*, NY: Oxford University Press, 1976: 134–64.

GUTTMAN, SAMUEL A., et al., *The Concordance to The Standard Edition of The Complete Psychological Works of Sigmund Freud.* 6 volumes. Boston: G. K. Hall, 1960.

HAAG, PAMELA S. "In Search of 'The Real Thing': Ideologies of Love, Modern Romance, and Women's Sexual Subjectivity in the United States, 1920–40." *Journal of the History of Sexuality* 2:4 (1992); reprinted in Fout and Tantillo: 161–91.

HACKING, IAN. "The Invention of Split Personalities." In Alan Donagan, et al., eds. *Nature and Natural Knowledge.* Dordrecht: D. Reidel, 1986: 63–85.

——. "Making Up People." In Thomas Heller, et al., eds., *Reconstructing Individualism: Autonomy, Individuality, and the Self in Western Thought.* Stanford: Stanford University Press, 1986: 222–36; reprinted in Stein, ed.

HALE, NATHAN G., JR. *Freud and the Americans: The Beginnings of Psychoanalysis in the United States, 1876–1917.* NY: Oxford University Press, 1971.

HALL, DIANA LONG. "Biology, Sex Hormones, and Sexism in the 1920s." In Carol Gould and Marx Wartofsky, eds., *Women and Philosophy: Toward a Theory of Liberation.* NY: G. P. Putnam's, 1979: 81–96.

HALL, JACQUELINE DOWD. "'The Mind That Burns in Each Body': Women, Rape, and Racial Violence." In Snitow, et al.: 328–49.

HALL, LESLIE A. *Male Anxieties: Male Sexuality, 1900–1950.* Cambridge, MA: Polity Press/Basil Blackwell, 1991.

HALLER, JOHN S. "From Maidenhead to Menopause: Sex Education for Women in Victorian America." *Journal of Popular Culture* 6:1 (Summer 1972): 49–70.

——. *Outcasts from Evolution: Scientific Attitudes of Racial Inferiority, 1859–1900.* Urbana: University of Illinois Press, 1971.

——, and ROBIN M. HALLER. *The Physician and Sexuality in Victorian America.* Urbana, IL: University of Illinois Press, 1974; reprinted NY: W. W. Norton, 1977.

HALLER, MARK H. *Eugenics: Hereditarian Attitudes in American Thought.* NJ: Rutgers University Press, 1963.

HALLEY, JANET E. "Bowers v. Hardwick in the Renaissance." In Goldberg, ed.: 15–39.

————. "The Construction of **Heterosexuality**." *Stanford Journal of Law, Gender and Sexual Orientation* 1 (1991). In Warner, ed.: 82–99.

————. "Misreading Sodomy: A Critique of the Classification of 'Homosexuals' in Federal Equal Protection Law." In Epstein and Straub: 351–77.

————. "The Politics of the Closet: Towards Equal Protection for Gay, Lesbian, and Bisexual Identity." *UCLA Law Review* 36:5 (June 1989): 915–76.

————. "Reasoning About Sodomy: Act and Identity in and After *Bowers v. Hardwick*." *Virginia Law Review* 79:7 (Oct. 1993): 1721–80.

————. "Sexual Orientation and the Politics of Biology: A Critique of the Argument from Immutability." *Stanford Law Review* 46:3 (Feb. 1994): 503–68.

HALPERIN, DAVID M. "The Describable Life of Michel Foucault" and "The Queer Politics of Michel Foucault." Forthcoming.

————. *One Hundred Years of Homosexuality And Other Essays on Greek Love.* NY: Routledge, 1990.

————, JOHN J. WINKLER, and FROMA I. ZEITLIN, eds. *Before Sexuality: The Construction of Erotic Experience in the Ancient Greek World.* Princeton: Princeton University Press, 1990.

HALTTUNEN, KAREN. *Confidence Men and Painted Women: A Study of Middle Class Culture in America, 1830–1870.* New Haven: Yale University Press, 1982.

HAMILL, PETE. "American Journal: Confessions of a **Heterosexual**." *Esquire* (Aug. 1990): 55–57.

HANSCOMBE, GILLIAN E., and MARTIN HUMPHRIES, eds. *Heterosexuality*. London: GMP Publishers, 1987. (See especially Jon Ward's "The Nature of **Heterosexuality**": 145–69.)

HANSEN, BERT. "American Physicians' 'Discovery' of the Homosexual, 1880–1900: A New Diagnosis in a Changing Society." In Charles Rosenberg and Janet Golden, eds., *Framing Disease: Studies in Cultural History.* New Brunswick, NJ: Rutgers University Press, 1992.

————. "The Historical Construction of Homosexuality" (review of Jeffery Weeks's *Coming Out*), *Radical History Review* No. 20 (Spring/Summer 1979): 66–73.

HARRIS, DAVID. *From Class Struggle to the Politics of Pleasure: The Effects of Gramscianism on Cultural Studies.* NY: Routledge, 1992.

HARWOOD, VICTORIA, et al., eds. *Pleasure Principles: Politics, Sexuality and Ethics.* London: Lawrence & Wishart, 1993.

HEKMA, GERT. " 'A Female Soul in a Male Body': Sexual Inversion as Gender Inversion in Nineteenth-Century Sexology." In Herdt, ed.: 213–40.

———. "A History of Sexology: Social and Historical Aspects of Sexuality." In Jan Bremmer, ed., *From Sappho to De Sade: Moments in the History of Sexuality.* NY: Routledge, 1989: 173–93.

HENRY, GEORGE W. *Sex Variants: A Study of Homosexual Patterns.* 2-volume ed. NY: Paul B. Hoeber, 1941.

HERDT, GILBERT, ed. *Third Sex, Third Gender: Beyond Sexual Dimorphism in Culture and History.* NY: Zone Books, 1994.

HERTZ, NIEL, ed. Special Issue: "Freud and Dora." *Diacritics* (Spring 1983.)

HERZER, MANFRED. "Kertbeny and the Nameless Love." *Journal of Homosexuality* 12:1 (Fall 1985): 1–25.

———. "Ein Brief von Kertbeny in Hannover an Ulrichs in Wurzburg." *Capri: Zeitschrift für Geschichte* 1 (1987): 25–35.

HIGGINBOTHAM, EVELYN BROOKS. "African-American Women's History and the Metalanguage of Race." *Signs* 17:2 (Winter 1992): 251–74.

HIGHAM, JOHN. "The Reorientation of American Culture in the 1890s." In his *Writing American History: Essays in Modern Scholarship.* Bloomington: Indiana University Press, 1970.

HOBSBAWM, ERIC, and TERENCE RANGER, eds. *The Invention of Tradition.* London: Cambridge University Press, 1983.

HOLE, JUDITH, and ELLEN LEVINE. *The Rebirth of Feminism.* NY: Quadrangle, 1971. (See especially "The 'Sexual Revolution,' " 218–21, "The Politics of Language," 222–24, and **"heterosexuals"** in index.)

HOLLIBAUGH, AMBER. "Desire for the Future: Radical Hope in Passion and Pleasure." In Vance, ed.: 401–10.

———, and CHERIE MORAGA. "What We're Rollin Around in Bed With: Sexual Silences in Feminism." In Snitow, et al.: 394–405.

HOLT, ROBERT. *Abstracts of the Standard Edition of the Complete Psychological Works of Sigmund Freud.* NY: Jason Arons, 1976.

HONIG, J. "Sigmund Freud's Views on the Sexual Disorders in Historical Perspective." *British Journal of Psychiatry* 129 (1976): 193–200.

HOOKS, BELL. *Talking Back: Thinking Feminist, Thinking Black.* Boston: South End Press, 1989.

HORNBLOW, ARTHUR. "Mr. Hornblow Goes to the Play." *Theatre Magazine* (April 1923). (See **"heterosexual,"** 68.)

HOUPAERT, KAREN. (*Review of Heterosexuals in Crisis*). *Village Voice* (April 16, 1989): 18–20.

HUGHES, CHARLES H. "Erotopathia—Morbid Eroticism." *Alienist and Neurologist* 14:1 (Oct. 1893): 531–78. (See **"heterosexual,"** 563.)

HULL, GLORIA T., PATRICIA BELL SCOTT, and BARBARA SMITH, eds. *All of the Women Are White, All the Blacks Are Men, But Some of Us Are Brave: Black Women's Studies.* Old Westbury, NY: Feminist Press, 1982.

IRVINE, JANICE. *Disorders of Desire: Sex and Gender in Modern American Sexology.* Philadelphia: Temple University Press, 1990.

———. "From Difference to Sameness: Gender Ideology in Sexual Science." *Journal of Sex Research* 27:1 (Feb. 1990): 7–24.

JACKSON, MARGARET. " 'Facts of Life' or the Eroticization of Women's Oppression? Sexology and the Social Construction of **Heterosexuality**." In Pat Caplan, ed. *The Cultural Construction of Sexuality.* London: Tavistock, 1987: 22–81.

JAY, KARLA, and ALLEN YOUNG. *Out of the Closets: Voices of Gay Liberation.* NY: Douglas Book Corp. 1972.

JEFFRIES, SHIELA. *Anticlimax: A Feminist Perspective on the Sexual Revolution.* NY: New York University Press, 1990. (See **"hetero-reality," "heterosexual** desire," and **"heterosexuality"** in index.)

———. *The Spinster and Her Enemies: Feminism and Sexuality 1880–1930.* London: Pandora, 1985. (See **"heterosexuality"** in index.)

JOHNSTON, JILL. *Lesbian Nation.* NY: Simon and Schuster, 1973.

KAPLAN, CORA. "Wild Nights: Pleasure/Sexuality/Feminism" (in section on "Feminism and Compulsory **Heterosexuality:** Adrienne Rich"). In Formations Editorial Collective, eds. *Formations of Pleasure.* Boston: Routledge, 1983: 15–25.

KATZ, JONATHAN NED. "Coming Out Fighting" (reviews of Altman's *Homosexual Oppression* and Karla Jay and Allen Young, eds., *Out of the Closets: Voices of Gay Liberation), The Nation,* July 2, 1973.

———. *Gay American History: Lesbians and Gay Men in the U.S.A.* NY: T. Y. Crowell, 1976; reprinted NY: New American Library, 1992.

———. *Gay/Lesbian Almanac: A New Documentary.* NY: Harper and Row, 1983; reprinted NY: Richard Gallen, 1994. (See especially the essays "Lesbian and Gay History: Theory and Practice"; "The Age of Sodomitical Sin"; and "The Invention of the Homosexual." See also **"heterosexuality"** in index.)

———. "Homosexual History: Its Import and Implications." Keynote address, conference, "Constructing a History of Power and Sexuality," sponsored by New York University Graduate History Society and NYU Women's Center, March 31, 1978. Revised as "Why Gay History?" *The Body Politic* (Aug. 1979): 19–20.

———. "The Invention of **Heterosexuality**." *Socialist Review* 20:1. (Jan.-Mar. 1990): 7–34.

———. "The Invention of **Heterosexuality,** 1892–1982. In Supplement

II, papers of the conference Among Men, Among Women, University of Amsterdam, 1983.

———. "Melville's Secret Sex Text" (on the novel *Redburn*). *Village Voice Literary Supplement* (April 1992): 10–12.

———. "True Lust" (review of Snitow, et al.) *Village Voice* (Oct. 18, 1983): 50, 52–53.

———. "Womanhood in America" (review of Mary P. Ryan's book of that title). *The Body Politic* (Dec. 1977/Jan. 1978): 19, 21.

KATZ, MICHAEL B., and MARK J. STERN. "Fertility, Class, and Industrial Capitalism: Erie County, New York, 1855–1915." *American Quarterly* 33 (Spring 1981): 63–70

KELEMAN, STANLEY. *In Defense of* **Heterosexuality.** Berkeley: Center Press, 1982.

KELLY, JOAN. "The Social Relations of the Sexes: Methodological Implications of Women's History." *Signs* 1:4 (Summer 1976): 809–23; reprinted in her *Women, History, and Theory.* Chicago: University of Chicago Press, 1984.

KENDRICK, NEIL M. "Sex and Married Victorians" (review of Peter Gay's *Education of the Senses* I). *New York Times Book Review* (Jan. 8, 1984): 1, 35.

KENDRICK, WALTER. *The Secret Museum: Pornography in Modern Culture.* NY: Viking/Penguin, 1987.

KENNEDY, DAVID M. "The Nineteenth-Century Heritage: The Family, Feminism, and Sex." In *Birth Control in America: The Career of Margaret Sanger.* New Haven: Yale University Press, 1970: 36–39.

KENNEDY, ELIZABETH L., and MADELINE D. DAVIS. *Boots of Leather, Slippers of Gold: The History of a Lesbian Community.* NY: Routledge, 1993. (See "**Straight** life" in index.)

KENNEDY, HUBERT C. "The 'Third Sex' Theory of Karl Heinrich Ulrichs." *Journal of Homosexuality* 6:1–1 (Fall/Winter 1980/81): 103–12.

———. *Ulrichs: The Life and Works of Karl Heinrich Ulrichs, Pioneer of the Modern Gay Movement.* Boston: Alyson, 1988.

KESSLER, SUZANNE J. "The Medical Construction of Gender: Case Management of Intersexed Infants." *Signs* 16 (1990): 3–26.

———, and WENDY MCKENNA. *Gender: An Ethnomethodological Approach.* NY: John Wiley, 1978; Chicago: University of Chicago Press, 1985.

KIERNAN, JAMES G. "Responsibility in Sexual Perversion." *Chicago Medical Recorder* 3 (May 1892): 185–210.

KING, KATIE. "The Situation of Lesbianism as Feminism's Magical Sign: Contests for Meaning and the U.S. Women's Movement, 1968–1972." *Communications* 9 (1986).

KINSEY, ALFRED. "Concepts of Normality and Abnormality in Sexual Behavior." In P. Hoch and J. Zubin, eds., *Psychosexual Development in Health and Disease.* NY: Grune and Stratton, 1949.

———, et al. *Sexual Behavior in the Human Female.* Philadelphia: W. B. Saunders, 1953. (See **"heterosexual"** in index.)

———, et al. *Sexual Behavior in the Human Male.* Philadelphia: W. B. Saunders, 1948. (See **"heterosexual"** in index.)

KINSMAN, GARY. " 'Homosexuality' Historically Reconsidered Challenges **Heterosexual** Hegemony." *Journal of Historical Sociology* 4:2 (June 1991): 89–111.

———. *The Regulation of Desire: Sexuality in Canada.* Montréal: Black Rose Books, 1987. (See especially "The Historical Emergence of Homosexuality and **Heterosexuality**": 37–64.)

KITZINGER, CELIA, et al., eds. (Special Issue) **"Heterosexuality."** *Feminism & Psychology* 2:3 (October 1992).

KOEDT, ANNE. "Lesbianism and Feminism." In Koedt, Levine, and Rapone eds. (1973): 246–58.

———. "The Myth of the Vaginal Orgasm" (June 1968). In Koedt, Levine, and Rapone, eds. (1973): 198–207.

[———]. "Politics of the Ego: A Manifesto for N.Y. Radical Feminists." In Koedt, Levine, and Rapone eds. (1973): 379–83.

———, ELLEN LEVINE and ANITA RAPONE, eds. *Radical Feminism.* NY: Quadrangle, 1973.

———, ANITA RAPONE and ELLEN LEVINE, eds. *Notes from the Third Year: Women's Liberation.* NY: Radical Feminists, 1971.

KOEHLER, LYLE. *A Search for Power: The "Weaker Sex" in Seventeenth-Century New England.* Urbana: University of Illinois Press, 1990.

KRAFFT-EBING, RICHARD VON. *Psychopathia Sexualis, with Especial Reference to Contrary Sexual Instinct: A Medico-Legal Study.* Trans. by Gilbert Chaddock. Philadelphia: F. A. Davis, 1893.

KUSHNER, HOWARD I. "Nineteenth Century Sexuality and the 'Sexual Revolution' of the Progressive Era." *Canadian Review of American Studies* 9 (1978): 34–49.

LAPORTE, RITA. "The Causes and Cures of **Heterosexuality**." In Barbara Grier and Coletta Reid, eds. *The Lavender Herring: Lesbian and Gay Essays from The Ladder.* Baltimore: Diana Press, 1976: 43–49.

LAQUEUR, THOMAS. *Making Sex: Body and Gender from the Greeks to Freud.* Cambridge: Harvard University Press, 1990.

LASCH, CHRISTOPHER. *The Culture of Narcissism.* NY: W. W. Norton, 1979.

LAURITSEN, JOHN, and DAVID THORSTAD. *The Early Homosexual Rights Movment (1864–1935).* NY: Times Change Press, 1974.

LEONARD, VICKIE. "No Apologies from a **Heterosexual**." *off our backs* 4:9 (Oct. 1979): 13.

LEVINE, JUDITH. *My Enemy, My Love: Man-Hating and Ambivalence in Women's Lives.* NY: Doubleday, 1992.

LEWES, KENNETH. *The Psychoanalytic Theory of Male Homosexuality.* NY: Simon and Schuster, 1988.

LEWIN, MIRIAM, ed. *In the Shadow of the Past: Psychology Portrays the Sexes, A Social and Intellectual History.* NY: Columbia University Press, 1984.

LEWIS, JAN. "Mother's Love: The Construction of an Emotion in Nineteenth-Century America." In Andrew Baines and Peter Stearns, eds., *Social History and Issues in Human Consciousness.* NY: New York University Press, 1989.

LICHTMAN, RICHARD. *The Production of Desire: The Integration of Psychoanalysis Into Marxist Theory.* NY: The Free Press, 1982. (See esp. "5. Clinical Practice: The Case of Dora.")

LORDE, AUDRE. *Sister Outsider: Essays and Speeches.* Freedom, CA: The Crossing Press, 1984. (See especially "The Master's Tools Will Never Dismantle the Master's House," 110–14; "Scratching the Surface: Some Barriers to Women and Loving," 45–52; and "Uses of the Erotic: The Erotic as Power," 53–59.)

LOTH, DAVID. *The Erotic in Literature: A Historical Survey of Pornography as Delightful as it is Indiscreet.* London: Secker & Warburg, 1962.

LOTT, TOMMY L. "Du Bois on the Invention of Race." *The Philosophical Forum* 24:1/3 (Fall/Spring 1992–1993): 166–87.

LUNDBERG, FERDINAND, and MARYNIA F. FARNHAM. *Modern Woman the Lost Sex.* NY: Harper, 1947.

LYNCH, MICHAEL. " 'Here Is Adhesiveness': From Friendship to Homosexuality." *Victorian Studies* 29:1 (Autumn 1985): 67–96.

———. "New York Sodomy, 1796–1873." Paper presented at the New York Institute for the Humanities (Feb. 1, 1985).

LYSTRA, KAREN. *Searching the Heart: Women, Men, and Romantic Love in Nineteenth Century America.* NY: Oxford University Press, 1989.

MACDONALD, ROBERT H. "The Frightful Consequences of Onanism: Notes on the History of a Delusion." *Journal of the History of Ideas* 28 (July-Sept. 1967): 423–31.

MACEY, DAVID. *The Lives of Michel Foucault: A Biography.* NY: Pantheon, 1993.

MACKINNON, CATHERINE A. *Feminism Unmodified: Discourses on Life and Law.* Cambridge, MA: Harvard University Press, 1987.

———. *Sexual Harassment of Working Women: A Case of Sex Discrimination.* NY: Yale University Press, 1979.

————. *Towards a Feminist Theory of the State.* Cambridge, MA: Harvard University Press, 1989. (See **"heterosexuality"** in index.)

MANGAN, J.A. and JAMES WALVIN, eds. *Manliness and Morality: Middle Class Masculinity in Britain and America, 1800–1940.* NY: St. Martin's Press, 1987.

MARCUS, STEVEN. *The Other Victorians: A Study of Sexuality and Pornography in Nineteenth-Century England.* NY: Basic Books, 1966.

MARMOR, JUDD. " 'Normal and Deviant' Sexual Behavior." *Journal of the American Medical Association* No. 217 (1971): 165–70.

MARTIN, KARIN. "Gender and Sexuality: Medical Opinion on Homosexuality, 1900–1950." *Gender and Society* 7 (1993): 246–60.

MASS, LAWRENCE. *Homosexuality as Behavior and Identity: Dialogues of the Sexual Revolution.* Binghamton, NY: Harrington Park Press, 1990. 2 vols.

MASTERS, WILLIAM H., VIRGINIA JOHNSON, and ROBERT KOLODNY. *Crisis: **Heterosexual** Behavior in the Age of AIDS.* NY: Grove Press, 1989.

————. *Heterosexuality.* NY: HarperCollins, 1994.

MATTHEWS, FRED H. "The Americanization of Sigmund Freud." *Journal of American Studies* 1 (1967): 39–62.

MAY, ELAINE. *Great Expectations: Marriage and Divorce in Post-Victorian America.* Chicago: University of Chicago Press, 1980.

MCGOVERN, JAMES R. "The American Woman's Pre-World War I Freedom in Manners and Morals." *Journal of American History* 55 (Sept. 1968): 315–33.

MCINTOSH, MARY. "The Homosexual Role." *Social Problems* 16 (1968): 182–92; reprinted with postscript in Plummer, ed.: 30–49; reprinted without postscript in Stein, ed.

MCLAREN, ANGUS. *Reproductive Rituals: The Perception of Fertility in England from the Sixteenth Century to the Nineteenth Century.* London: Methuen, 1984.

————. *Sexuality and Social Order: The Debate Over the Fertility of Women and Workers in France, 1770–1920.* NY: Holmes and Meier, 1983.

MCWHIRTER, DAVID P., et al. *Homosexuality/**Heterosexuality**: Concepts of Sexual Orientation.* NY: Oxford University Press, 1990.

MEYEROWITZ, JOANNE J. *Women Adrift: Independent Wage Earners in Chicago, 1880–1930.* Chicago: Chicago University Press, 1988.

MILLER, JAMES. *The Passion of Michel Foucault.* NY: Simon and Schuster, 1993.

MILLETT, KATE. *Sexual Politics.* Garden City, NY: Doubleday, 1970.

MITCHELL, JULIET. *Psychoanalysis and Feminism.* NY: Pantheon, 1974.

————. *Woman's Estate.* NY: Pantheon, 1972.

MONEY, JOHN. *Gay, Straight, and In-Between: The Sexology of Erotic Orientation.* NY: Oxford University Press, 1988.

MORAGA, CHERIÉ, and GLORIA ANZALDUA, eds. *This Bridge Called My Back: Writings by Radical Women of Color.* Watertown, MA: Persephone Press, 1981.

MORANTZ, REGINA. "The Scientist as Sex Crusader: Alfred Kinsey and American Culture." *American Quarterly* 29 (Winter 1977): 519–46.

MORGAN, ROBIN, ed. *Going Too Far.* NY: Random House, 1978.

———. *Sisterhood Is Powerful: An Anthology of Writings from the Women's Liberation Movement.* NY: Vintage, 1970. (See especially Susan Lydon, "The Politics of Women's Orgasm"; Mary Jane Sherfey, "A Theory of Female Sexuality"; Naomi Weisstein, " 'Kinder, Kuche, Kirche' as Scientific Law: Psychology Constructs the Female.")

MORT, FRANK. *Dangerous Sexualities: Medico-Moral Politics in England Since 1830.* London: Routledge, 1987. (See **"heterosexuality"** in index.)

MOSHER, CLELIA D. *The Mosher Survey: Sexual Attitudes of 45 Victorian Women.* Eds. James Mattood and Kristine Wenburg. NY: Arno Press, 1980.

MOSSE, GEORGE L. "Nationalism and Respectability: Normal and Abnormal Sexuality in the Nineteenth Century." *Journal of Contemporary History* 17 (1982).

———. *Nationalism and Sexuality: Respectability and Abnormal Sexuality in Modern Europe.* NY: Howard Fertig, 1985.

MURPHY, TIMOTHY. "Freud Reconsidered: Bisexuality, Homosexuality, and Moral Judgment." *Journal of Homosexuality* 9:2/3 (1984), 65–77.

———. "Freud and Sexual Reorientation Therapy." *Journal of Homosexuality* 23:3 (1992): 21–38.

MURRAY, ROBERT K. *The Politics of Normalcy: Governmental Theory and Practice in the Harding-Coolidge Era.* NY: W. W. Norton, 1973.

MYRON, NANCY, and CHARLOTTE BUNCH, eds. *Lesbianism and the Women's Movement.* Baltimore: Diana Press, 1975.

NESTLE, JOAN. *A Restricted Country.* Ithaca, NY: Firebrand Books, 1987.

———, ed. *The Persistent Desire: A Femme-Butch Reader.* Boston: Alyson, 1992.

NEUMAN, R. P. "Masturbation, Madness, and the Modern Concepts of Childhood and Adolescence." *Journal of Social History* 8 (Spring 1975): 1–27.

NEWTON, ESTHER. *Cherry Grove, Fire Island: Sixty Years in America's First Gay and Lesbian Town.* Boston: Beacon Press, 1993.

———. "The Mythic Mannish Lesbian: Radclyffe Hall and the New Woman." *Signs* 9:4 (Summer 1984): 557–75.

[NEW YORK RADICAL WOMEN.] *Notes from the First Year: Women's Liberation.* NY: New York Radical Women, June 1968. (See also Firestone, ed., *Notes from the Second Year;* and Koedt, ed., *Notes from the Third Year.*)

NIEKERK, ANJA VAN KOOTEN, and THEO VAN DER MEER, eds. *Homosexuality, Which Homosexuality?* London: GMP, 1989. (Often mistakenly listed under the names of the authors included: Altman, et al.)

OOSTERHUIS, HARRY, "Richard von Krafft-Ebing's Step-Children of Nature: Psychiatry and the Making of Modern Sexual Identity." Presented at Second Carleton Conference on the History of the Family, May 12, 1994.

ORTNER, SHERRY B., and HARRIET WHITEHEAD, eds. *Sexual Meanings: The Cultural Construction of Gender and Sexuality.* NY: Oxford University Press, 1981.

Oxford English Dictionary Supplement. Oxford: Clarendon Press, 1933. (See **"heterosexual,"** 460).

Oxford English Dictionary Supplement. Vol. II, H-N. Oxford: Clarendon Press, 1976. (See **"heterosexual,"** 85.)

PADGUG, ROBERT. "Sexual Matters: On Conceptualizing Sexuality in History." *Radical History Review* 20 (Spring/Summer 1979): 3–23; rev. in Duberman, et al.: 54–64; in Peiss, et al.: 14–31; in Stein, ed.

PALMER, BRYAN D. *Descent Into Discourse: The Reification of Language and the Writing of Social History.* Philadelphia: Temple University Press, 1990. (On **heterosexual**/homosexual and on gender history see 161–86.)

PARSONS, GAIL PAT. "Equal Treatment for All: American Medical Remedies for Male Sexual Problems: 1850–1900." *Journal of the History of Medicine* 32 (Jan. 1977): 55–71.

PATTON, CINDY. "Tremble, **Hetero** Swine." In Warner, ed.: 143–77.

PEISS, KATHY. " 'Charity Girls' and City Pleasures: Historical Notes on Working Class Sexuality, 1880–1920." In Snitow, et al.: 74–87; in Peiss and Simmons: 57–69.

————. *Cheap Amusements: Working Women and Leisure in Turn-of-the-Century New York.* Philadelphia: Temple University Press, 1986.

————, and CHRISTINA SIMMONS, with ROBERT A. PADGUG, eds. *Passion and Power: Sexuality in History.* Philadelphia: Temple University Press, 1989. (See especially Ch. 1, "Passion and Power: An Introduction" by Peiss and Simmons.)

PERRY, LEWIS. " 'Progress, Not Pleasure, Is Our Aim': The Sexual Advice of an Antebellum Radical." *Journal of Social History* 12 (Spring 1979): 354–66.

PHILIPSON, ILENE. "**Heterosexual** Antagonisms and the Politics of Mothering." *Socialist Review* 12:6, No. 66 (Nov.-Dec. 1982): 55–77.

──────. "The Social Construction of Sexuality" (review of Weeks, *Sex, Politics and Society*), *Socialist Review* 13:6, No. 72 (Nov.-Dec. 1983): 133–37.

PIVAR, DAVID J. *Purity Crusade: Sexual Morality and Social Control, 1868–1900.* Westport, CT: Greenwood Press, 1973.

PLECK, ELIZABETH H. and JOSEPH H. PLECK, eds. *The American Man.* Englewood Cliffs, NJ: Prentice-Hall, 1980.

PLUMMER, KENNETH, ed. *The Making of the Modern Homosexual.* Totowa, NJ: Barnes and Noble, 1981. (See **"heterosexuality"** in index.)

PONSE, BARBARA. *Identities in the Lesbian World: The Social Construction of Self.* Westport, CT: Greenwood Press, 1978.

POSNER, RICHARD A. *Sex and Reason.* Cambridge: Harvard University Press, 1992. (See Ch. 1, "Theoretical Sexology" and **"heterosexuality"** in the index. He rejects the idea that "**heterosexuality** is itself a male invention and imposition," calling this view, "the reductio ad absurdum of social constructionism": 33, 29.)

PUGH, DAVID G. *Sons of Liberty: The Masculine Mind in Nineteenth-Century America.* Westport, CT: Greenwood Press, 1983.

PURPLE SEPTEMBER STAFF. "The Normative Status of **Heterosexuality**." In Myron and Bunch, eds. (1975): 79–83.

RADICALESBIANS. "The Woman-Identified Woman." In Koedt, Levine, and Rapone, eds. (1973): 240–45.

RAFFALOVICH, MARC-ANDRÉ. "Uranism, Congenital Sexual Inversion. Observations and Recommendations." *Journal of Comparative Neurology* 5 (March 1889): 33–65.

RAFFEL, BURTON. *Politicians, Poets and Con Men: Emotional History in Late Victorian America.* Hamden, CT: Archon, 1986.

RAMAS, MARIA. "Freud's Dora, Dora's Hysteria: The Negation of a Woman's Rebellion." *Feminist Studies* 6:3 (Fall 1980): 472–510. Reprinted abridged in Bernheimer.

RAPP, RAYNA, and ELLEN ROSS. "The Twenties Backlash: Compulsory **Heterosexuality**, the Consumer Family, and the Waning of Feminism." In Swerdlow: 92–107

REDSTOCKINGS, ed. *Feminist Revolution.* New Paltz, NY: Redstockings, 1975. Revised ed., NY: Random House, 1978.

REICH, WILHELM. *Sex-Pol: Essays 1919–1934.* Ed. by Lee Baxandall. Trans. Anna Bostock, Tom DuBose, Lee Baxandall. NY: Vintage Books/ Random House, 1972.

──────. *The Sexual Revolution: Toward a Self-Governing Character Structure.* Rev. ed. trans. by Theodore P. Wolfe. NY: Farrar Straus and Giroux, 1969.

REID, COLETTA. "Coming Out in the Women's Movement." In Myron and Bunch (1975): 91–103.

RICH, ADRIENNE. *Blood, Bread and Poetry.* NY: Norton, 1986. (Includes reprint of "Compulsory **Heterosexuality** and Lesbian Existence," Rich's correspondence with Snitow, Stansell, and Thompson in 1981, and a "Foreword" by Rich first published in 1982: 23–75.)

———. "Compulsory **Heterosexuality** and Lesbian Existence." *Signs* 5:4 (Summer 1980): 631–60. Reprinted in Rich, *Blood;* Snitow, et al.: 177–205.

———. *Of Woman Born: Motherhood as Experience and Institution.* NY: W. W. Norton, Oct. 1976. (See "**heterosexuality,** institutionalized," in index.)

RICHARDSON, DIANE. "The Dilemma of Essentiality in Homosexual Theory." *Journal of Homosexuality* 9:2/3 (Winter 1983/Spring 1984): 79–90.

RIEFF, PHILIP. *Freud: The Mind of the Moralist.* 3rd ed. Chicago: University of Chicago Press, 1979.

RIEGEL, ROBERT E. "Changing American Attitudes Toward Prostitution." *Journal of the History of Ideas* 29 (July-Sept. 1968): 437–52.

RILEY, DENISE. *"Am I That Name?" Feminism and the Category of "Women" in History.* Minneapolis: University of Minnesota Press, 1988. (See especially "Does Sex Have a History?")

ROBERTSON, E. ARNOT. *Ordinary Families.* London: Jonathan Cape, 1933. Reprinted London: Virago Press, 1982. (See " 'hetero,' " 272.)

ROBINSON, PAUL. *The Modernization of Sex: Havelock Ellis, Alfred Kinsey, William Masters and Virginia Johnson.* NY: Harper and Row, 1976.

ROEDIGER, DAVID R. *The Wages of Whiteness: Race and the Making of the American Working Class.* NY: Verso, 1991.

ROPER, MICHAEL, and JOHN TOSH, eds. *Manful Assertions: Masculinities in Britain Since 1800.* NY: Routledge, 1991.

ROSENBERG, CHARLES E. *No Other Gods: On Science and American Social Thought.* Baltimore: Johns Hopkins University Press, 1976.

———. "Sexuality, Class and Role in 19th-Century America." *American Quarterly* 25:2 (May 1973): 131–53.

ROSENBERG, ROSALIND. *Beyond Separate Spheres: Intellectual Roots of Modern Feminism.* New Haven: Yale University Press, 1982. (See especially Ch. 7, "The Reluctant Revolutionaries," on sexuality 178–206 [particularly 204–06]; and Ch. 8, "Beyond Separate Spheres": 207–37).

ROSS, ELLEN, and RAYNA RAPP. "Sex and Society: A Research Note from Social History and Anthropology" (1981). In Snitow, et al.: 51–73.

ROTHMAN, ELLEN K., *Hands and Hearts: A History of Courtship in America.* NY: Basic Books, 1984.

———. "Sex and Self-Control: Middle-Class Courtship in America, 1790–1870." In Michael Gordon, ed., *The American Family in Social-Historical Perspective.* NY: St. Martin's Press, 1983.

ROTHMAN, SHEILA. *Woman's Proper Place: A History of Changing Ideals and Practices, 1870 to the Present.* NY: Basic Books, 1978.

ROTUNDO, ANTHONY E. *American Manhood: Transformations in Masculinity from the Revolution to the Modern Era.* NY: Basic Books, 1993.

ROUSSEAU, G. S. "The Pursuit of Homosexuality in the Eighteenth Century: 'Uterly Confeused Category' or Rich Repository." *Eighteenth-Century Life* 10 (1985–86): 132–68.

RUBIN, GAYLE. "Thinking Sex: Notes for a Radical Theory of the Politics of Sexuality." In Vance, ed.: 267–319.

———. "The Traffic in Women: Notes on the 'Political Economy' of Sex." In Rayna R. Reiter, ed., *Toward an Anthropology of Women.* NY: Monthly Review Press, 1975: 157–210. (See "compulsory **heterosexuality**," 198).

RUPP, LEILA J. " 'Imagine My Surprise': Women's Relationships in Historical Perspective." *Frontiers* 5 (Fall 1980): 61–70.

RUSSELL, DIANA, and NICOLE VAN DEN VENS, eds. *Proceedings of the International Tribunal on Crimes Against Women.* Millbrae, CA: Les Femmes, 1976. (See "compulsory **heterosexuality**," 42–43, 56–57.)

RUSSETT, CYNTHIA EAGLE. *Sexual Science: The Victorian Construction of Womanhood.* NY: Cambridge University Press, 1989.

RYAN, MARY P. *The Cradle of the Middle Class: The Family in Oneida County, New York, 1790–1865.* Cambridge, MA: Harvard University Press, 1981.

———. "Political Space: Of Prostitutes and Politicians." In her *Women in Public: Between Banners and Ballots, 1825–1880.* Baltimore: Johns Hopkins University Press, 1990: 94–129, 188–91.

———. *Womanhood in America: From Colonial Times to the Present.* NY: Franklin Watts, 1975 (1st ed.); 1979 (2nd ed.); 1983 (3rd ed.). Third ed. includes: "The Sexy Saleslady: Psychology, **Heterosexuality,** and Consumption in the Twentieth Century," 151–182.

SAHLI, NANCY. "Sexuality in Nineteenth and Twentieth Century America: The Sources and Their Problems." *Radical History Review* 20 (Spring/Summer 1979): 89–96.

———. "Smashing: Women's Relationships Before the Fall." *Chrysalis* 8 (Summer 1979): 17–28.

SCOTT, JOAN. "Gender: A Useful Category of Historical Analysis." *Ameri-*

can Historical Review No. 91 (Dec. 1986); in her *Gender and the Politics of History.* NY: Columbia University Press, 1988: 28–50.

SEARS, HAL D. *The Sex Radicals: Free Love in High Victorian America.* Lawrence, KS: The Regents Press of Kansas, 1977.

SEDGWICK, EVE KOSOFSKY. *Between Men: English Literature and Male Homosexual Desire.* NY: Columbia University Press, 1985.

———. *Epistemology of the Closet.* Berkeley: University of California Press, 1990. (See especially Introduction and Ch. 1, and **"heterosexuality"** in index).

———. *Tendencies.* Durham, NC: Duke University Press, 1993. (See **"heterosexuality"** in index.)

SEGAL, LYNN, and MARY MCINTOSH. *Sex Exposed: Sexuality and the Pornography Debate.* New Brunswick, NJ: Rutgers University Press, 1993.

SEIDMAN, STEVEN. *Embattled Eros: Sexual Politics and Ethics in Contemporary America.* NY: Routledge, 1992. (See **"heterosexuality"** in index.)

———. *Romantic Longings: Love in America, 1830–1980* (NY: Routledge, 1991). (See **"heterosexuality"** in index.)

———. "Sexual Attitudes of Victorian and Post-Victorian Women: Another Look at the Mosher Survey." *Journal of American Studies* (Spring 1989).

SHADE, WILLIAM. "A Mental Passion: Female Sexuality in Victorian America." *International Journal of Women's Studies* 1:1 (Jan.-Feb. 1978): 13–29.

SHERFEY, MARY JANE. *The Nature & Evolution of Female Sexuality.* NY: Random House, 1972.

———. "A Theory of Female Sexuality." *Journal of the American Psychoanalytical Association* (1966). In Morgan, *Sisterhood:* 220–29.

SHORTER, EDWARD. *The Making of the Modern Family.* NY: Basic Books, 1975. (See "Sexual revolution," "Sexual roles," and "Sexuality" in index.)

SIMMONS, CHRISTINA. "Companionate Marriage and the Lesbian Threat." *Frontiers* 4:3 (Fall 1978): 54–59.

———. "Marriage in the Modern Manner: Sexual Radicalism and Reform, 1914–1941." Ph.D. diss., Brown University, 1982.

———. "Modern Sexuality and the Myth of Victorian Repression." In Peis, et al., *Passion and Power* (See Peis above.)

SIMSON, RENNIE. "The Afro-American Female: The Historical Context of the Construction of Sexual Identity." In Snitow, et al.: 229–35.

SMALL, MARGARET, "Lesbians and the Class Position of Women." In Myron and Bunch (1975): 49–62.

SMITH, BARBARA. "Towards a Black Feminist Criticism." *Conditions* 1:2

(Oct. 1977); reprinted in Judith Newton and Deborah Rosenfelt, eds., *Feminist Criticism and Social Change: Sex, Class and Race in Literature and Culture.* NY: Methuen, 1985: 3–18.

———, ed. *Home Girls: A Black Feminist Anthology.* NY: Kitchen Table Press, 1985.

SMITH, DANIEL SCOTT. "The Dating of the American Sexual Revolution: Evidence and Interpretation." In Michael Gordon, ed., *The American Family in Social-Historical Perspective.* NY: St. Martin's Press, 1978: 426–38.

———. "Family Limitation, Sexual Control, and Domestic Feminism: An Interpretation of Victorian Sexual Ideology, 1790–1850." In Mary Hartman and Lois Banner, eds., *Cleio's Consciousness Raised: New Perspectives on the History of Women.* NY: Harper & Row, 1974: 119–36.

SMITH-ROSENBERG, CARROLL. *Disorderly Conduct: Visions of Gender in Victorian America.* NY: Alfred A. Knopf, 1985.

———. "Sex as Symbol in Victorian Purity: An Ethnohistorical Analysis of Jacksonian America." In John Demos and Sarane S. Boocock, eds., *Turning Points: Historical and Sociological Essays on the Family. American Journal of Sociology* 84, Supplement. Chicago: 1978.

———, and CHARLES ROSENBERG. "The Female Animal: Medical and Biological Views of Women and Her Role in 19th Century America." *Journal of American History* 59 (Sept. 1973): 331–56.

SNITOW, ANN BARR. "Mass Market Romance: Pornography for Women Is Different." In Snitow, et al.: 245–63.

———, CHRISTINE STANSELL and SHARON THOMPSON, eds. (Correspondence with Adrienne Rich, April 19, 1981.) In Rich, *Blood.*

———; *Powers of Desire: The Politics of Sexuality.* NY: Monthly Review Press, 1983. (See "The Institution of **Heterosexuality**": 177–279.

SOKOLOW, JAYME. *Eros and Modernization: Sylvester Graham, Health Reform, and the Origins of Victorian Sexuality in America.* Rutherford, NJ: Fairleigh Dickinson University Press, 1983.

SPURLOCK, JOHN. *Free Love, Marriage and Middle Class Radicalism in America, 1820–1860.* NY: New York University Press, 1983.

———. "The Free Love Network in America, 1850 to 1860." *Journal of Social History* 21 (Summer 1988).

STAGE, SARAH. "Out of the Attic: Studies in Victorian Sexuality." *American Quarterly* 27:4 (Oct. 1975): 480–85.

STANSELL, CHRISTINE. *City of Women: Sex and Class in New York, 1789–1860.* New York: Alfred A. Knopf, 1986.

STEAKLEY, JAMES D. *The Homosexual Emancipation Movement in Germany.* NY: Arno Press, 1975.

STEARNS, CAROL Z., and PETER N. STEARNS. "Victorian Sexuality: Can Historians Do It Better?" *Journal of Social History* 18 (Summer 1985): 625–34.

STEARNS, PETER N., and CAROL Z. STEARNS. "Emotionology: Clarifying the History of Emotions and Emotional Standards." *American Historical Review* 90 (Oct. 1985): 813–36.

STEIN, ARLENE. "Three Models of Sexuality: Drives, Identities, and Practices." *Sociological Theory* 7 (1989): 1–13.

STEIN, EDWARD, ed. *Forms of Desire: The Sexual Orientation and the Social Constructionist Controversy.* NY: Garland, 1990.

STIMPSON, CATHARINE R. *Where the Meanings Are: Feminism and Cultural Spaces.* NY: Methuen, 1988.

———, and ETHEL SPECTOR PERSON, eds. *Women, Sex, and Sexuality.* Chicago: University of Chicago Press, 1980.

STONE, LAWRENCE. *The Family, Sex and Marriage in England, 1500–1800.* NY: Harper and Row, 1977.

———. "Sexuality" in *Past and Present Revisited.* NY: Routledge, 1987: 344–82.

STRONG, BRYAN. "Ideas of the Early Sex Education Movement in America, 1890–1920." *History of Education Quarterly* (Summer 1972).

SULLOWAY, FRANK J. *Freud: Biologist of the Mind.* NY: Basic Books, 1979.

SWERDLOW, AMY, and HANNA LESSINGER, eds. *Class, Race, and Sex: The Dynamics of Control.* Boston: G. K. Hall, 1983.

SZASZ, THOMAS. *The Myth of Mental Illness: Foundations of a Theory of Personal Conduct.* NY: Harper and Row, 1974.

TEAL, DONN. *The Gay Militants.* NY: Stein and Day, 1971.

TERMAN, LEWIS, and C. C. MILES. *Sex and Personality: Studies in Femininity and Masculinity.* NY: McGraw-Hill, 1936.

TERRY, JENNIFER. "Anxious Slippages Between 'Us' and 'Them': A Brief History of the Scientific Search for Homosexual Bodies." Forthcoming in Terry and Jacqueline Urla, eds., *Deviant Bodies.* Bloomington: Indiana University Press.

———. "Lesbians Under the Medical Gaze: Scientists Search for Remarkable Differences." *Journal of Sex Research* 27 (1990): 317–40.

———. "Theorizing Deviant Historiography." *differences* 3:2 (1991): 55–74.

THOMAS, KEITH. "The Double Standard." *Journal of the History of Ideas* 20:2 (April 1959): 195–216.

THOMAS, KENDALL. "Corpus Juris (**Hetero**)sexualis: Doctrine, Discourse, and Desire in *Bowers v. Hardwick.*" *GLQ: A Journal of Lesbian and Gay Studies* 1:1 (1993): 33–51.

THOMPSON, MARTHA E. "Comment on Rich's 'Compulsory **Heterosexuality** and Lesbian Existence.' " *Signs* 6:4 (Summer 1981): 790–94.

THOMPSON, SHARON. "Search for Tomorrow: On Feminism and the Reconstruction of Teen Romance." In Vance, ed.: 350–84.

TIEFER, LEONORE. "Social Constructionism and the Study of Human Sexuality." In P. Shaver and C. Hendrick, eds., *Review of Personality and Social Psychology* 7 (1987): 70–94; reprinted in Stein, ed.

TRIMBERGER, ELLEN KAY. "Feminism, Men, and Modern Love: Greenwich Village, 1900–1925." In Snitow, et al.: 121–52.

TRIPP, PAUL. *The Homosexual Matrix.* NY: McGraw-Hill, 1975. (See especially Ch. 4, "The Origins of **Heterosexuality**.")

TRUMBACH, RANDOLPH. "The Birth of the Queen: Sodomy and the Emergence of Gender Equality in Modern Culture, 1660–1750," in Duberman et al.: 129–40.

———. "Gender and the Homosexual Role in Modern Western Culture: The 18th and 19th Centuries Compared." In Niekerk and van der Meer: 149–70

———. "London's Sapphists: From Three Sexes to Four Genders in the Making of Modern Culture." In Epstein and Straub, eds.: 112–41; in Herdt, ed.: 111–36.

———. "London's Sodomites: Homosexual Behavior and Western Culture in the Eighteenth Century." *Journal of Social History* 11 (1977): 1–33.

———. *The Rise of the Equalitarian Family: Aristocratic Kinship and Domestic Relations in Eighteenth-Century England.* NY: Academic Press, 1978.

———, ed. *Select Trials at the Sessions-House in the Old-Bailey.* 2 vols. NY: Garland, 1986.

———. "Sodomitical Assaults, Gender Role, and Sexual Development in Eighteenth-Century London." *Journal of Homosexuality* 16:1/2 (1988): 407–29.

———. "Sodomitical Subcultures, Sodomitical Roles, and the Gender Revolution of the Eighteenth Century: The Recent Historiography." *Eighteenth Century Life* 9 (1985): 109–21.

———, ed. *Sodomy Trials: Seven Documents.* NY: Garland, 1986.

VALVERDE, MARIANA. *Sex, Power, and Pleasure.* Philadelphia: New Society Publishers, 1987. (See Chapter 2, "**Heterosexuality:** Contested Ground": 47–74; and Chapter 3, especially "A Bit of History" and "Making **Heterosexuality** Compulsory": 77–87.

VANCE, CAROLE S. "Anthropology Rediscovers Sexuality: A Theoretical Comment." *Social Science and Medicine* 38:8 (1991): 875–84.

————. "Gender Systems, Ideology, and Sex Research." In Snitow, et al.: 371–84.

————, ed. *Pleasure and Danger: Exploring Female Sexuality.* Boston: Routledge, 1984; reprinted London: Pandora Press, 1992, with new introduction. (See **"heterosexuality"** in index.)

————. "Social Construction Theory: Problems in the History of Sexuality." In Niekerk: 13–34.

VANN, RICHARD T. "The Youth of *Centuries of Childhood.*" *History and Theory* 21:2 (May 1982): 2279–97.

VICINUS, MARTHA, ed. *Suffer and Be Still: Women in the Victorian Age.* Bloomington: Indiana University Press, 1972.

————. *A Widening Sphere: Changing Roles of Victorian Women.* Bloomington: Indiana University Press, 1977.

————. " 'They Wonder to Which Sex I Belong': The Historical Roots of the Modern Lesbian Identity." In Niekerk: 171–98.

VIDAL, GORE. "Someone to Laugh at the Squares With [Tennessee Williams]." *New York Review of Books* (June 13, 1985); reprinted in *At Home: Essays, 1982–1988.* NY: Random House, 1988; and *United States: Essays, 1952–1992.* NY: Random House, 1993.

————. "The Tree of Liberty: Notes on Our Patriarchal State." *The Nation* (Aug. 27/Sept. 3, 1990): 1, 202, 204.

WALKOWITZ, JUDITH R. *City of Dreadful Delight: Narratives of Sexual Danger in Late-Victorian London.* Chicago: University of Chicago Press, 1992. (See **"heterosexuality"** in index.)

————. *Prostitution and Victorian Society: Women, Class, and the State.* NY: Cambridge University Press, 1980.

WALLACE, MICHELE. *Black Macho and the Myth of the Superwoman.* NY: Dial Press, 1978.

WALLER, ALTINA L. *Reverend Beecher and Mrs. Tilton: Sex and Class in Victorian America.* Amherst, MA: University of Massachusetts Press, 1982.

WALTERS, RONALD G. "The Erotic South: Civilization and Sexuality in American Abolitionism." *American Quarterly* 25 (May 1973), 177–201.

————. *Primers for Prudery: Sexual Advice in Victorian America.* Englewood Cliffs, NJ: Prentice-Hall, 1974.

WARD, JON. "The Nature of **Heterosexuality**." In Hanscombe and Humphries: 145–70.

WARNER, MICHAEL. *Fear of a Queer Planet: Queer Politics and Social Theory.* Minneapolis: University of Minnesota Press, 1993. (See Part I on "**hetero**theory" and **"heterosexuality"** in index.)

————. "New English Sodom." In Jonathan Goldberg, ed., *Queering the Renaissance:* 330–58.

Webster's New International Dictionary. First ed. Springfield, MA: G. & C. Merriam Company, 1909 (see **"heterosexual,"** 1030). *Supplement.* Same, 1923 (see **"heterosexual,"** xcii). Second ed. Same, 1934 (see **"heterosexual,"** 1173).

WEEKS, JEFFREY. *Against Nature: Essays on History, Sexuality and Identity.* London: Rivers Oram Press, 1991.

———. *Coming Out: Homosexual Politics in Britain, from the Nineteenth Century to the Present.* London: Quartet Books, 1977; rev. 1990.

———. "Foucault for Historians." *History Workshop,* No. 14, Autumn 1982: 106–19.

———. *Sex, Politics and Society: The Regulation of Sexuality Since 1800.* London: Longman, Harlow, 1981. (See **"heterosexuality"** in index.)

———. *Sexuality.* NY: Tavistock, 1986. (See especially 83 and **"heterosexuality"** in index.)

———. *Sexuality and Its Discontents: Meanings, Myths & Modern Sexualities.* London: Routledge, 1981. (See **"heterosexuality"** in index.)

———. "Values in an Age of Uncertainty." In Donna C. Stanton, *Discourses of Sexuality: From Aristotle to AIDS.* Ann Arbor: University of Michigan Press, 1992: 389–411.

WEISSTEIN, NAOMI. "Kinder, Kuche, Kirche as Scientific Law: Psychology Constructs the Female." (Pamphlet) Boston: New England Free Press, 1968. In Morgan, *Sisterhood;* revised and reprinted in Koedt, Levine, and Rapone, eds. (1973): 178–97.

WELTER, BARBARA. "The Cult of True Womanhood: 1820–1860," *American Quarterly* 18 (Summer 1966): 150–74. In Michael Gordon, ed., *The American Family in Social-Historical Perspective.* Third ed. NY: St. Martin's Press, 1983: 372–92.

WESTPHAL, KARL FRIEDRICH OTTO. *"Die conträre Sexualempfindung."* *Archiv für Psychiatrie und Nervenkrankheiten* 2:1 (August 1869): 73–108.

WHITE, KEVIN. *The First Sexual Revolution: The Emergence of Male **Heterosexuality** in Modern America.* NY: New York University Press, 1993.

WHITMAN, WALT. *Leaves of Grass: Facsimile Edition of the 1860 Text.* Ithaca: Cornell University Press, 1961.

WIEBE, ROBERT H. *The Search for Order 1877–1920.* NY: Hill and Wang, 1967.

WILLIAMS, RAYMOND. *Keywords: A Vocabulary of Culture and Society.* NY: Oxford University Press, 1976.

WILLIS, ELLEN. *Beginning to See the Light.* NY: Alfred A. Knopf, 1981.

———. "Radical Feminism and Feminist Radicalism." In Sayres, Sohnya, et al., eds., *The '60s without Apology.* Minneapolis: University of Minnesota Press, 1984.

WINKLER, JOHN J. *The Constraints of Desire: The Anthropology of Sex and Gender in Ancient Greece.* NY: Routledge, 1990.

WITTIG, MONIQUE. "Paradigm." In George Stambolian and Elaine Marks, eds., *Homosexualities and French Literature: Culture Contexts/Critical Texts.* Ithaca: Cornell University Press, 1979: 114–21.

————. *The **Straight** Mind and Other Essays.* Boston: Beacon Press, 1992.

WYDEN, PETER and BARBARA. *Growing Up **Straight**: What Every Thoughtful Parent Should Know About Homosexuality.* NY: Stein and Day, 1968

YOUNG, ALLEN, "Out of the Closets, Into the Streets," in Jay and Young: 6–31.

INDEX

A NOTE ON THE TYPE

The typeface used in this book is a version of Baskerville, originally designed by John Baskerville (1706-1775) and considered to be one of the first "transitional" typefaces between the "old style" of the Continental humanist printers and the "modern" style of the nineteenth century. With a determination bordering on the eccentric to produce the finest possible printing, Baskerville set out at age forty-five and with no previous experience to become a typefounder and printer (his first fourteen letters took him two years). Besides the letter forms, his innovations included an improved printing press, smoother paper, and better inks, all of which made Baskerville decidedly uncompetitive as a businessman. Franklin, Beaumarchais, and Bodoni were among his admirers, but his typeface had to wait for the twentieth century to achieve its due.